Playing With Fire
(Tales of Duality)

by
Ano Nimmus

Grosvenor House
Publishing Limited

This book is published by
Grosvenor House Publishing Ltd
Link House
140 The Broadway, Tolworth, Surrey, KT6 7HT.
www.grosvenorhousepublishing.co.uk

A CIP record for this book
is available from the British Library

ISBN 978-1-83975-044-1

Disclaimer
This story is based upon actual events. However, some of the characters and
incidents portrayed and some of the names herein are fictitious, and with
respect to such characters and incidents, any similarity to the name, character
or history of any person, living or dead, or any actual event is entirely
coincidental and unintentional. This is to protect the innocent and also to
some extent the guilty.

Dedication page

For Benjamin.

INTRODUCTION

Once a mind is opened, it can never be closed.

I was about thirty-four, I was two years into sorting myself out, again. I was doing a lot of deep work on myself. My eyes were opening, wide. My heart was beginning to heal, but in order to heal it must first release the pain; pain that it had been carrying for most of my life. I was on an emotional and spiritual quest. I was hunting for answers, the answers to life's big questions, I just wasn't sure what the questions were. I was exploring various alternative ideology groups, I was mixing with free-thinking people, I was attending meetings and I was practicing daily meditation. I'd heard this could be simultaneously both guiding and healing. I was also slowly 'working' my way through a very profound book on 'Inner Child' healing. As I released my old trapped pain, some of my lost innocence was beginning to return. I was cleansing myself. I was in the process of some truly agonising healing. I was walking my own path, parallel to 'the steps'. I felt shunned by some of my peers, but I knew I was doing the right thing. I'd learnt to be guided by my heart, and my gut instinct. I was experiencing tremendous synchronicities that confirmed to me that I was heading the right way. This time I was taking it very seriously; I'd been here before. I knew I needed to strip myself bare in order to fully recover. I knew I needed to plunge to the deepest of depths, in order to heal. It was a brave decision, but I had nothing left to lose.

One morning I'd been affected by a deep conversation, following some intimacy with my then partner. It touched me deeply and I felt my emotional axis change. Suddenly I started to feel peculiar, unlike anything I had ever experienced before. It was dramatic and powerful. I was due to travel to Preston and beyond, but I felt too sensitive. Raw, but in a good way. Everything around me was vibrating in an awe inspiring and beautiful way. It started with sounds at first. Every noise I heard was resonating powerfully within me. I could feel it all; traffic, foot-steps, a child laughing. I became overwhelmed by a feeling of deep unconditional love. I could see it, hear it, feel it. I walked past a lamp post and I could literally sense and psychically see its inner vibrations. My overly analytical mind desperately trying to make sense of it all, but failing miserably. I knew I wasn't going mad. I knew I was experiencing reality, only from an altered perspective, a different dimension. I was in the midst of a psychic, spiritual experience. This vibration screamed a positive creative power of unconditional love.

I walked to the train station in St Anne's, before boarding the rickety old train. All the while, my head overloaded with sights, sounds, vibrations and colours. I'd hear a child laugh and the love, joy and purity of it would make me weep. Tears of joy; tears brimming with true unconditional love. Burning down my barriers, melting away the ice surrounding my soul. It felt as if my frequency had come into alignment with everything around me, and together we were producing a powerful resonance. I believe that on that day, I caught a tiny miniscule glimpse of the supreme universal force. It was too much for me to take in and felt like an overwhelming, immensely powerful, unbearable love.

I was studying art at the time and I had my sketch book with me. I started to draw, in an attempt to capture what I was feeling. It seemed impossible, but I managed to rough out a silhouette of myself, with a glow of warm vibration emanating from the centre of me in light, and from everything else around me. At that time, I was using my art as an outlet, an expression, and a healing tool.

The train arrived at Preston Station, a big, old steel structure. I was weeping with tears of pure joy and unworthiness at the same time, trying to avoid the eyes of other passengers, who were simply going about their daily business. I stood on the draughty platform and looked up. I could sense and feel the entire steel structure vibrating and pulsating. The same was true of the glass, the light, the people, myself, and the stone underneath my feet. I could feel the power, it was 'in' everything. The prevailing unifying force of creation and love. Again, I broke down overwhelmed by painfully joyful tears of bliss and love. I eased into and hid in quiet corner and let the tears fall freely. Unsure of what was happening. There was such relief in the release I was experiencing.

I was only slightly afraid; the supernatural dimension was both baffling and bewildering to my analytical mind. Any fear seemed trivial, when compared to the awe-inspiring love that was coursing through my every molecule. It felt at times too much to tolerate; I had no choice but to sob. I watched others in their oblivion, unable to communicate with them, or stop my tears.

I was experiencing the awesome power and love of the universe.

I have since tried to make of sense of this experience but may never know why. I just know I can never deny that this presence exists, for me it was an experience of biblical proportions.

"If you want to find the secrets of the universe, think in terms of energy, frequency and vibration". **Nikola Tesla**

"The more I study science, the more I believe in God". **Albert Einstein**

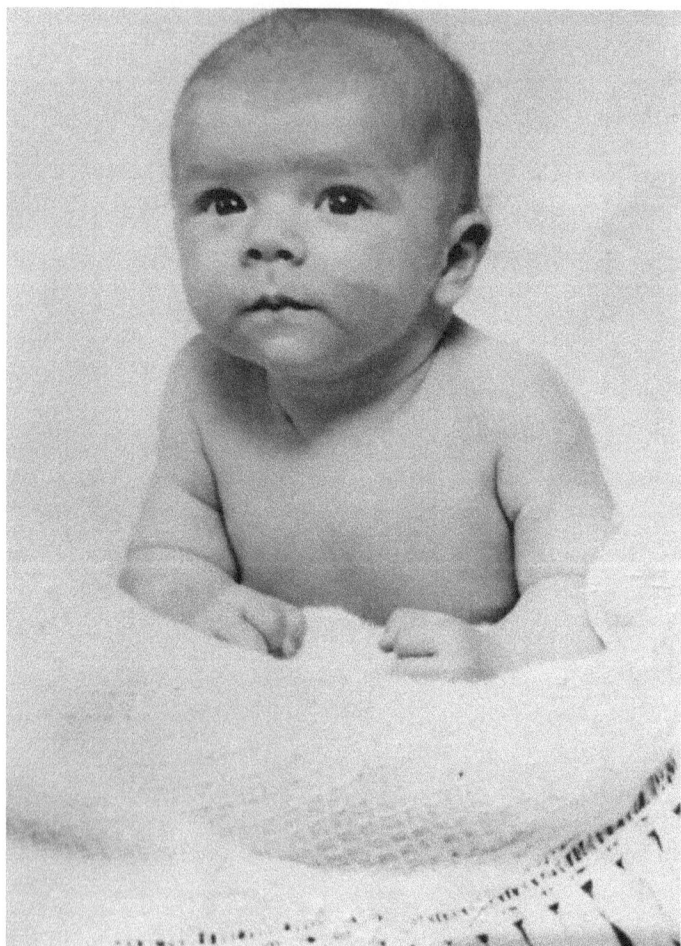

Me Born Summer 1966

Chapter One

The Tin House

Fate can be so fickle, destiny so delicate. Before I was born, the decision was made: I was to be adopted. It was the mid-sixties, a time when single motherhood was taboo, even in the midst of a psychedelic revolution. But as the story goes, once they saw my helpless innocent face gazing up, they couldn't send me away, couldn't sign those papers. My mother and my grandparents decided to keep me and take me home. I didn't know any of this until my early teens. I was oblivious to the mystery surrounding my father, oblivious to the fact that my life could have been so very different. So I was taken home with my mother and her parents. Home, to a prefab bungalow made of corrugated tin, in Hereford, England. It was the summer of 1966. I was a Midsummer's Eve baby, blissfully ignorant to the harsh vicissitudes of life.

Born into a humble single-storey post-war tin house. It stood on land that was originally an apple orchard. A small cluster of prefabs had been constructed after the war. No real roads or fences had existed when they were first built, and pigs had roamed free in the orchard. By the time of my arrival there were boundary fences in place, and a road.

My earliest vivid memory is quite magical. I was lying in my pram by the big lilac tree on a hazy summer's day. A butterfly fluttered above my face, buoyant in the clear blue sky. I remember looking in awe and innocence at its delicate wings and the way it moved. I could feel it flutter, and sense and see its vibration. It tickled me and made me giggle with joy. I was fully tuned in, my senses unadulterated. I didn't know it then, but I was born with an innate sensitivity. This sensitivity has brought with it immense pain and intense joy.

In winter the house was bitterly cold and the windows would ice solid, inside and out. In the mornings we'd wait patiently for the newspaper and twigs to catch the coal fire alight. Finally, the flames would take hold and the heat would permeate the room, slowly warming us through. Now, it seems primitive and basic but I recall the comforting feeling of the fire; it was an era when simple things were still savoured. I can remember the rustle of the newspaper, the smell, and the patient, trembling anticipation to get warm. I remember the shed in the garden too, filled with treasures. Jars and tubs of nuts and bolts, nails and screws, tools and tangled things. Looking back, it felt like something of historic fascination and intrigue, captured in time. I loved all that old stuff and the musty smell of the place. There was an old Belfast sink dug into the lawn for me to paddle in during the summer. I would explore the garden and climb the trees – for which I was always scolded. That bungalow was my whole world, my place of adventure, exploration and safety.

I have memories of watching people and characters walk by on the footpath just beyond the garden hedge. These would include the pretty lady from around the corner, the two tramps that stayed at the Polish monastery up the Straight Mile and the rag and bone man with a horse and cart, ringing a bell and calling out.

Winifred and Walter, my grandparents, played a central role in my childhood. Winifred wore the trousers with flair. Walter was a quiet, passive man who wore a flat cap and suffered from shrapnel wounds and shell shock after serving in the Second World War. He had the nickname of Badger but nobody ever told me why. Winifred always sported a wig when she was out in public, despite having a full head of her own hair. When not in use, it rested on a mannequin's head in the bedroom, beside the glass containing her soaking spare false teeth. I gave her the nickname of Wiggy as I grew up. Winifred and Walter had grown up as stepbrother and stepsister. Walter, from a family of ten, had somehow been adopted into Winifred's family as a teenager. As they grew older, love had blossomed. Walter returned from his time as a military policeman during the war, having faced his own mortality, and wanted to marry Winifred. Having grown up almost as brother and sister but not being blood related, they needed to apply for a special licence in order to wed. The marriage seemed a happy one, prone to harmless bickering but generally one of kindness and happy companionship. They were to be a valuable and loving influence in my life.

I was the baby, unaware that I should have had a father. It was just the six of us – me, mother, grandmother, grandfather, auntie and uncle.

I was in my early teens when my younger brother came bounding down the stairs and gleefully announced that I was adopted, he had found the papers. I remember feeling shocked, lost and speechless. Initially my mother told me my father had died and was buried in a local graveyard. I remember wandering about that graveyard from time to time. However, it turned out that this was another untruth, hidden amid many others. My mother simply didn't know where my father was, or who he was. She'd gone out on the town one night and enjoyed a drunken romantic encounter with a man from 'the regiment'. The SAS were based in Hereford at Bradbury Lines. It was my stepfather who vaguely remembered that he was in the regiment and was of Scottish origin. The secrecy around this regiment prevents me from hunting down any further information. I've often wondered if he knows that I exist, or even cares? I spent many years resenting my mother for these mistakes and lies, for not being able to provide more information and for living a lie for so many years. It wasn't an easy thing to come to terms with, but slowly I've come to accept that it wasn't personal. I'm not unique. People have one-night stands, mistakes are made, life goes on. It was a mistake and my mother did the best she could, she had her own struggles. My stepfather adopted me from about the age of two and those were the papers that had been found. He was also from the regiment.

After a couple of years in the tin house, my mother and I moved into a flat above a shop, in the city centre. Hereford is more like a town and is classified as a city purely due to its dominant Cathedral. So for a very short while it was just the two of us. I remember my first encounter with the man who was to become my 'father'. He wore army greens and a red beret. He'd brought with him an army ration pack and provided me with my very first taste of chocolate. It was strong, rich and bitter but I loved its intensity. He seemed friendly and I was deeply fascinated by his ration pack. He stepped straight into the role of teacher and began teaching me new words, the alphabet and numbers. I could feel his robust and powerful male presence.

Soon after that my younger brother, Alan, was born. A brother who would also have many interesting tales to tell as the years rolled by. I remember going around the town in an old pram with big rubber wheels. In those days it was common to leave a pram outside while popping into the shops. I remember encounters with random strangers, who paused to say hello. I could sense their energy, feel their imprints. From this upstairs flat I could also watch the busy street below. The new-born Alan was getting a lot of the attention I was used to having all to myself. I don't know why but one day I decided to hold my hand over his mouth, purely on instinct I think. I'm not sure if I wanted simply to shut him up, or something more sinister. I succeeded in shutting him up at least. It could well have been more permanent had my mother not intervened and seriously rebuked me, explaining that it was a very wrong thing to do! We often seemed to be in competition – some things never change.

There was an asbestos roof out the back with a washing line strung above it. My mother used to climb through the first-floor window onto it to hang the washing out. One day I heard a loud crash and a piercing scream. She'd fallen through the roof and sustained serious injuries that left her with significant lifelong pain. She was by then heavily pregnant with Teddy, who luckily was born unscathed as far as we knew. Yet another brother who later lived a life very much on the wild side. We were all very young when one day we somehow managed to start a fire in a cupboard using a box of matches. The fire took hold and did some damage to the bedroom. Our father managed to prevent it from spreading any further. I sometimes wonder if this incident is what sparked Teddy's dangerous fascination with fire. So we were three brothers, with two years between each of us. All three of us crazy and wild from the very beginning.

A much talked about story within the family was my intrepid trip across town as a toddler. I was familiar with the buses and one day I decided I wanted to visit my grandmother. So I toddled off the few hundred yards to the bus stop and got on the bus. By sheer chance, the driver was my uncle. He could not leave me alone on the street, so he let me ride the bus to the required stop. Before the age of mobile phones, his options were limited. Apparently, he dropped me as near to the house as he could. I then made my way up the road to the tin house and knocked at the door. Much to everyone's surprise and amazement I had navigated my way from one side of town to the other, back to the tin bungalow. Unbeknown to me, it was a quite an achievement for a toddler. I always have loved any adventure, big or small.

My familiarity with the buses in part came from going to work with my grandmother. She was a bus conductress, had been through the war and she used to take me to work with her, something that would never be allowed now. I would sit at the front or back of the buses and travel around the city, soaking up the sights and sounds. I would be introduced to passengers and always received plenty of attention. I remember these days fondly. I grew up on my grandmother's stories of manning the buses throughout the war. During the blackouts they would continue the required journeys but with the lights off, navigating the dark streets at slow speeds and with great care. I was struck by the bravery and adventure of those times and loved to hear her stories and tour the city by her side. She remained a consistent and loving influence in my life for many years to come, as did my grandfather.

Chapter Two

Plas Madoc

When I was about four, we moved to Wales, to a council housing estate called Plas Madoc, near Llangollen. It was a large estate, surrounded by fields and woodlands. My father (or stepfather) had left the army, and after initially doing manual labour at a mill, he gained employment as an electrical engineer for a TV repair shop. The shop was in Chester and he worked long days away from home. I have some happy memories of that place; the countryside, the woods, togged out in waterproofs and splashing in deep puddles. It was Wales after all, a place famous for its plentiful rainfall. I enjoyed an innocence that would not last forever.

I recall my first day at school. The school was a couple of miles from the house. I felt fearful and intimidated; I didn't want my mother to leave me there. I don't know how, but within a few hours I had found my way back home. Evidently, I had remembered the route we had walked and retraced our steps. This was a common pattern for me, retreating to somewhere I felt safe and secure. In this sense, I vaguely resembled a homing pigeon. As the years went on, I regularly returned to my grandparent's house, a sanctuary of picture-perfect safety and comfort. It also highlighted my inclination to wander and explore, as well as the fact that I felt more at home in nature than in the 'safe' confines of a school. I felt safe in the wild, in the woodlands and fields.

Our little house had three bedrooms and to begin with I had a room all to myself. The two youngest shared a bed at first, but this was less than ideal for Alan. Teddy, the youngest, was a bed wetter all the way through until his teens. Eventually they graduated to two single beds, with Teddy's mattress being wrapped in a thick rubber sheet. Poor Teddy faced regular and severe punishment for this night time behaviour, even though he was not doing it on purpose. In hindsight, this chastisement probably only made his predicament worse. Teddy was already caught up in a destructive vicious cycle.

At school I seemed to be born with the desire to be a leader, to be popular and to mix with the cool kids. I was also bright and possessed an enquiring mind. I was good at writing and spelling – I'm sure I had my father's constant tutoring to thank for this skill. I loved art and had a natural ability; it was one of the few things that I really wanted to do well at. I recall the little bottles of milk we used to get mid-morning, a straw poked into the tin-foil lid. Later those heady days of milk ceased due to government policy. I recall a rhyme, "Maggie Thatcher, the milk bottle snatcher" which reflected the politics of the Prime Minister at the time. Games were simple affairs like hopscotch and tick. We played mainly in our group or gang, and one member springs to mind, Dwayne Elwood. A statue of him was later erected; he'd joined the army and suffered the unhappy misfortune of being one of the first to be killed in the Falklands Conflict. Back then, none of us knew what the future would hold.

Not long after we moved to Wales, I was taken out into the fields by my babysitter, the teenage daughter of one of my mother's friends. She built a circle of straw bales, two bales high so that I couldn't escape. She then told me I couldn't go home until I kissed her private parts. I wanted to run, I felt terrified and even frightened for my life. I was her prisoner, but I desperately wanted to go home to my mother. Even as a young child, I sensed something was wrong with this entrapment and I knew I didn't want to kiss her 'down there'. I think in the end I carried out the required deed but soon broke down in heavy, sobbing tears, crying for my mother. She softened and began comforting me, it had all been just a game she said. I was too young to know any different, I didn't really understand what had happened. She told me I could go home, but only if I promised not to tell anyone about the game we'd played. Knowing what I now know, I have my suspicions that she herself had suffered abuse, it was possibly part of some kind of re-enactment. With hindsight I feel sadness, my childlike innocence had been jeopardised. A precious innocence had been tainted.

Possibly my main trait was my adventurous nature, my love of climbing and exploring. We'd spend hours out in the countryside playing Cowboys and Injuns or swinging on ropes in the woods. I was drawn to the wilds and loved feeling a connection with nature, although it was never a conscious thing back then. I revered its rawness, power and simplicity. I felt safe somehow and would take huge risks climbing tall trees. I knew from experience that it was often far more hazardous to descend, but that never stopped my ascending to the highest reaches. Many times, I found myself in peril, either climbing trees or clambering around derelict buildings. Making dens and crafting weapons was another preferred enterprise. We'd set booby traps to protect our territory, digging holes and filling them with nettles or broken glass to deter intruders. Playing could be a very serious business.

We'd wander miles as relatively young children, living purely in the moment, without worrying about time or where the next meal was coming from. We'd scavenge blackberries or apples and drink water from streams – swimming too, if the weather was good. It was a life of back to basics, primal and innocent. If it rained, we'd build shelters under trees or find caves to rest in, running feral and free for the whole day. On other days we'd find scrap and build go-carts to race on, or play Soldiers. At this I found my calling; I was very good at acting shot or mortally wounded. Whoever 'died' the best won the game and I was a frequent victor. Later we graduated onto pellet guns and things got a bit more serious as numerous injuries were sustained. Injury was something we expected and even thrived on and these were what could be called council estate games.

As well as these innocent memories, there was a much darker side to my childhood years in Wales. There was a lot of violence at home. As far as I recollect, this escalated as the years went by. Something would go wrong, something broken or something stolen, and no-one would own up. This always resulted in all three of us being punished.

Sometimes just sent to bed, other times whipped heavily with a leather belt. My father was a disciplined man, he worked hard and kept himself in good shape but he also liked a drink. I've questioned since if he was an alcoholic, or just a very heavy drinker. It's a question I've never found the answer to. Addiction and alcoholism run strong within the family and it can sometimes be a very blurry line. No doubt alcohol helped him to cope with the pressures of life, but it also contributed to his temper.

For some reason my mother wasn't well enough to work at that time, so he shouldered the financial responsibility for all five of us. To keep fit, he'd run tirelessly around a wooded track with the family dog Waldo, an obedient and well-trained black and white mongrel, named after Mr. Magoo's nephew in an old cartoon. No doubt his obedience can be attributed to my highly regimented father. He was an unaffectionate man, both physically and verbally. Typical no doubt of men of his time, particularly those from a military background. Looking back, he showed his care through teaching and doing. "Good lad" was the highest accolade we could expect. But as a child I craved more, partly due to my own insatiable nature, I suspect. I craved something that I would never really get.

He hailed from the slums of Liverpool's Scotty Road, and was of Irish descent and from a large family of seven or eight children. His father was also a very heavy drinker and likewise prone to violence. These things so often run in cycles. Whenever we were taken there as children, I never liked it. It felt dirty and we always seemed to come away with lice or worse. My mother, who had always been verging on obsessive regarding hygiene, most certainly did not enjoy those visits. She would now be described as an obsessive-compulsive cleaner, but it was an oppressive fixation even back then. Scotty Road must have been her worst nightmare. He really had come from the bowels of the city.

My father was an intelligent man and he'd climbed his way out. He'd been offered a place at grammar school as a boy, but didn't go because his family couldn't afford the uniform. I believe his family delivered coal around the city using a horse and cart. Finally, he escaped the slums by joining the army. From there he made it into the Parachute Regiment and ultimately into the SAS. He'd passed a brutal and elite selection process, an impressive achievement in itself and one that very few accomplish. On one occasion, while training in the Black Mountains, he was out on manoeuvre for days, in freezing conditions. Desperate to survive, he'd killed and skinned a sheep, using its skin and fleece for shelter and warmth. He was a striver and also a survivor, a very tough, clever and capable man. Assets that, as children, we paid for dearly at times.

As an ex-SAS soldier, my father's focus was primarily on teaching skills and instilling discipline. He still had connections with the army and later joined the Territorial Army. Our childhood holidays were always very budget friendly and normally consisted of us camping at the side of a river or a mountain. I have fond and vivid memories of wild camping in Scotland, Wales, Devon and Cornwall. My father was a serious mountaineer and rock climber and he taught us his skills from a young age. We were often out on the hills. I recall trudging to the top of Snowdon, crying and miserably cold, enviously watching the summit train glide effortlessly by. Or clambering fearfully along The Horseshoe Pass, frantic to keep up with my father. It was tough going as a youngster, but there was also a great sense of achievement at the end of a long, tough day. I was also desperate to earn his approval, an approval that felt predominantly unattainable. On the odd occasion when I felt I had achieved it, I felt like I'd struck gold and hit the jackpot all at the same time. He taught me many skills and helped to instil a sense of purpose and discipline within me. Without him, I wouldn't have a lot of my abilities and attitudes. Whatever else happened, he did show care, and he showed it through teaching. For this I will always be grateful.

Once, there were just the two of us out climbing. He'd tied a rope around my waist and then around a nearby rock. He took me to the cliff edge and told me to lean forward as far as I could. As I leant forward he let out the rope, until I pivoted at a perilous angle over the edge of the cliff. I was terrified that he was going to let me go. My life was flashing before me, balancing delicately in his hands. After a few minutes, when I had acclimatised to my predicament, he drew me back up. Whether he wanted to cure my fear of heights or build my trust, I have no idea, I never did ask. His motive remains a mystery.

You could think this crazy but those were the kind of things we did, normal father and son activities. In that moment he meant me no harm. I'm glad I had those experiences, they built me up. We did a lot of river and lake swimming too. He'd always check that the currents weren't too strong and we trusted him to save us if things went wrong. In some ways he was a great father figure, he taught us skills and helped us to mature and grow up. His wildness taught me a lot and it's never left me.

I've always been drawn to danger; leaning over the metaphorical cliff, swimming the deep waters, climbing to great heights.

We never went without food or clothing. Christmases were always good. Big bags of presents, full of everything from books to toys to sweets. Once I received a book on unexplained mysteries, ghosts and the supernatural. For some reason it grabbed me and I was hooked. I read it from cover to cover in one sitting. I was intrigued by the fact that the world had hidden dimensions and I acquired a fascination and hunger for knowledge about the extraordinary and the paranormal. It's a fascination that has remained with me ever since.

I'd also get big bags of presents from my grandparents. I was close to them and I loved them. Rightly or wrongly I felt I was their favourite, maybe because I lived with them as a baby. We used to travel several times a year to see them. I loved that picturesque journey, through the Shropshire Hills on the A49, often in the evenings. This strong relationship with my grandparents continued for many years. I have plenty of happy memories of being cherished, loved and cared for. When I was with them, I felt emotionally well-nourished and free.

I was close to my mother too. She was our nurturer and she cared deeply for us all. I have hugely happy memories of her loving and gentle encouragement. She was an attractive woman with long dark hair, slightly overweight, her size being something that she has always battled with. She is a very sociable person, a great cook and homemaker. Unlike my father, she could be physically affectionate and very warm, with a deep heart. She was always there for us, but she had her own demons to deal with in what was an at times very turbulent marriage. Due to these stresses she could be prone to bouts of rage.

On the wrong day, she'd chase us round the house with a broom – and if she caught us, she meant it. Maybe I inherited my interest in the paranormal and the spiritual from her too. She has certain abilities and has always felt things, with many of her pre-monitions coming true over the years. She used to do tarot cards and read runes for people from the estate. She'd regularly have visitors around the kitchen table, cups of tea and cigarettes, engrossed in a reading. This ability may have been passed down but I'm no card reader. My mother hails from a long line of women who just knew things.

I have many memories of a far more fractious nature; arguments, shouting and violence. During these Plas Madoc years, my father started having affairs. On one occasion my mother came home and found him in bed with a neighbour. I think in this instance, she left home for a few days. I felt terrified that she had abandoned us all. I kept asking my father if she would return, he simply replied that he didn't know. What a horrible feeling that was. On other occasions she would take me with her and we would take refuge at my grandparent's house after long train journeys through the night. I can't put these memories into any kind of sequence, I just know that these incidents were not uncommon. Any stability was beginning to crumble away.

My father would go out drinking and this would make my mother deeply unhappy. I was by now her confidant, a position I felt privileged to hold. Being the eldest, I was allowed to stay up with her, watching TV while she vented about what a bastard he was. These were not the happiest or healthiest of times, thinking back. I was permitted to watch TV shows too old for my years, like *The Sweeney* and *Tales of the Unexpected*, both iconic 1970s shows, but not always well suited to my already overactive imagination. No doubt as a reaction to her stress, my mother's cleaning obsession accelerated. It became a daily thing, with full spring cleans escalating into weekly affairs. We were required to help and were regular- ly trapped in the house most of the day to assist with these chores when we were off school. I felt stifled and imprisoned. Sometimes we'd sneak out first thing to avoid it, risking hefty consequences later. Any punishment was worth an occasional day of running free.

There was also an escalation in my father's violence and aggression. He became far more active with his faithful leather belt. My mother's temper spiralled too; she could be very hostile and frightening. Mainly she used words to injure and maim but on occasion she could get physical as well. Neither were happy, and arguments and atmospheres were fraught and frequent. Fights between them would break out, both of them being equally culpable.

It was a house full of tensions and worries, pain and fear and unpredictable safety and security. I began to become fearful and acutely aware of the atmosphere.

I'm sure my own conduct wasn't beyond reproach either. I lost the privilege of having my own room due to my unruly ways, although I can't recall exactly why this transpired. It was awarded to Alan, the middle brother. Thinking back, that house was very small. The three bedrooms were cramped, with a small living room and kitchen downstairs. The disturbing din of domestic violence regularly resounded around the confines of the tiny abode, both parents being armed with increasingly explosive tempers. Sometimes it felt like there was nowhere to hide and I sometimes I felt like didn't want to return home. It was a complex and perplexing environment.

Bad times were interspersed with times of happiness and harmony. There were car journeys and camping holidays, when mum would be singing Dolly Parton and we'd all be laughing. Embarrassing yes, but also happy. In some respect this contrast heightened my anxiety, I never knew what atmosphere to expect and I found myself constantly hoping for the best but bracing myself for the worst, wondering what mood the house would be in each time I returned home. It was about other people's moods and I was a sponge.

My mother's words could hurt more than any leather belt. She called me evil on occasion and this was only compounded by our Catholic faith. It had a long-term impact on my psychology and internal dialogue. As I suffered from psychosis in later years, these words returned repeatedly to haunt me. Please don't think badly of my mother. She was living with a heavy drinking adulterer, had three wild children to raise, in a climate of breadline finances. She had a huge amount of warmth and love to give as well. Everyone always loves my mother; she's funny, warm and real. She was always there for us, she wiped away our tears, cleaned us up, hugged us and loved us. We're still close to this day. She's a strong and remarkable woman.

As children, we had a habit of sneaking downstairs at night and helping ourselves to the treats such as biscuits and sweets. This was an ongoing crusade. In the end, bolts were fitted to the outside of our bedroom doors. At weekends we were trapped in our bedrooms until we were let out. We were all in the grip of a sugar addiction, I'm certain of it. As you will see, all three of us have what could politely be called addictive personalities. Our relentless quest for anything sweet caused a lot of trouble in that house. My father would buy bulk packs of sweets to bring the cost down, then he'd have to hide them. But we would hunt them down. I became very sneaky at a young age. If he'd hidden them in the car, I'd pinch the keys and grab some of the stash, polishing it off in one sitting. It was a game of cat and mouse, with extremely painful consequences. Somehow the thrashings could never deter me fully. It was all about the high, the thrill of the chase.

During this time, I graduated from infants to junior school. The new big school involved a daily bus journey into Wrexham. It was a Catholic school and I was now required to learn the Welsh language. Sadly, my only interest lay in learning swear words. I have happy memories of playing football – I was good at it and enjoyed being one of the better players. We played another version of it in the sports hall using a beanbag instead of a ball. This was also the venue for my very first fight. I punched a boy and made his nose pour with blood. It felt great, I'd won! The simple fact that he was a nice lad mattered little to me at the time. It must have been over something minor because I've no idea what sparked the scrap. Sadly, I spared little empathy for him at the time.

I also recollect another boy who had come over from South Africa. He told stories of fighting in a war and being given a gun. He couldn't have been more than twelve years old. Looking back, I'm not sure if it was true, but I do remember being hugely impressed and intrigued by him. It made me wonder what else went on in the wider world and it sparked my imagination. The school was run by very strict nuns; church attendance and hymn singing were compulsory. Unusually, I think my behaviour was fairly good at St. Mary's. I did however continue my, by now characteristic and undesirable, habit of stealing. The easiest pickings came from other pupils' pockets. I'd rifle through the coats in the cloakroom, sometimes chancing across some loose change or even the odd conker. I also stole some crystals from a display in the science class. After the teacher offered a reward, I 'found' them – but it was a trap. I pretended that I'd found them somewhere, but in hindsight, I'm sure the teacher knew that I'd stolen them.

On one occasion I stole one of my father's military medals and swapped it for a pile of conkers and marbles. It became the lucky recipient's prized possession before it was spotted by a teacher, who called my father into the school. I was steeped in shame and expected very unpleasant repercussions, but they never came. If only my father's more compassionate approach could have continued. The bad habits and dishonesty had started young.

At some point the whole school was relocated to new premises. I remember with fondness playing football, marbles and conkers in the new school yard. Far tougher times lay ahead.

I was taken fishing by my father's friend, Nigel and I loved it. I felt very privileged and all grown up. We'd hunt rabbits with air rifles and I loved the buzz of hunting and the thrill of the kill, but I especially took to fishing. I recall with pride catching my first fish, a nice fat trout. It had a big impact on me, from that moment on I was hooked. I continued with my passion for fishing for many years, I loved being out on the riverbanks, in the wilds, at one with nature. Before long I had my own fishing rod and air rifle and I felt like I'd won the lottery. I used to fire pellets at the cars on the street from my window, pretending I was a sniper, narrowly missing people on occasion. I was not the kind of boy who could be trusted with a pellet gun or to stay out of trouble for long. It was this same gun that my father shot Waldo with. I think it was a Sunday morning and Waldo was barking and being boisterous. Our father shot him bang in the arse. Poor Waldo ran off and didn't come back. We did go looking for him but my father assured us he would return when he was hungry enough – which he did.

Then came the arrival of a local supermarket and leisure centre. All very modern and fashionable, the pool even had a wave machine! A siren would blare to warn when the waves were about to start. We loved it. Of course, the new supermarket sold plenty of sweets and biscuits and I soon took to stealing these frequently. The first thing I stole was a packet of marshmallow biscuits. I'd planned it out and I got away with it too. I made off with my haul, filled with a mixture of pride and guilt. It gave me a thrill, a buzz, again I was hooked.

We were crazy kids, getting up to all sorts of misdemeanours. There was a railway line nearby and we used to pile stones onto the tracks. The experiment was to see if the train would crush the rocks. I think there was also the added excitement of wondering what would happen if the rocks came off best. Luckily the rocks were always crushed and the trains and passengers escaping unscathed. Soon planks of wood and bricks joined the pile, as we and other kids upped the ante. Thankfully we stopped doing it before disaster struck, but this was more by luck than judgement I suspect. Yet again I was drawn to danger, drawn to walking near the edge, we all were, with total disregard for the potentially deadly consequences. A pattern was forming.

At some point my Auntie Lidia came to live with us. She was my father's youngest sister and somehow she'd ended up in care. My father took her out of care and brought her into the household, almost as if she were his adopted daughter. Having lost two other sisters in childhood, one to leukaemia and another in a fire, he possibility felt a desire to help or save

Lidia. She was therefore my auntie, but also a sort-of sister, it was a strange set-up. There was even less space in the already small house, with me and my two brothers now needing to share a room. I think she was with us for about two years.

I found it difficult and challenging. I felt infuriated that she didn't seem to be punished to the same degree that we were. She was disciplined with the leather strap I think, but she was always taken to another room, so I never saw it happen. Either way it was a strange state of affairs; he was either pretending to punish her, or he was thrashing his own sister in private. Even in my naivety, it seemed like an odd arrangement. Lidia and I also used to mess around, kissing and touching. I carried shame around this, feeling like I had committed incest of some sort. I'm sure I was, in part, echoing my earlier encounter with the babysitter. Later it transpired that we were not blood related at all and I felt some reprieve from the shame that had clung to me. I was not to see Lidia again for nearly forty years.

To add to my various reputable little hobbies, I also started smoking. I've no idea why it seemed like a good idea but I pinched a cigarette and took it out to the railway tracks. It made me sick as a dog, I heaved up strange vomit and felt utterly horrible. However, this was not about to deter me; they were minor details. It had given me a new buzz so I persevered, and in no time became a hardened smoker. And a thieving smoker at that. With no means to buy cigarettes, my only option was to steal from any unattended packet. My mother would be beside herself without her cigarettes, so having an opportunistic thief about didn't help. She'd really lose her marbles if deprived of nicotine, and if she then found even a speck of dust, it was game over. It was not uncommon to see an airborne can of Mr Sheen furniture polish spinning towards my head. One day she raided our piggy banks for fag money. We'd saved for months to buy a kite on holiday, then watched as our kite dreams literally went up in smoke. She never did pay us back fully as promised. Maybe she just forgot, she had bigger problems to deal with, I'm sure. A big thing though, when you're a kid and money is scarce.

One day Alan somehow managed to pour white spirit all over his school trousers. In a panic he decided to dry them off by standing close to the fire. It was the seventies, everything was made of nylon and this was an electric bar heater. He went up in a big whoosh of furious flames, screaming out in pain as the flames took hold. I didn't know what to do. Luckily my father was upstairs and heard the screams. Stark bollock naked, he took off from the top of the stairs in one leap landing at the bottom. In one fluid motion he wrapped Alan in a thick rug to stop the fire in its tracks. Knowing not to remove the melted fabric he kept him tightly wrapped. He drove the eight miles to Wrexham Hospital, Alan still swaddled in the rug, his feet sticking out of the open window to keep them cool. Alan spent weeks and weeks in hospital, having skin grafts and acute pain medication. A very painful lesson for Alan, but it taught Teddy nothing.

Teddy was possibly the most problematic of us all and he continued to possess an enduring fascination with fire. He'd regularly start cupboard fires, normally choosing cupboards that held items which were seldom used, such as tents and old clothing. Sometimes we'd catch it early and put it out before our parents found out, other times we couldn't. I've no idea why he kept doing this, he just did. I can imagine it must have been very concerning on many levels for our parents. He knew he'd get a good hiding for it, but he continued undeterred. This soon developed into a full-time hobby, and he began dropping matches into car petrol tanks as well. I don't know how long this little phase lasted for, but I do remember seeing a car completely burnt out down our street and Alan telling me "that's our Teddy." Back then not all cars had locks on petrol tanks and you could unscrew them. Teddy would unscrew them, drop a match in and run. Easy as one, two, three and crazy behaviour for a boy of his age. He couldn't have been more than six or seven. Teddy's dangerous conduct escalated further as the years went by. Later we realised that he had serious mental health problems, but at that time he was receiving punishment as opposed to treatment. Sometimes I wonder what difference the right help might have made. I wish I could say that Teddy's story had a happy ending.

I too had my own dalliances with fire, just not as regularly as Teddy. Once I doused an abandoned building in petrol, before sitting back and watching the flames spread and take hold. It was mesmerising. I'd also set fire to the dry grass on the wastelands in summer, waiting patiently for the fire to spread. I was always up to some variety of misbehaviour. I remember one day finding a perfectly symmetrical forked thin tree in the woods. On closer inspection I noted that it was especially springy, perfect as a catapult. After pridefully constructing the inventive and powerful weapon, I decided it was a good idea to fire rocks at passing cars on the main road. Having missed several times, I made a direct hit. As my eyes focused in on the car as luck would have it, and to my horror, I realised that it was a police car. All bravery evaporated, and I legged it deep into the woods, hiding for hours in a cramped and sodden underground den left long abandoned. That night I went home pretending everything was normal, all the while worried that there might be a knock at the door. Thankfully the knock never came, not that time anyway.

We regularly climbed over a ten-foot-high stone wall that dropped down onto this same fast-moving main road. We needed to cross that road to get deeper into the woods and ponds. I always found the woods enticing and magical; exploring them was endlessly exciting. On one occasion I didn't want to go, I wanted to play football with my brothers. So the rest of the gang set off, among them a good friend called Simon, a younger boy from an Italian family. Later, news spread that he had been killed, hit by a car after scaling the wall. I don't know what transpired that day, but whatever happened, he was gone and he wouldn't be coming back. I was aware that if I had gone with them, maybe I could have prevented it. In some sense I felt guilty and res-ponsible. I also knew that it could have been me killed that day. It was the first time I'd experienced death at close quarters. I remember seeing his sister, whom I quite liked, being very tearful and clearly upset on the bus to school. It could have been a wake-up call, but it passed by unheeded. It never stopped us using the same route again.

Another little habit I had was also an omen of what the future was to hold. I would be taken on TV repair call-outs with my father. Sometimes 'foreigners' at night, sometimes long boring days, driving miles in between customers. I'd be left waiting in the car, sometimes for a very long time. I'd always liked the smell of the solvent he kept in his toolbox. By chance, one night, I discovered that sniffing the stuff produced a heady and intense buzz. Sometimes I'd sniff so much I'd totally trip out and not have a clue where or who I was. It was pokey stuff and you only needed a small squib. A couple of times I had comedowns, although I was too young to know what they were. I'd feel low and depressed, without really knowing why. Minor blips, but I loved sniffing those moreish aromatic vapours.

My father had a bar in our sitting room, it was always well stocked for their frequent parties and gatherings. We'd already started sneaking caps of whisky and other spirits. This went unnoticed for a while but my consumption must have increased over time. One day my Godfather Brummie had come over with his new girlfriend. He knew my father from the SAS and he was also a mountaineer, somewhat famous at that time for climbing Mount Everest and losing his toes to frostbite. Then I made a spectacle of myself by trying, and failing, to ride my push-bike. I think my parents were amused at first, but this quickly turned to concern as I became violently ill. I was struck down by a ruthless headache and vomiting. The next day I promised my mother that I would never drink again, and I remember her saying "I hope you've learnt your lesson." I said, "I have," and I meant it.

Chapter Three

Chester

Our move to Chester hailed the beginning of a new era. I was growing up and times were changing. My innocence was in rapid decline, as was the family unit. The move was due to my father's employment as a TV engineer and we found ourselves living on a different council housing estate, on the edge of the city, again surrounded by countryside. The whole family was excited. A fresh start – new house, new job, new school, new city, new beginnings. The pinnacle of my excitement was the rumour of an adventure playground, built like a giant fortress. I ended up spending many hours there, honing my climbing and adventure skills. The move was both exciting and daunting.

Chester was far bigger than Plas Madoc and it felt huge and intimidating to me. We knew no-one. Luckily, I enjoyed my new school, St Theresa's, where I was to finish my junior school years. Yet again it was a Catholic school and church-going was compulsory. I also had a confirmation ceremony where I had to pick an additional name for myself. Foolishly I choose 'James', the name of a classmate who I must have idolised to some extent. I don't think this is how I was meant to pick a name, and it somewhat backfired. I ended up detesting him and for a long time felt stupid for naming myself after him. A real schoolboy error, however I like the name now.

Bizarrely this school put on random lunchtime discos with the latest pop music and flashy disco lighting, which we each paid two whole pence to attend. By now I was starting to notice girls. Boys and girls would meet at the discos, or in the woods after school. It was here that I enjoyed my very first kiss. When I say 'enjoyed', I mean I ran off into the woods as soon as it was over. It was an unbearably big deal to me; I didn't know how to behave, so I retreated rapidly.

There is one teacher who I will never forget. I liked her, she was one of the good ones, she was kind and she cared. Then she started talking to herself and behaving oddly. She'd be teaching one minute and then seconds later she'd do these strange aside comments like "I wish I was dead and so were you". She rarely bothered to lower her voice and her behaviour became more and more erratic. Eventually news of her curious behaviour must have filtered up to the powers that be and some of us were called to the headmistress's office. I said I'd heard her saying these unusual things. I can only assume that she'd had some sort of breakdown or mental health crisis. We never saw that teacher again and I have no idea what became of her. Sad really. Overall, my memories of that school are good. My conduct wasn't too bad, bar the odd roof climbing exploit.

I was enjoying meeting new people, exploring a new environment and finding my feet. We found a canal not far from the house and we'd go swimming in summer, even though the water was filthy. In winter, if it froze over, we'd go 'shoe skating'.

Sometimes we'd skate for miles, listening avidly for cracking sounds and avoiding the danger areas. Miraculously we never fell through and I loved the buzz of literally skating on thin ice. Flirting with death and danger, yet again.

It was around this age that me and my brothers started growing apart; I wanted to play with the bigger lads. Teddy was always a problem child and sadly still a bed wetter. I started to feel embarrassed about him. He was always a very loveable, sensitive, crazy kid and I feel sad that I was ever embarrassed about him, but I was. There was a jealousy issue developing between Alan and me. It'd been brewing for a long while. He was a more aggressive kid and he felt our grandparents favoured me, so there was a competitive and jealous vibe between us, which worsened over the ensuing years.

Alan is blessed with a wicked sense of humour though. He's as dry as a fossilised femur, and we used to have some real fun too. We'd frequently be in hysterics, impersonating people, doubled over in belly laughs. The laughs kept us sane to some extent. By now I had started to become aware that our home life was far darker and very different to the home life of most of my friends. I wanted to distance myself from it as much as possible. A sense of shame had started to develop.

I also rekindled my love for fishing on the canals and waterways of Chester. I'd been given a rod for Christmas, so I'd take myself off exploring the fishing territories. I wasn't very good to begin with, but slowly I learnt that it was a skill, an art, and I loved it. I spent hundreds of hours honing my expertise and refining my art. Slowly over time I increased my equipment supplies; a basket here, a new reel there. I enjoyed meeting older fishermen and learning from them. It was an uncharacteristically sensible pastime, I suppose. To me, it felt like freedom.

At some point came the bombshell that rocked my already wobbly foundations to the core. Alan came running down the stairs one summer afternoon, full of glee. He was shouting "you're not one of us, our dad's not your dad, you're not one of us!" At first, I wasn't bothered, I assumed he was lying, but then he said, "I have proof," and my inner alarm bell jingled loudly. He'd found my adoption papers! Alan took great pleasure in taunting me, his submerged jealousy jubilant at last. Eventually I was reduced to tears. Only then did he stop his unremitting cruelty. I waited anxiously to ask my parents when they got home. My mother tried to make light of it, saying, "it's not important, John is the only father you've ever had." She said, "your real father is buried in a churchyard in Hereford," Her comforting helped but it didn't abolish my fear and alienation.

I used to look over at that churchyard when we drove by when visiting Hereford, but the sense of my absent heritage didn't really hit me until I had emerged from many more bad chapters of my life. I had many unanswered questions and unproven theories. I went looking for answers that would prove very elusive. Answers that I still hope to find.

At home, the same dynamics continued. Things would go wrong, no-one would own up, so we would all be punished. My father's faithful leather belt was in more frequent use now. The level of punishment was often baffling, depending on his mood, rather than the severity of the offence. Like Pavlov's dogs I'd automatically become anxious at the mere sight of his car, or the sound of his car door closing, developing a primal fear of him and even his car. That car is still seared into my memory, a white Escort estate with the registration PFR 92M. I was on constant bad mood alert, knowing that his mood dictated the atmosphere of the entire house. If we were lucky, we'd be sent to bed early without any tea. I remember watching children playing out on summer evenings while we'd be locked in. I found that almost as torturous as physical punishment.

I didn't like feeling trapped or having my wings clipped. I remember being grounded for the whole summer holidays once. A whole summer of being imprisoned and watching out the window while helping with my mother's never-ending household chores. The doorstep became my boundary. If I crossed that, the belt would come out, so I was terrified to even go into the garden. On occasion my mother would let me out for a couple of hours, putting herself on the line for me. We were both fearful that he might return home from work early. That was not a happy summer. I can't remember what I'd done, but I do know that I was a bit of a thief. I'd steal sweets, cigarettes and money. In fact, I was a lot of a thief, especially with money. I knew that if I got caught, I'd get a severe belting, but I'd still do it.

I'd sneak into my parent's bedroom and dip his pockets from time to time, my heart pounding from sheer terror and adrenaline. Maybe I need to explain just how close to the wind I was sailing when I performed this fearsome exploit. Bear in mind they'd be asleep in bed when I undertook this most tactical of manoeuvres. I'd carefully plotted a cunning technique which included added subterfuge. Armed with cups of tea, brewed with love, care and cunning, I'd enter their room in the morning, under the guise of this kindly gesture. Then I'd try to dip his jacket pocket in split seconds on my way past, my hands shaking from adrenaline overload. If they stirred, I'd have the pre-prepared excuse that I was bringing them tea; what a good son I was. Carefully thought out as it was, it was a nauseatingly risky pursuit. The consequences of being caught were unbearably painful, but the buzz of a successful mission was thrillingly addictive. I suppose it was one of the few ways I could get one over on this formidable opponent too. I think the satisfaction of success was as important to me as the monetary reward it brought. A fix more potent than any narcotic. One of my first addictions was stealing.

A similar exploit involved stealing from the payphone he'd installed in the hallway downstairs. It was a proper payphone with a lockable cash drawer. This replaced the usual circular dial phone which had been over-used due to the fact that calls could be made when it was locked. We had learned that we could tap the two pins that the receiver would sit on equal to the number we wanted to dial. For instance if we wanted the number 4 we would tap four times, this way we could call other phones. This was called tapping and any self-respecting credibility aspiring juvenile knew how to do this. The problem then was though that the bills were off the scale and arguments would ensue when they came in.

He'd installed it to keep on top of the bills. I've no idea where he got it from, but the lockable drawer was used to store additional money that would go toward all of the household bills. I saw a tiny window of opportunity and on occasion braved another highly tactical manoeuvre. It was best carried out when the whole family was watching *Star Trek*. It was his favourite programme, so I could be more confident that he would stay glued to the TV. He bore an uncanny resemblance to William Shatner's Captain Kirk and maybe this was why he loved the show so much. I'd ask if anyone wanted a cup of tea, giving myself a chink of opportunity. First task – put the kettle on while rooting through his pockets in the hallway for the key. If they were there it was game on! Grabbing the key from his jacket pocket, I'd quickly unlock the box. My whole body would tremble with anxiety. If I'd been caught with my hands in the cookie jar it was game over, never mind game on! Then I'd re-enter the TV room while the kettle boiled, acting all casual. Second task – put the tea in to brew while raiding the cash drawer, for a tenner maybe. Then re-enter the living room as the tea brewed, nonchalant and relaxed yet again. Third task – retrieve the perfectly brewed tea while locking the box on the way past. An anxiety inducing trio of terrifying tactics.

My ears would be straining to pick up any movement from the living room. A couple of times he got up to go to the loo during this lengthy process, leaving me vulnerable to discovery. My little heart would be pounding to breaking point. Discovery was unimaginable. I never got caught doing this, although money was discovered missing several times. The mystery remained unsolved but it caused added tension between my parents. He and my mother were the only ones who had keys, and it created arguments and mistrust between them. After a successful mission the thrill of the score was incredible, not unlike the thrill of the drug chase in later years. Then I'd be on edge for days and the acting would need to continue consistently. I couldn't let my brothers know I had money either but thankfully my acting skills were pretty good by that age. Over time I gradually became a more elusive and accomplished thief and I found it addictive. It was also a means to an end, worth the constant fear. Money meant a kind of freedom, a commodity I had little of.

I'd spend this hard-won cash on bus rides out with my friends, cigarettes and sweets. Or I copied the older kids and developed a taste for gaming machines like *Space Invaders* and *Pacman*. I didn't limit my light-fingered activities to the home either. I was caught stealing a brooch from Woolworths and ended up in Juvenile Court that time. We also used to regularly hit the gift shop in the cathedral, where I'd taken a liking to some large handcrafted leather crosses. They'd looked very expensive to my magpie-like eyes. I squeezed in over the locked arched gates and stole a big pile of them, before foolishly attempting to sell them at school. Somehow, I got caught and it brought much shame upon the family. Of course, a good leathering followed shortly after. Stealing crosses from the cathedral was considered a lowly deed within a Catholic school and family, the police being involved was just an added calamity. I can't say I was God-fearing at that time – and if I was, I did not care

I remember thinking 'where is this God?', when all this abuse is happening at home, 'where is he?', 'where is the justice?' Once, after being beaten and banished to my room without tea yet again, I watched the other kids playing in the street and became angry at this so-called God. I decided to make a pact with his enemy the devil. I spoke out loud to him, promising my soul to him if he would release me from this living hell. This connection I felt to the dark side was to haunt me for many years. Later, in a drug addled psychosis I recall begging a priest to exorcise me. I'd become convinced that being born in the sixth month of 1966 was of grave and dark significance. I believe my upbringing, the harsh contrast between being God-fearing and the apparent Godlessness, contributed to these later traumas. It took many years for me to reconnect with faith.

After the initial honeymoon period of Chester, the domestic violence at home started to escalate. It seemed to spring out of nowhere and became more regular and more severe. I was constantly on edge, never knowing what to expect, or when to expect it. Home felt far from a safe haven. My mother was no angel, but no-one was a match for my formidable father. He suffered from terrifying rages. In addition, he began taunting me that I was a "bastard", which of course stung me hard, and I began to develop a deep sense of shame about it. Even my mother would call me the same, when she flew into one of her tempers. On one occasion we both ended up hurt. We were huddled together in the bathroom, her mouth was bleeding and I felt so broken. I think she had tried to defend me but was powerless against a trained, powerful and furious opponent. It hurt physically but the emotional damage was far more brutal.

It disturbed me to watch my mother being brutalised and abused. It haunted me. Sometimes she'd lash out at him too, she could be feisty and foolish. The violence wasn't always one-sided. Knowing what I know now, I'm certain his rages sprang from his own trauma and PTSD. Probably being formed in his own violent childhood and intensified through his experiences in combat. He wouldn't have known this, he had only focused on bettering himself and escaping that life – and he had succeeded, oblivious to the fact that he had brought his old traumas along for the ride, ready to inflict them upon the next generation. As a child, I understood none of this, he was simply an infallible adversary. I was too young to understand these cycles as a child, but as soon as I was old enough, I could see them plain as day. I later made a commitment to break the cycle, stop the loop, which also included the responsibility of me addressing my own acting out of the vicious cycle of abuse.

By now I was at a Catholic high school, on the other side of the city. It seemed very far away and the commute consisted of two sizeable bus journeys. There was a school bus but we used to miss it frequently. Some days I'd get a lift with my father. On other days, I'd have spent my bus fare in the tuck shop and I'd have to walk for the rest of the week. I'd walk it regularly, it took about an hour. Sometimes I'd go off into the city centre to pinch sweets from shops on route to school. I'd happily cross the city on foot. Back then, if you wanted to see a friend you'd have to walk. It was years before the dawn of the mobile phone and it was common to walk for miles only to find no-one was home. It seems crazy now, but back then it was the way things were done. Walking didn't bother me, I was a very fit kid, most kids were.

Some of the characters from that school really stuck in my mind. One poor lad was riddled with chronic eczema and his skin would dislodge in chunks every time he scratched. He was an incredibly bright lad and I'm relieved to report that no-one picked on the poor sod. We must have felt sorry for him, and he was shown a rare bout of compassion in a dog eat dog school. Before long I was moved down from the top class, I suspect due to my disruptive tendencies and class clown persona. With shame and dread I'd trudge home with damning report cards, marking me out as a clown or as not trying. These crippled me; my father was a highly intelligent man with qualifications in electronic engineering, maths and astrophysics. The consequences of a bad report could therefore be brutally painful. Would it just be a telling off, or the dreaded belt? Sometimes we were even threatened with the buckle end.   The suspense was agonising.

The violence at home continued to worsen. It was starting to concern my mother too, who frequently tried to intervene, only to find herself powerless to help us. Father used to say that I was old enough to be beaten like a man and he started to use his fists. Cleverly, he struck areas that couldn't be seen, maybe a punch or two to the stomach. Often it was a painful mixture of this and the belt as well. I regularly feared for my life. He suffered from a deep and petrifying rage and I never knew when he would stop. One time I felt like I'd had the life beaten out of me, quite literally. I was covered in bruises and welts all over my legs and back. Shortly after, we went to visit my grandparents. My grandmother knew that something wasn't right, she could see that my spirit was broken. Somehow, she discovered my injuries. Mortified, she put me to bed and cuddled me to sleep. The next day she spoke to my parents and there was uproar. By this stage I was utterly terrified of him, he seemed to be an indestructible and merciless force with an unforgiving rage. I wished that I would never be sent back with them, but I was.

As if we three brothers didn't have enough violence to contend with, we also used to fight amongst ourselves. As the eldest, to some extent, I was held responsible for keeping the others in check. An impossible task, seeing as they were both as crazy as me. Accidents and misdemeanours would happen frequently and I usually bore the brunt of the responsibility. Often it wasn't even my fault and it felt painfully unfair. The three of us would get into real scraps which frequently ended in something in the house being broken. Then the fear would kick in, real, crippling fear.

Once, I was held up by my throat against the wall and savagely strangled, somehow my shoulder was dislocated too. At times like this I had a genuine fear that I would be killed. I never knew when his rage would subside or how far he would go. This brutality was deeply traumatic and instilled a morbid fear of dying in me. I was a young teenager at the mercy of a trained, angry and brutal man. He was a brute, a bully. I don't think he could control his rage though, it came from a very deep and scary place. He was a trained soldier and a good one, having served in Northern Ireland and Aden. A formidable opponent for anyone to face, let alone a child.

In the hallway of that house hung a big jungle knife, maybe about eighteen inches long. It was the real deal, the size of a small sword and razor sharp. I spent many a night seriously contemplating and fantasising about plunging it into his chest while he slept. I desperately wanted him dead so I could feel safe. By now, I hated him with my every fibre. While this desire was very strong, my fear of failing and getting caught was even stronger. It was not my morals that stopped me but my paralysing fear. A testament to my desperation, distress and hatred. Once, a drinking party at our house got out of hand and I heard a commotion outside. I watched him holding my mother down in the garden while he ripped her clothes off, screaming "is this what you want?" I was shouting for him to get off her, but I could nothing to help her. I was so tired of feeling weak and powerless.

Their relationship was getting ever more toxic and violent. I'm sure our behaviour didn't help matters either. We were all on the slippery slope towards the dark years that lay ahead. My bad behaviour at school started to escalate; frequently I'd be in detention or get the cane. The cane was little deterrent for me, it was nothing compared to what I endured at home. Mainly we found it laughable, deeming certain teachers wimps. Sometimes we'd put books down our trousers and wouldn't feel it at all. Overall, it wasn't a sufficient deterrent to end my unruly ways. One teacher did however command respect, the dreaded maths teacher. I always wanted to make people laugh, desperate for the good attention. I also figured that if I made people laugh, then I wouldn't be bullied. Bullying was commonplace and cruel.

So in my attempt to win class approval, I was caught out by this fearsome maths teacher and I paid a painfully high price. He had three canes, and on this occasion, he sadistically selected his medium-weight one. I held my hand out while he took a run up, and that cane came down with such force the pain was almost indescribable. I was reduced to tears and the ends of my fingers later became swollen and bruised. I didn't tell my parents, that would just lead to more misfortune. One thing's for sure, I didn't mess about in his lessons ever again. Unsurprisingly, maths was never my favourite subject.

As I grew older, I began absconding from school. I'd go AWOL habitually, with a boy called Britty from a different school, who lived down the road from me. He was a tall thin lad, with big ears that stuck out through his black pudding bowl haircut. I liked him because he had a very quick wit. We shared an adventurous spirit and spent a lot of time together. His parents had split up and he lived with his dad, who had an ice cream van but also claimed benefits on the side. He was mostly left to his own devices and we'd spend our schooldays down on another council house estate with an older woman, whom he was somehow related to. Strangely, she had her own kids and she knew we were skiving, but she happily supplied us with fags and cups of tea. Many days were spent there, smoking fags, drinking tea and chatting shit. She was involved with a drinker, and she was probably a drinker herself, looking back. Later, I became aware that he was a criminal and involved in heroin. Unknowingly, I'd entered a much darker world.

On our estate, gangs of kids would gather round on the streets. We called them grebos, they were into rock music and motorbikes. Half of me wanted to be in their gang and the other half was afraid of being bullied by them. A couple of them had bullied me in the past, so they made me feel on edge. These were tricky times for me. Alan was better at standing his own ground, suffered less bullying, and was far more popular in these circles. I never really felt like I fitted in, yet I wanted to be out of the house as much as possible. Some of the grebo's gave me the nickname Quee, short for queer. It's just what kids do but I found it shameful and demoralising. At other times, I'd feel part of the gang and then I felt great, bullet-proof and safe. It still felt like a perilous existence.

Most of the time we were preoccupied with smoking fags, scrounging fags or stealing the money to buy fags. At school there was a crevice behind the sports hall called smoker's corner. Someone would keep watch for patrolling teachers. It was safe, unless the teachers combined forces and organised a pincer movement. The deputy head, nicknamed Killer, took matters further though, he'd climb up onto the roof to photograph us. At his leaving assembly, the photos he'd taken of us were displayed on a big screen in the main hall. We watched in amazement as his revealing collection of photos was broadcast to the whole school. It was like an homage to his skills and diligence as a teacher. We all feared the possible repercussions but they never came.

At this school there was a big craze for running up to people and kicking them hard in the bollocks. I seemed to be on the receiving end a lot, and it goes without saying that it hurt. It meant you always had to be on guard. Sometimes I thought I'd made a new friend, then all of sudden, they'd kick me in the bollocks and run off laughing. It was a trust no-one atmosphere. If I got a bigger lad back, I'd get a leathering for it, so occasionally I ended up picking on the weaker boys. A tough life in a cruel dog eat dog world.

I played on the school football team for a while, mainly as a sub, but I enjoyed it. I loved the camaraderie of football. Everyone supported different teams. I supported Liverpool, the team passed down through the family. I remember getting the Liverpool strip for my birthday and being thrilled. My parents, for all their flaws, always did their very best at Christmas and birthdays. We usually got what we'd asked for, which can't have been easy for them. We'd always celebrate with nice family meals, friendly and bountiful and in blunt contrast to the commonplace brutality. I never knew what to expect, never felt I could properly relax. It was a life of stark duality.

To highlight this contrast, I would frequently spend the summer holidays at my grandparents in Hereford. Often, it would just be me who went. My poor brothers would not get the same holiday. The thought of going there was more exciting than any Christmas or birthday and I would relish the thought of escaping into the freedom of a loving home. I loved every day I was there. I had friends there too, who I could play out with until dark, which was late in the summer months. We'd go adventuring all day, maybe going fishing or playing footy. I would return in the evenings without worry about what awaited me. I could choose what I wanted to eat, sometimes I'd even be given money to go down to the local chippy as a treat. Then I could sit in front of the TV and eat my chippy tea, feeling relaxed and at peace. I could flourish, make choices and be free. I didn't need to live in fear. Grandmother would make big huge jars of pickled onions and I could help myself without fear of retribution. All my needs were met and I had the care and space to be me.

I suppose in some ways my grandparents spoilt me, either way this nurturing significantly improved my behaviour. My desire to rebel and act out faded away. My good behaviour was rewarded; it wasn't just my bad behaviour that was punished. I wasn't scrutinised to the same extent if I was slightly late home. I wouldn't be grounded for a week, it was no big deal. Both my grandparents were good, decent and very kind folk. My grandfather was a peaceful and passive man. He did, however, possess a very unusual quirk. He had suffered a serious injury in the war, after serving in the Military Police. He had a huge wound on his leg that never healed and required constant treatment. It was a deep shrapnel wound caused by a landmine explosion, in which two fellow soldiers had been killed. As a result of this, he would become very effected by certain TV programmes. He loved western films, especially a John Wayne classic, or occasionally a war film. Very often at the sound of the gunfire he would rise rapidly from his chair, draw his imaginary pistol, and fire it vigorously at the screen. He'd even make gunfire sound effects, "pow, pow, pow". Then he'd freeze, posed, guns still aimed at the TV, like a statue. It was so normal to us, we used to say "granddad's off again" and get on with our lives. Sometimes he'd be frozen there for an age. We were told that it was his shellshock and we were trained, from a young age, not to walk up behind him, as he might attack. Eventually he'd revert to normal granddad and act as if nothing had happened. I don't even think he remembered what he'd just done. He'd been completely somewhere else. It was funny, strange and sad, all at the same time.

Hereford was more spacious and spread out than Chester. I loved it. It wasn't as built up as the council estates I was used to. It felt like home, and I dreaded going back to my actual home, where I was no was longer allowed to breathe as a child. My summers of bliss would always have to come to an end. Returning to Chester was tearful and always a very painful shock to my system. My father didn't like me going away, believing they were too soft on me. I probably returned rejuvenated (literally) and he resented the change in my attitude. However, the happy child would not endure for long. Instinctively, I knew that this home life was wrong and my life at my grandparents' house was right. This contrast and duality heightened my awareness, and I would return home more defiant and cheeky. I'd found my voice and that was not allowed.

At home we were also subjected to the regular sound of our parents having sex. Our bedrooms were close and the walls thin. It used to disturb me occasionally. Sometimes she'd be screaming "you're hurting me" and we'd feel really distressed, wondering for hours if she was all right. Often, she'd emerge happy and smiling; it was both confusing and troubling. We also found his porno mag collection stashed in the bottom of his wardrobe, some of them a long way from mainstream. It left me with confused and conflicting attitudes towards sex.

Alan and Teddy were as badly beaten as me at times and I hated listening to them being beaten too. Even though the three of us led more separate lives by now, we were united and had a strong bond forged from the violence at home. Their screams and their pleadings, their cries for help, "please, please Dad don't!" would deeply torment me. I couldn't bear it, it haunted me yet I was powerless to help. My father's rage and strength were so extreme that it literally sounded like they were pleading for their lives, tantamount to listening to someone being tortured. All I could do was try not to imagine what was happening and cover my ears. That too left its emotional mark.

Poor Teddy, who was only about eight or nine at this point, seemed especially vulnerable. He was the smallest and even back then we all knew he was the most mentally fragile, yet he was granted no mercy. Later, he was to be diagnosed with schizophrenia, which I'm sure was worsened by his childhood. He also maintained his fascination with fire. There was always something very unpredictable about Teddy's behaviour and I never knew what he would do next. He also struggled at school, as he was poor at reading and writing, which led to him becoming frustrated. Apparently, he could remember whole books if they were read to him, yet he was well behind with his reading skills. This was before dyslexia was commonly picked up but it seems very likely that he had this as well. One day, in a fit of frustration, he had thrown his chair across the classroom. He was taken aside to discuss his behaviour and somehow the school became aware that he was covered in deep strap marks. Even in an era when a good thrashing was commonplace, the teachers were horrified. I can understand my father's desire to instil discipline, but when I consider the brutality and cruelty of his actions I cannot reconcile the two.

He was a bully, who transferred his own damage onto his children.

Due to this incident at Teddy's school, Social Services were alerted. We were all ushered into a meeting and questioned about our family life. My mother whispered to me "be honest". My father was in the spotlight. I felt afraid to be truthful and felt some strange misguided loyalty to him too. I timidly answered their questions, although I'm sure I minimised the truth. His behaviour within the family had been exposed and the beatings stopped. He'd obviously received a pretty serious warning. Keeping his temper constrained must have been tough for him, but for the time being he managed it. There was more harmony in the house at long last. I felt that there was a glimmer of hope and a chink of justice.

I felt vindicated. What had been going on was wrong, just as I inherently knew it had been. Our behaviour improved and as a result of being treated with more compassion, our desire to rebel and lash out was reduced. He couldn't keep it up for ever though, one day his temper would crack. His free rein over the home was lessened for the time being. He was under pressure and I enjoyed it greatly. My sense of despair and powerlessness diminished; that same sense of despair that had led me to make my pact with the devil. My life lightened, just a shade.

Slowly though, the thrashing crept back into our lives and I concocted a plan with my friend Britty. His dad had an ice-cream van and he could always pinch cash with relative ease. I had access to my mother's family allowance book, which I knew would be my most serious offence to date. The consequences being so dire, I couldn't even contemplate them, but the plan was to finally escape and was rebellious. My father was away in Germany on a Territorial Army climbing expedition. So we gathered our financial resources and ran away. We had cash but hadn't even thought to take warm coats. It really was a good example of piss poor preparation. Somehow, we caught several trains and ended up in the bright lights of Blackpool. We wandered the streets before sitting on a wall to eat our chips, as we watched the fairground rides swirling by. A child's paradise, or so we thought.

Then it dawned on us, "where are we going to sleep?" Our money was already starting to run low and our grand plans were suddenly reduced to a painfully sharp focus. After rummaging through the back streets near the prom, we found an open storage shed. We tried to sleep in there but it was freezing and dirty, so we started yet again to roam the streets. Somehow, we were lucky enough to bump into

Patrick, a filthy dirty chronic alcoholic. He said we could stay with him and we followed him to his grimy, foul-smelling flat. He offered us his luxurious floor and we slept amid the discarded beer cans and fag burns. He gave us a few fags but refused to share his drink with us. We didn't want to be there at all. Freedom had started to look a bit grim. The next morning, we left in a hurry, anxious to escape the filth. By now our money had gone and we were beginning to feel very vulnerable. I decided we should go to my grandparents, always a haven of safety for me. We'd realised our grand plan had been fatally flawed. The big wide world suddenly seemed a very scary place and we were on the run.

Going back home to the consequences was not an option; even the thought terrified me. The new plan required us to dodge the train all the way down to Hereford and we eventually made it, kipping in public toilets overnight. We crossed the fields towards my grandparent's house as the sun was rising and the grass was dewy. I was so relieved, so cold. We ended up hiding in their shed for a couple of days, pinching bits of food from the kitchen when opportunity arose. It felt good to have safety close by at least. When we were finally discovered, my grandmother refused us sanctuary and called my parents. I'm guessing she didn't want to get involved with the whole situation, which was also a legal matter by then. We were after all teenagers, so we bolted. I felt shocked and rejected; I didn't understand.

I couldn't go home, it was unthinkable, so we decided to go to Britty's Aunty in Birmingham. We got there and were fed a big meal, which we wolfed down with sheer delight. I sat back thinking everything was great, thinking we could stay long term and wondering what my new school would be like. I was oblivious to the seriousness of the situation. Before long there was a loud knock at the door. The police had arrived and off to the police station we went. The gravity of our plight slowly dawned on us as we sat in our cells at the station. They'd left the cell doors open, but it still wasn't a good feeling. We weren't under arrest but we were in trouble. It was to be my first of many visits to the nick.

Unbeknown to me, my father had to cancel his entire mountaineering trip to Germany, letting the whole team down. Things were not looking good at all! He stormed in, my mother trailing in his wake. He was very angry. Eventually we were dragged out of the station and into the car. As we took off home, I was more terrified than I have ever been in my entire life. He'd already made it crystal clear that I'd be getting the hiding of my life when we got home. Sporadically, he'd spin round in his seat to punch and threaten me. I was beyond petrified, in genuine fear for my life. It was the longest drive of my life. I was sent straight upstairs when we got home. Waiting, wondering and then more waiting.

The waiting was worse than the beatings sometimes.

I think my mother was trying to negotiate my reprieve, but on this occasion she failed. Eventually he came up the stairs and gave me the worse beating I'd ever had. He kept saying that I was old enough to be hit like a man and it seemed to go on forever. Then he said his mate Gary was coming up to beat me too, as I'd ruined his trip as well. All Gary's abuse was verbal fortunately and he didn't hurt me physically, but it was disturbing all the same. I think sometimes my mother was genuinely worried that he was going to kill one of us. The screaming and pleadings that emanated from those beatings must have carried down the whole street. I later heard that Britty had barely gotten into any trouble at all, whereas I was lucky to be alive. Life felt bitterly unfair.

My father was continuing his extra-marital activities and had been caught numerous times. The marriage was in serious trouble but my mother was painfully co-dependent on him. He was away more and more, by now heavily involved in the Territorial Army, having risen through the ranks rapidly. My mother was in the grips of an all-consuming insecurity but still remained desperate to keep him. His dominance was yet again palpable; he held all of the power. In later years, she became remorseful that she had stayed with him for so long, but at the time she feared being alone and being unable to support her children. Things broke down further and he started to stay away more. I've no idea where he went; I didn't care.

I was glad he was gone, most of the time.

One evening I was out with him looking for Teddy and he said to me, "Your mother and me are getting divorced." I was floored – good floored and bad floored, all at the same time. Then he went on, "It's all your fault, you're to blame." He landed that one straight into my gut and I really felt its weight. I was stunned and emotionally winded. Suddenly I felt responsible. I knew I was a naughty kid, but I didn't understand how I could be responsible for it all. What about his adultery, heavy drinking, wife beating and violence? Then it hit me like a heavenly tidal wave. I would be free, not just from the beatings (I was used to them), but free to do what I wanted. I could sail my own ship at long last.

By the end, family life had spiralled out of control, but I also have no doubt that both of my parents did their best, with the capabilities that they possessed. My mother was a good mother and possessed a warmth and kindness. However, she had a temper and didn't always make the right decisions and her choice in men was far from ideal. We all paid a price for the errors of judgement she made as a young woman.

My father had many good qualities too. He wasn't an evil man. He'd had a tough start in life and he'd used his brains and resilience to carve himself out a new place in the world. He'd escaped the slums of Liverpool and travelled the world with the SAS. He had taught us many skills and spent many hours doing things with us. He showed his love by 'doing' but struggled to show any affection or warmth. He undoubtedly had his own wounds from his abusive childhood, which left him prone to bouts of fearsome rage and cruelty. I think he was a man under intense pressure, struggling to cope, and this pressure could erupt unfairly and without warning. His drug of choice was alcohol, a substance which certainly didn't help the situation. I hated him for a very long time, but intensive emotional work, the gift of time and healing has provided me with a far more forgiving and empathic perspective. Those were very different times; times when thrashings and hidings were perfectly normal, both at school and at home. When my father had been a child, life would have been even tougher. He spoke little of it.

I remember vividly the day he gathered together his remaining possessions and left the house for the last time. My mother was crying and begging him not to go, clinging onto his leg as he struggled towards the door. She was screaming, pleading "please, please don't leave me, please," as she was dragged along the floor behind him. I was profoundly relieved that he was going, but I also felt my mother's humiliation deeply. It was an intensely sad sight. I didn't understand the power of my mother's pain back then, and on occasion I felt ashamed about a mother who seemed pathetic and pitiful. My mother retreated to her bedroom for days after that, consumed by unremitting tears. I'd visit her with cups of tea, my feelings fluctuating between sadness and disdain. I see this in a different light too now, with the benefit of healing and hindsight. I now feel sadness and compassion for a woman broken by a deep and desperate dependency. Selfishly, I was internally jubilant that he had finally gone, once and for all.

I was free to do whatever the fuck I wanted!

Chapter Four

A Kind of New-Found Freedom

Would I spend this new-found freedom wisely? I can't say I gave it much thought at the time, but my life was now in my own hands. Soon after the divorce I went to live with my grandparents in Hereford, to complete my last year of high school. I think this was arranged to take some of the pressure off my now struggling mother. Social Services were involved in some capacity but the details escape me. It was another Catholic school, this time just outside Hereford. I didn't make many friends and I felt very much like an outsider, as other kids had formed strong friendships already. Surprisingly, I didn't get bullied there, though I'm not quite sure why. Yet again, I proved to be a bit of an attention seeker and soon began getting into trouble regularly. Some weeks I barely went to school and I became a regular absconder, with my now good friend Sniff who was at a different school to me. He was a loyal and solid friend and we formed an almost instant bond. He was very well liked and he could handle himself. I felt safer and more respected with him by my side. We looked alike, thought alike and laughed a lot. He was a skinhead and we both had all the right clobber, although we weren't stereotypical skinheads either, mostly listening to Two Tone and reggae music. It was an era when most young people identified with one of three distinct factions, either as a skinhead, a rocker or a new romantic.

My skinhead uniform consisted of Doctor Marten boots and shoes, brogues, cut-off jeans with braces, Fred Perry T-shirts, Sta-Prest trousers, Harrington jacket and a flight jacket or a full-length Crombie coat. We all looked the part and used to go to the football matches, giving it plenty of mouth and attitude. I was never an instigator. I'd get in a sneaky kick in the fighting and I was good with my mouth, but I erred on the cowardly side. I never really stepped up and proved myself, or earned my stripes, so to speak. I was always a bit fearful of the violence and for that reason I was never held in high regard within the skinhead circles. When it came to a physical fight I wasn't as tough as most. Occasionally I'd pick on people I felt confident I could beat. From time to time I'd target lads I considered might be gay, assuming that I would win. Once I spotted a couple of men on the street. I'd been drinking which was rarely good, and I decided they might be gay and therefore would make ideal targets. I smacked one of them right in the head after mouthing abuse and without giving any warning. The next thing I knew I was pinned to the floor in a vice-like grip, with the guy telling me that he was a Kung Fu expert and could kill me in heartbeat. He meant it and I believed him. However, never one to learn a lesson easily, I continued to behave like a twat whenever I had too much to drink, I'm sure to compensate for the inadequacy I felt deep down and also my growing adolescent pains and insecurity around my own sexuality. I enjoyed being part of

'Frankie Lord's Black and White Army' at Hereford United FC. Yet again I drank a lot and was great with my mouth but less so with my fists. Drink gave me the confidence I otherwise lacked and reversed the fears and anxieties.

In contrast, Sniff was a great scrapper. He was a bit of a mad bastard, I suppose. We were best mates, often being mistaken for brothers. At one point we actually became blood brothers, after we'd cut deeply into our palms and let the blood merge by holding hands. Sniff was tougher and more established than I was, so I admired him and felt safer when I was with him. He said he liked me because I was crazy and always up for doing stupid shit. Whatever the bond, it worked, we loved each other. We used to hang out with the older skinheads in 'our' local pub.

It was all about territory and fighting, back then.

One day, a group of away fans came into our pub. The tension was palpable but an air of fake friendliness prevailed for a time. After a couple of quick, edgy pints the away fans decided to leave, but our gang grabbed the very last one as they filed out, dragging him back inside and closing the door before beating and glassing him to a pulp. A very cowardly and underhand move. Windows were smashing all around me as the away fans went ballistic outside, trying to get back in to save their man. I was shocked and terrified. I legged it down into the cellar to hide while the beating continued. The solitary victim was eventually hospitalised and the cowardly nature of this incident repulsed and haunted me.

It seemed that anything went in those territorial tribal days.

Luckily, Sniff and I were more into alternative pastimes and fighting wasn't really our calling. We liked listening to ska, sniffing glue and getting drunk far too much. Sniff was into tattoos and he'd ink me using a pin and Indian ink, while we were both off our heads. He's still a tattoo artist all these years later and we remain friends to this day. Twenty years on, he ended up covering up some of this shoddy early work with his much-improved workmanship. Getting laid was also high up on our to-do list. We liked to think we'd even had an orgy on one occasion. We all had different girls, at the same time, but in different rooms of his parents' house while skiving off school. In our minds it was an orgy – we'd somewhat misunderstood the concept. We'd spend our days drinking and sniffing, then we'd brush ourselves down, put our school uniforms back on and pretend we'd been at school all day. I was on a slippery slope, idealising it as a hedonistic lifestyle. In reality, I was already beginning my descent into addiction. This was before the days of legislation, when glue was easy to get hold of and much cheaper than beer. It really wasn't very glamorous when I think back. Those heady days of Evo-stik and Thixofix glue.

It wasn't all about cider, glue and fighting. I also rekindled my passion for fishing, and night fishing in particular. I spent many a night camped up on a riverbank with my fishing friends. I loved the peace and magic of nature and the honing of my skills. It kept us out of a lot of trouble, because if we weren't fishing, we'd usually be up to some sort of mischief. Myself and another good friend, called Stan the Man, had found a way through a fence into a truck storage yard. It felt heaven sent. The trucks would be parked up overnight, loaded with pop and cider. We'd sneak in and help ourselves regularly to a few bottles, the most sought-after loot being 'GL' or Gold Label cider. Any self-respecting skinhead loved a few pints of GL, it was part of the culture, like the uniform. Getting hold of a good stash for free was manna from heaven.

In the end, I was suspended from school for letting down a teacher's car tyre; as usual it was my desperation for attention that had landed me in trouble. I only went in for two of my final exams, art and history. I'd failed to gain any worthwhile qualifications but I didn't care about any of this. I knew that I was a clever fucker and I wanted to turn my attention to things that really mattered. Things like alcohol, glue and girls. Alcohol was the preferred choice, but if I couldn't afford that, glue was an adequate alternative. I could lose a whole afternoon on the glue, as well as a few million brain cells no doubt. I'd often regain consciousness sitting on a riverbank, with no idea of how I'd got there or what I'd done all afternoon. Many a day was lost to the glue.

Later, when Teddy began his own descent into addiction, he got into the glue and gas in a big way. I doubt it did his already diminishing sanity any favours at all. Additionally, due to his mental health issues, he was a target for cruelty at times. Once he was spiked with very strong acid. I guess they wanted to see the mad kid tripping. He was arrested by the police after he had broken into someone's house and was found praying frantically at the foot of the stairs. The large dose of acid had left him seriously distur-bed. Again, such incidents, would only have damaged his fragile mind still further. To this day I'm angry at the people who did that to him and would disclose their names if I did not believe it would serve their egos. Drugs, trauma and mental fragility are a dangerous combination.

By now, regrettably, I'd started stealing from my grandparents as well. I'd do anything to get my alcohol, fags and glue money. There was a favourite pub called The Sun where you could buy rough cider from a cask and they'd happily serve us all under-age as we were no questions asked. Hereford is a huge cider producing county and this brew came in barrels and was often produced on local farms as rough cider or scrumpy. It was viciously strong, harsh on the stomach and cheap; three pints would blow my mind. I did have the odd job at times, helping local farmers at baling time, known as bale hauling. It was hard work but provided much needed drinking funds. More money meant more beer and more glue. That was as far as my ambitions stretched back then.

There was also a weekly disco at a place called Scouts' Corner, a large scout hut that still stands to this day. The primary reason to frequent these discos was to get off with girls, and we looked forward to the mere possibility of 'getting a shag' or 'sticky fingers'. It was the early eighties, the days of Madness, The Specials and Bad Manners; music was an identity. The disco wasn't a peaceful and serene affair as we had our rivals The New Romantics to contend with. They preferred the music of Duran Duran and Spandau Ballet and liked to wear pointy shoes and floaty scarves. We dressed differently, didn't get on, and there was usually trouble. Everyone travelled in packs, the last thing you wanted was to be outnumbered. It was always edgy, like the wild west, or cowboys and Indians. Once I was down at the disco and the place started filling up, but not with my tribe. There wasn't a skinhead in sight. I was dancing with some girls but slowly it dawned on me that I was in big trouble. I was going to get a good kicking, like it or not. I could feel it in the air.

The organisers sensed my predicament and tried to guide me to safety, via the front door. But it became clear that I was going to be followed, so they hatched another plan and ended up helping me escape through the kitchen. I vaulted over the serving tables and out of the kitchen window and ran like crazy down the lane. They'd spotted my escape and twenty New Romantics were chasing behind me. Comical in hindsight, frightening at the time. I knew that if they caught me, my life would be in danger. I also knew that if I made it across the river to the south side I'd be safe, the river marking an important territorial boundary. Senseless but true. I outran them, fuelled by the adrenaline that surged through my petrified veins. Luckily, I survived to tell the tale and made sure never to make that mortal error again. Having such clearly demarcated enemies seems mad thinking back, but at the time none of us knew any better and if I'm honest I did kind of like their music. We were all kids, playing dangerous games. Not long after this, one of the group was imprisoned for a tragic death that happened due to a man hitting his head on a kerb during a fight.

There was another tribe called the Rockabillies, but they were in the background and we didn't have much trouble with them, but some serious fighting and violence took place, based purely on what side of the river you lived on, and what clothes you wore. People were beaten to within an inch of their lives, based simply on what attire they preferred to wear. These were the days of drink, and this alcohol added much fuel to the fire. Eventually, the drugs mellowed us out and preoccupied us more and more, and the strict boundaries started to blur and things like glue were a distant memory.

I loved the sense of belonging, being part of something. The sense of freedom I felt, after years of oppression, was beyond words or comprehension. I was filled with excitement for my future, albeit misplaced. It was a time before addiction, when I could spread my wings and enjoy myself. For these few short years I was free to be me. At the time I was oblivious to the damage that I was carrying or the pain that lived within me after suffering years of trauma. Unconsciously this concealed and congealed pain silently guided me to seek an escape. My drinking was steadily increasing, as was my unruly behaviour. I wanted little more than daily oblivion.

To add to this new-found autonomy, I'd got myself a 49cc Puch Maxi moped. You could ride one legally with a provisional driving licence, so I was road legal and free! As was Stan the Man. We'd bomb around, sometimes drunk and far too daring, causing chaos and disorder wherever we went. We'd taken the baffles out of the exhausts and we made a formidable racket – we could be heard coming from half a mile away. I felt like I was doing eighty mph on a Harley – in reality, I was doing about twenty-eight mph on something more akin to a push-bike. A comedy value that escaped me at the time as I thought I was flying!

Whatever the reality, I loved that moped, loved the chasing around, off roading, exploring. By now I'd developed a slot machine problem too, to add to my financial 'responsibilities'. I could get through all of my money in one night, drinking and literally throwing the rest of it into a bandit, chasing the big score. I'd feel so depressed when I lost but couldn't stop the compulsion to chase a big win. Life was getting expensive. All of these little problems led to a much bigger issue; I needed a lot more money. There was only one obvious solution. I needed to start thieving, and quickly.

It started off with minor crimes. The milkman was my first target and I became the Butch Cassidy of doorstep milk thefts, often taking so much I couldn't drink it all. Orange juice was always a top find, and once I sat on the riverbank with such a big stash I didn't know what to do with it. I liked the buzz more than the actual milk and orange juice, the same old familiar story. Then it progressed to opportunistic thefts, like squeezing through the open window of a pub in the middle of the night and making off with a sizeable stash of tobacco, cigarettes and alcohol. That was a particularly good haul and it felt like Christmas had come early. Foolishly, I'd hidden it all in my grandparents' shed and it was found by them in the morning. When questioned, my claims that I'd found it went unheeded and the police were called. My grandparents were law-abiding citizens, there was no grey area for them where morals were concerned. I was mortified and ended up getting nicked. Even with such undesirable consequences, I was swept along on a tide of adrenaline and excitement. Undeterred, I wanted more.

On one memorable occasion, I'd pulled up at a cottage outside of town with the singular intention of robbing the place. Happy to discover no-one was home, I popped a back window and made my way inside, several pints to the wind. I was rooting around upstairs when I heard a neighbour shouting "who's there?" Now that really spooked me! In my wisdom I grabbed a pair of tights and squeezed them over my head, rendering myself reassuringly invisible. I ran out of the house and grabbed my moped, scaring the neighbour as he scrambled to safety. I'm un-recognisable, I reassured myself, as I screeched through the country lanes with the tights over my head on my Puch Maxi, feeling like I'd made the great escape. It didn't cross my drink-addled mind that the neighbour might have my number plate jotted down. And to add insult to injury, I hadn't even made off with any loot! The police came knocking and off to court I went. I ended up being sent to an Assessment Centre near Crewe called Redsands, a residential centre for troubled children. I was playing about in an adult world, equipped only with the mind of a child. Thinking about it now, I really was fucking clueless.

I was sentenced to six weeks in Redsands and told that I wasn't allowed to come back into the county of Herefordshire. When I told my friends about this, I made it sound like I was some kind of Dick Turpin outlaw, but internally I felt uprooted and devastated. Redsands was in the middle of nowhere and I missed my grandparents and the security they provided. It was an institution and it felt very alien to me. It was split into two halves; one side was locked-down and contained the more serious felons. I was on the open side and we enjoyed a lot more freedom. Rumours abounded about those in lock-down – one had apparently set an entire school alight – but we had little contact with the 'other side'. Lots of activities were put on for us, so that we could be observed. We were aware that bad behaviour could lead to a stint in an actual detention centre. It wasn't a bad place though and my time there seemed to pass quite quickly. One night a few of us escaped and did glue in a farmer's barn. I ended up sleeping with one of the female inmates in a field somewhere. I felt pretty chuffed with myself. Glue and girls; what a life!

The experience of Redsands did help me to straighten out my thinking somewhat, albeit temporarily. I felt clearer in the head and my behaviour became less chaotic. In some respects, I responded well to the routine and structure that it offered. Still grieving the loss of living with my grandparents, I went back to live with my mother in Chester once I'd done my time. My two brothers were still at home, and I rejoined the household once again. I started doing a Vocational Foundation course at college, which aimed to introduce me into the world of employment. I didn't learn a huge amount, because by now I'd started smoking dope. Lunch break consisted of a chippy meal and a fat joint.

However, for a while I did straighten out and I also got my first proper job at a fishmonger's shop in the city centre. The owner, Mr Mentor, was a genuinely nice chap and a decent employer. He taught me all the required skills and treated me very well. I used to nip out at lunchtime and smoke a joint, but other than that it was a more stable time. I enjoyed my job, I liked learning new skills, and I enjoyed feeling grown up and responsible. Regrettably, I also stole from this most kindly of bosses; tenners from the till to buy my drugs and fish from the storeroom too sometimes. He was a good man and it's a sorry I never got to say. I was smoking far too much dope and spent a lot of time stoned and listening to music. I remember buying my first albums; *Wilder* by The Teardrop Explodes and *The Final Cut* by Pink Floyd. Music had become a passion for me with the amplified sonic of my cannabis use.

Before long, we started to get the overspill of heroin coming in from Birkenhead, as Merseyside was suffering a serious epidemic. Heroin started to infiltrate around the Blacon Estate and a few dealers set themselves up locally. I became intrigued by this new dark and mysterious sub-culture. I found the lawlessness of it all deeply attractive, and it seemed that this drug had immense and almost mythical powers. This was before it gained widespread negative news coverage, although I doubt that would have put me off the idea either.

Before long I approached a lad I knew, asking him to sell me some. He gave me a short lecture about how I should stay away and then administered me a small scoop onto a sheet of tin foil. I was instantly captivated and intrigued by the ritual of this new drug, the fascination fuelling my need. The burning of the foil, the making of the tube, the running of the brown beetle and the sucking up of those pungent fishy fumes. I loved the whole procedure and all of the paraphernalia. Chasing the dragon sounded so exotic and I read deeply into it. I'd only had a small amount, but I felt impenetrable, shielded, fearless, warm and glowing. The sharp edges of life melted away, even the itchiness and slight nausea in no way dampened my delight. I felt like I'd crawled back into a warm and welcoming womb.

Like a moth to a flame, I wanted to understand the power of this drug more deeply. Why were people taking it, if it was so very bad? But now I understood. It felt so good, better than anything else I'd ever taken. It was the deadly Holy Grail of drugs and I knew I wanted more. I went home that day and I felt invincible, nothing in the world could bother me. I was carefree and coddled by an invisible warm protective blanket. As it wore off, that beautiful feeling faded and I felt stripped and vulnerable yet again. With a pang of guilt. I knew I wanted more. I knew it was rumoured to destroy lives but I was confident that it wouldn't destroy mine. I knew I was a clever fucker, remember?

The following Friday, I was back for more, wages in hand. For a while I would smoke it, but the older ones had started injecting it by now and they would be huddled in the kitchen. Again, I became fascinated and intrigued by a new ritual. Eventually, I persuaded them to inject me too, with half a bag, but of course I wanted a whole bag. I felt it, but it merely teased me into wanting more. I became determined to have a proper hit; I was chasing my Utopian hidden kingdom, always striving for the ultimate high. Same as every other junkie on the planet. These Fridays continued for some time. I was in no way physically dependent, but mentally it had me by the balls. My whole week was geared towards that fabulous Friday feeling.

I was smoking dope during the week, keeping my Friday ritual a secret, as heroin was despised by most of my friends and most of the estate too. Alan had warned me off it. Although he took other drugs, he'd managed to keep his distance from the smack. Poor Teddy was already into glue and lighter gas. All three of us already drug users in our different ways. The heroin had started to cause a serious spike in the crime rate, with many addicts becoming prolific burglars etc. Groups of vigilantes would target dealers and users, in retribution for the crimes and burglaries. The impact of the heroin epidemic effected the entire estate, times were changing, in the wake of this new drug. Sometimes retributions were serious, with kidnappings and beatings starting to become commonplace. It was the start of a very dark time.

This all added to the incredibly dark reputation of this new drug, but it did nothing to deter me and in fact made it more dangerously attractive. My fascination deepened. It was a tough environment. Some very hard men were involved on both sides of this new divide. I wasn't fully immersed in that world just yet. It was playing the long game with me, but my involvement in this dark subculture had begun.

In the meantime, I had a few more adventures ahead of me, of the more trippy variety. One day Alan and his friend went out mushrooming and returned with a very healthy haul, filling a carrier bag. I'd never heard of magic mushrooms and had no idea what they did, but the name was intriguing enough – I didn't even know what 'tripping' was. They said it's just that everything changes and I was sold. I needed to experience this different reality for myself. I scoffed down about forty raw, soggy, disgusting mushrooms, chewing the fleshy pulp down with difficulty, cynical about any possible effects. After about half an hour I was proven right, I could feel nothing at all, so I forced down another hefty handful. I sat down against a gable-end of a row of houses, dejected and disappointed, looking up at the stars, when suddenly I started to feel very peculiar. Hold on tight, it had begun! Giggles, colours, feelings, shadows, objects, movement and much more. Suddenly I was feeling so, so high! My cynicism melted away, I was tripping.

Amazed and transfixed, I had a powerful realisation. What's wrong with people? Why doesn't everyone do this all the fucking time? I couldn't understand why they didn't, the weirdness of this new world hit me like a juggernaut. It was a revelation, I'd found the solution to the world's problems; tripping was the answer. Then suddenly the darkness of the night turned into bright daylight (in my mind at least) and everything went weird. I kept blacking out and I'm unsure of the finer details, but I felt compelled to take action. I fancied the daughter of one of my mother's friends and thought this would be an ideal time to pay a visit. It was the middle of the night and I knocked on the door to ask for the girl. What could possibly go wrong? My confidence was sky high. Unfortunately, I'd also decided that it was a good idea to pull down my trousers and pants while I did this, but I've no idea what thought process led to this brave decision. I vaguely remember the door opening and me standing there bollock naked, pants around my ankles. I had no idea why so I can't imagine what they thought. Needless to say, they didn't welcome me in and my mother was called to come and fetch me!

Eventually I managed to find my way home, my mother asking me, "what's wrong with you, what're you on?" I replied, "Nothing, everything's great!" Then I went upstairs and tipped my wardrobe onto its back, opened its door and crawled inside, thinking it was a coffin. All perfectly normal, I think you'll find. My poor horrified mother tried to extricate me but I was too busy riding my motorbike, or at least making the noises as if I was. I got out and headed towards the window, convinced that I could "float like a butterfly and sting like a bee". My mother was becoming concerned, but I remained convinced of my butterfly-like abilities. Below me stood a spiked garden fence and my mother must have panicked and called my father, who came storming round for the first time in a long time. Alan, who was tripping his nuts off downstairs, managed to run away up the street at the sight of our father, only to spend the next four hours hiding in terror under a car. I failed to make a timely escape and sustained a winding blow to the stomach, which to some extent shocked me back into reality. It wasn't my best trip, that's for sure, as he was the very last person I wanted to see.

After he left, I managed to get some sleep, but the next day I felt so hung over, groggy and ashamed I could hardly cope. News had spread about the doorstep flasher and I felt utterly humiliated. I vowed then that this was not my kind of drug. It was one of the most powerful experiences of my life, but I didn't like the loss of control I had experienced. It was my first trip. Outside of the beautiful moments of truth and perception, I'd stripped, believed I could fly, and I'd been punched back down to earth. Trust me, that's one man you don't want to encounter when you're high as a butterfly. However, my vow to steer clear of hallucinogens would not last and many more adventures were to come. I was never very good at keeping to my vows.

Time moved on and I was working, I convinced my father and he agreed to be a guarantor so that I could buy a motorbike in instalments. He was trying to see me right I think, despite being with a new partner by now. I managed to buy a brand-new Yamaha DT50, which I rolled straight off the shiny showroom floor. It was one of my happiest days, I loved that bike. I had a passion for bikes then and I still do now, but it also provided me with freedom and social status. I managed to leave the heroin alone, I knew deep down that I was dicing with the devil. I kept my job, kept up my bike payments and made a concerted effort to stick to pot and lager. I'd still have a flirt with the devil on the occasional Friday, but I needed to keep it a closely guarded secret. That drug, and all those who used it, had such a bad reputation. I needed to suppress the self-destructive streak that lurked within.

My new bike allowed me to make new friends and was also crucial for my esteem and standing in the community. It was a tough housing estate and I needed all the help I could get; I'd always felt like an outsider to some extent. My bike gained me a new friend in John, one of the toughest and most respected men on the estate, who had a much bigger 250cc bike. I was grateful for his friendship and felt protected by it. The drug scene was massive on the estate, with one pub in particular having a reputation that you could buy almost anything there. It was of course my favourite pub.

The relationship with my mother wasn't great by now, I was seventeen and I was determined to do exactly as I liked. I'd frequently arrive home drunk to a barrage of questions and we'd fall out often. Her futile attempts to keep us all in line were failing miserably; in hindsight, I feel for her. Sometimes I'd be locked out and have to sleep outside in the doghouse, quite literally. I had a tendency to get mouthy and aggressive on the booze and this got me into a lot of trouble. One time I came home drunk and found myself locked out. I punched and broke a piece of glass in the front door and Alan defended the house and my mother, so we had a scuffle and he ended up putting me on my arse. My ego landed with a crash too that night, I realised that I was no longer ruler of the roost. I'd been usurped by a young upstart; a real 'ouch' moment!

I was renowned for going off like a firework when I'd been drinking. I was often full of really bright ideas too, after a few beers. One cold winter's day, after a couple of pints and listening to Alan Ant music, I decided I wanted to visit my grandparents. Determined, I set off on the hundred-mile journey on my trusty 50cc bike. Warmed and inspired by the drink, I slipped on a set of very cheap waterproofs and, half-drunk, I headed off towards Hereford. My maximum speed was somewhere in the mid-30s and the A-road was a tough shout. Before long, my hands were frozen to the handle grips. I'd have to stop to thaw myself out regularly, but I eventually made it. It was pitch black by the time I arrived as the journey had taken me a mere five hours. I was half frozen, craving the warmth and safety of their house, but I was not welcomed with open arms. I think I was fed and warmed, but then I had to sleep in a derelict house down the road. I was shocked and dejected by this rejection, my sanctuary had shunned me. I suspect my grandmother didn't want to be complicit in me breaking my order to stay away from Hereford. I'm sure she had also sensed a change in me, too.

The next day I headed back to Chester. The weather was still brutal, but this time my tail was between my spokes, adding to my misery. I decided to stop en route to warm myself with a few dry sherries – I must have been feeling posh or something. I then had another genius idea for keeping myself alive during the arduous journey ahead. My bike had a breather tube coming from the petrol tank, which gave off strong fumes. I already knew that sucking the air from this tube resulted in a seriously altered mental state, similar to the hit from a premium strength glue. On this particular journey, I realised it could be done while riding. Fuelled by a warming and heady mixture of dry sherry and petrol, I braved the open road, breather tube clenched between my frozen teeth. The thing about being an addict is you don't know when to stop, and I did so much petrol fumes I repeatedly blacked out along the way. I have no idea how I managed to get myself back to Chester and came to my senses only as I rounded the corner into the housing estate. It's one of many miraculous survival tales which left me asking some serious questions later in life. It remains a mystery how the hell I survived.

Plenty more miracles were to come.

Over the years I repeatedly surprised my grandparents with unannounced visits to their land of milk and honey. One time I arrived on their doorstep with three random biker mates and was shocked to be turned away yet again. Another dishevelled and disappointed night was spent in an old derelict building, complete with rats and apparently ghosts. The new me and my new friends were not welcome at the place that I felt was my home. For all my bravado, the vulnerable inner me still craved the safety and security of their house and the warmth of their love. Sadly, I think my unpredictability had begun to cause them deep concern. Maybe they even felt fearful of me.

My bike meant everything to me, it was my absolute pride and joy, my status, my freedom, my life. But it also put a target on my head and was a real double-edged sword. Nothing was easy back then on that rough estate. I had something that other people wanted and sometimes it would be taken off me by older bullies, ridden roughly and broken. I hated those people with passion. I was also persuaded by another older lad who had the same, but much older, bike, to swap for a day. I always had a longing to befriend these older protective figures. Being fatherless, I now felt devoid of protection and safety. For all of my father's flaws, he was an invaluable and formidable protector, and now he was gone. Keen to make another useful friend, I handed over my bike, I felt I could trust this man but I soon learnt that I'd made a costly mistake. Somehow, he managed to strip down both engines, and swapped all of my new engine parts for his old engine parts. I received back a bike that had basically been thrashed. I was mortified and felt deeply betrayed. My perfect bike had become forever sullied.

I bubbled with a rare and powerful hatred for that man that stayed with me for many years. I never felt the same about my cherished bike and I ended up transferring the payments over to another lad I knew, he took the bike over from me. I was so wounded by that betrayal. In the end, its new owner realised it had been thrashed and dumped it, along with his responsibility, in the local canal and made a claim on the insurance. My beloved bike was no more.

I didn't like that council estate, it was rough and harsh, I always had to watch my back and hold my own. Inside I felt vulnerable and was I frequently targeted; it felt like people could sense this struggle from me. Like a wolf at the bottom of the pack, I was always in danger of being attacked. Fortunately, people like John with the big 250cc offered me a brief respite and a certain level of protection, when I was with them, at least, especially if I was providing the weed. I craved peace and safety, but they were a long way off.

Life at home was also difficult. Teddy had by now been hospitalised several times in the local psychiatric ward, called The Deva, or the County Asylum. He tended to get up to big mischief, like stealing a fire engine and driving it around the streets. His particular brand of bizarre behaviour was taken seriously by the police. He also broke into the Territorial Army base and stole some sort of military vehicle. Upon each arrest they realised he was mentally disturbed and he bounced in and out of institutions for years to come. Alan was just finishing school but was also very involved in the drugs scene. Most people were. Worrying times, I'm sure, for our poor, distraught mother. As brothers we had grown apart and our lives had scattered in different but equally debauched directions. My mother had a couple of flings, but none of them treated her well or hung about and she was struggling. It was not a harmonious household.

Sniff visited us in Chester. I missed having him around and enjoyed showing him the city. My mum liked him, he was straight, you knew what you were getting with Sniff. He had a solidity that deep down I felt I lacked. Sniff had grown up in a liberal household and had been granted the space to find himself, an alien concept for me. He'd got more into punk music by now, Johnny Rotten and the Sex Pistols, as had Alan. I never got into the punk scene, it was too loud and too hard for me. Secretly I much preferred other music, although I was careful to keep this to myself. I also loved Alan and the Ants and occasionally donned face stripes and lace cuffs. I was becoming a weird hybrid of skinhead, new romantic and hippy and didn't really identify fully with any one tribe. On Sniff's visit we were kind enough to make my family a curry. We made it with great care, leaving it on the side for them to enjoy later. We then went out, having rather selflessly not eaten any of it ourselves. It wasn't a chicken or a lamb curry though, it was made with Chappie, a particularly cheap brand of dog food. They ate the lot and of course we enjoyed enlightening them later. Pranks were a favourite pastime still.

Sniff made me realise that I missed Hereford, and I knew I needed to get away from the darker drugs that Chester had to offer. I missed him. This wasn't a time when you could keep in touch easily, it was mainly letter writing. House phones were expensive to use and mobile phones were yet to arrive. I'd lost my bike, left my job, and still had enough sense to realise that the heroin was very dangerous for me. Hereford was calling me back, I yearned for somewhere that felt safer and more secure. I had big plans.

Plans to turn my life around and put the dark drugs down.

Chapter Five

Hereford – Return, Ascent and Descent

Hereford beckoned me yet again. I had little left in Chester and the situation at home was far from ideal. I wanted to be nearer to Sniff and further away from the heroin. I knew that dabbling was akin to playing with fire. My plan was to smoke a lot of pot instead and stay well clear of any needles or smack. Initially I stayed with Sniff but then I got a B&B once my benefits were sorted. I was happy to immerse myself in the smoking culture, it seemed safer and I figured it posed little threat. Soon I rediscovered tripping, forgetting my previous vow to never go there again. We'd all hit the acid, and mushrooms too when the time was right. Somehow, we heard about a field near Weobley, a village twelve miles out of the city. We'd all hitchhike there during the infamous 'mushy season'.

The crew consisted of a core of random regulars including Sniff, Blocky, Simmo, Whacko and a few others. This magical place was quite literally carpeted with mushrooms. We'd spot one, and then when our eyes focused, we'd see it was a whole clump, then look beyond that clump to see it merged into further clumps that stretched on into the distance. So we'd fill our carrier bags full and graze on raw mushrooms as we picked. After an hour or so we'd all be tripping and picking happily, out in nature, laughing at nothing and wondering if the sheep ate them and were tripping too. Those were happy times. We'd often take a long trippy walk back to the city and set ourselves up in the High Town to sell our harvest for a small fee. We were led to believe that so long as they weren't processed in any way, this activity was perfectly legal. It felt great to be legally high – and better still, it was free of charge. I loved the freedom of some of those times, far from the constraints of society, and perceptions beyond the confines of my life's and society's conditioning. Sometimes I seemed to see things outside of its illusion and to have spiritual experience, truth and insight.

Whacko wasn't a skinhead or a punk but had been accepted into our fold for a very different reason. His music tastes didn't venture beyond purest Pink Floyd. He was a highly intelligent academic type, but he really loved to trip. He took a liking to Fly Agarics, the pretty red and white spotted toadstools, and did a lot of these when he could find them. Then one day he heard that Death Caps also had hallucinogenic possibilities. He decided the pay-off far outweighed the risk of liver failure followed by slow and agonising death. One night he could resist no longer and ate one or two sizeable toxic toadstools. He lived with his mother and found himself paralysed, while enduring a terrifyingly bad trip. Unsure if he would survive the night, he was unable to call his mother for help, as he was gripped by both physical and verbal paralysis. Apparently, she was shouting up the stairs "your tea's ready, son" before assuming that he'd gone out. He was upstairs in the grips of deathly powerful hallucinations, unable to respond or cry out for help.

He survived and suddenly he was one of us, a crazy bastard. We welcomed him into our crew with open arms. An unusual way to gain respect, but his stripes had been earned, although I'm sure it left him a little brain damaged.

At some point I'd been put on probation, after being nicked with cannabis. I'd been put into lodgings with a very liberal lady, who let me store my mushrooms in her freezer. She was a lovely woman who sadly had cancer and wasn't to live for long, but I felt safe in the granny flat at the bottom of her garden. She provided good meals but left me to my own devices, which suited me fine. It was three miles out of the city, with the result that I was fit as a fiddle as I never had money for bus fare. By now Sniff and me were part of a gang of like-minded pot heads and we'd hang around the High Town or frequent the local pubs that were popular with heads like us. We'd both met girlfriends too; Smithy's was blond, my Mitch had very dark hair. I had common ground with Mitch as she was also the daughter of an SAS soldier. She wasn't as wild as me, but she was happy to smoke dope and take the odd tab of acid and speed.

It's probably just as well she wasn't as wild as me.

Sniff was a proper punk by now, with spiked bright blond Sid Vicious hair and hand-bleached dungarees. He may not have taken drugs quite as much as me, but he still had a rebellious side. Once he went out to a small village picking mushrooms with his girlfriend and a group of others. For some reason they broke into the village church, maybe to fulfil their anarchic ideals, and Sniff had sex with his girlfriend on the altar. She fell pregnant with a child that may well have been conceived that night, but Sniff was certainly no choirboy. The girl had the child, but he didn't take too much responsibility around the situation and they drifted apart very quickly. He felt he had been trapped into fatherhood. That night remained one of his anarchic claims to fame. I'm not sure if they damaged the church too. However, these were not acts of pre-meditated destruction, but rather thoughtless, wild and childish exploits, with little (if any) malice. For once, I wasn't involved.

By now I'd evolved into some sort of punk-hippie hybrid, proudly sporting a spikey blond mullet and moccasins. I spent most of my time tripping on either acid or mushrooms, developing a bit of a tolerance in the end. It was rare that I wasn't high to some degree. Selling my mushroom harvests had the added bonus of providing me with much-needed beer and pot money. Tripping constantly consolidated my belief that I was happy to live on the outskirts of society. I had no interest in becoming a responsible adult, being chained down by the modern constraints of working, home buying and marriage. The unveiled insights that the hallucinogens provided seemed to back up this school of thought. I made a committed and concerted effort to drop out.

But I was not only a drop-out, I was also a fool, incapable staying out of trouble for more than a couple of months. One fateful day, me and Simmo were in Hereford Cathedral, having already had a few pints. From our naive and drunken haze, our eyes settled on the huge, heavy, wooden donation chest that stood in the cathedral. We pondered on how much money it might contain. With no planning and absolutely no forethought, we looked at each other and thought, fuck it! We hefted it up and began staggering towards the exit. We'd not made it ten yards when we were intercepted by a cathedral custodian, wondering what we were doing. Having not thought of a suitable response we claimed we were "just moving it for a chap over there". Unconvinced, he asked us to put the chest down, at which point we dropped it to the floor and bolted away. Foolishly we assumed we'd gotten away, oblivious to the fuss we had caused. I was very soon arrested, yet again.

Evidently the chap had gone through mug shots at the police station and we were both promptly pulled in. Unfortunately, we made it onto the front cover of the *Hereford Times*, our thoughtless stupidity sensationalised into "Criminals attempt serious theft from cathedral". Hereford Cathedral is a highly respected and powerful institution and such a crime was not taken lightly. We, of course, had considered none of this. We were portrayed as serious criminals performing a premeditated robbery. This was far from true. We were two daft drunken teenagers, up to reckless mischief. I don't even know where we expected to take the chest, had we escaped with it. It was huge and extremely heavy – were we going to trudge through the High Town with it? Whatever the truth, it brought shame and unwanted attention to our families. We went to court and I ended up in a detention centre in Usk, for three very long months. A tough time indeed, and the famous 'short, sharp, shock' of the 1980s actually straightened me out for a while.

The summer of 1984, and also the summer of my 18th birthday, Sniff and I decided to go to Glastonbury festival, the then called CND Festival. We got a few quid together and set off to hitchhike to Somerset, with little or no idea of where we were going. We made it through Offa's Dyke and as far as the Severn Bridge, which we then had to cross on foot. It was a blistering hot day, but we trudged onwards, Sniff in his bleached dungarees and me with my bleached blonde mullet. The bridge crossing seemed to take for ever. Finally, we made it to the festival, but had no intention of paying the £13 entrance fee. This was long before the big double fence. We made our way round the back, over a couple of cow fields and stone walls and suddenly, we were in. There's a lot to be said for the good old days.

I was mesmerised, surrounded by thousands of my people. Drugs were everywhere and everyone was taking them. I could hear people calling out 'speed', 'acid' and 'hash', their voices music to my ears. Again, it cemented my belief that I did not want to be part of mainstream society, I was surrounded by thousands who felt the same way and it was a real eye-opener. The first thing we did was score some acid and it was quality stuff too. I had arrived. The line-up included the likes of Black Uhuru, Ian Dury and Joan Baez. One wild hippy had climbed up the huge wall of speakers on the Pyramid Stage. He was clinging on, high up in the air, his hair blown back by the vibration and noise. I was mesmerised by him, the bass volume must have blown his ear drums to Babylon and beyond, he was out of his tiny mind. I sat up on a hill tripping my nuts off, watching laser beams cutting through the rain and sweeping the crowd, thinking this is me, this is the life. It was both liberating and bohemian.

I was always creative, but I lacked any sense of purpose. I had nowhere to put this creativity, so the lifestyle itself became my goal. I'd always felt like an outsider, so I was happy to cast myself adrift from society. I embraced it; we all shared that same feeling of freedom and rebellion. The speed started to creep in more and more and I started to inject it. The powdery variety of drugs in Hereford were cut to death and were of poor quality. To me, injecting them was the only sensible option. I knew it was dangerous and frowned upon and I felt shame, but I was perversely drawn to its high risk-reward status.

A favourite pub was The Saracen's Head, which was full of stoners, junkies and very heavy drinkers. Frenchie, Chinky Novello, Carrot, Razor and Yanna were a few of its regular characters. Yanna bore an uncanny resemblance to a Jesus who had lost his mind to acid. His eyes were like saucers and his attention span was short unless he was staring at something. A meaningful exchange was usually impossible. He'd play *Whiskey in the Jar* by Thin Lizzy repeatedly on the jukebox. Carrot sported a ginger moustache and matching hair and was also a heavy drinker and drug user. There were also a few pub hard nuts who commanded respect and fought hard if they weren't given their due. One was even lucky enough to have the surname of Hardman, a name he unquestionably lived up to. Razor was a biker and another extremely hard man. Tall, lean and tough as fuck.

I admired them all, even the chronic junkies.

I'd watch the acute alcoholics and the mess they were in. It made me feel better, seemed to justify my drug use all the more. My drugs seemed less damaging than their drink. These were the days when pubs closed in the afternoon and we would be turfed out until opening time again at seven. Diddy the Skinhead, another tough as fuck regular, would sit out in the street wearing only a T-shirt drinking his GL. Even in winter he was far too hard to wear a coat. These were the early days, before heroin had done its worst. Several of these pub regulars would not weather its storm and died with a needle in their arm.

Slowly, the speed started to take root in my life. I'd had a couple of busts for petty amounts of pot – the police had targets to reach and we were easy prey. Hereford had its own Crockett and Tubbs in the form of Bently and Robins, although they bore little resemblance to *Miami Vice*. Slightly chubby, scruffy jeans and taches, they were the ones to watch and everyone knew them. It was like cat and mouse, but I'd found a game I enjoyed and soon I was wise to them. Heroin started to trickle into town sporadically, I was managing to stay away from it, but only by the skin of my teeth. I'd never forgotten the warm bliss it offered, and it was still very much on my radar. It had already gotten me, I just didn't know it yet.

I was lucky enough to be accepted by a guy called Jam, who owned a hippy shop called The Qasaba in the city centre. Jam was an interesting character who ran an organised little business selling hippy clothes, joss sticks and accessories. He also sold great pot under the counter. He wouldn't serve many people, and acceptance into his exclusive club carried with it status and street cred. Once he had accepted you, he'd invite you behind a thick velvet curtain to smoke a pipe, drink tea and purchase your pot. If regular customers came in you'd have to be cool, as he put it, pretend you were browsing through his array of tie-dye shirts, or maybe buy a pack of joss sticks. He'd get busted from time to time but his stash place was so clever he rarely got caught. He had a purpose-built crevice within his hand-made wooden counter, so clever it baffled the bust-hungry coppers every time. He notched up a few minor possession charges over the years but nothing more.

Jam may have sold hippy clothes, but he didn't wear them. He was a fascinating and unusual contradiction. He was always well groomed and preferred to wear a cravat and waistcoat and he always carried a briefcase. He ran a tight ship too. There were rules to being a member of his inner circle and he took no nonsense. I'm not sure why he accepted us, but he did and we felt highly privileged. Jam was the ultimate heavy pot smoking businessman-about-town. Pipes and chillums were always on the go, but so were his potent joss sticks and his shop was constantly swathed in a heady mix of strong and moreish scents. His deals were a bit shy, but he was a very decent man, well connected and undeniably cool. I respected him and for some reason he trusted me.

The shop often hosted a rich tapestry of Hereford's underground characters, in all shapes and sizes. One such character was Frenchie, who'd been a prisoner of war in Auschwitz and had the dubious honour of also being a serious junkie back in his day. We had doubted the validity of his stories until we saw an article about his prisoner of war days in the *Hereford Times*. He was much older than us, greying, tall and broad with a big hooked nose. He had some amazing stories about his junkie days in London, I could listen to him for hours and he further deepened my fascination with heroin. He regaled me with endless tales of Harley Street junkie doctors and famous jazz musicians. He'd lived a life, that was for sure. Numerous other unusual waifs and strays were members of Jam's exclusive hand-picked private pot club. He was my main supplier of pot for many years. I knew I was going get good stuff from Jam – red seal black, Lebanese or on occasion Sensimellia. I learnt a lot about cannabis culture; I loved that club.

Jam was a reggae music connoisseur and authentic root reggae music always blared from his record player, maybe Peter Tosh or Steel Pulse. We'd hang out there for hours and I actually felt part of something. It was a rare and precious feeling for me, and it certainly wasn't a regular high street shop. You also never knew who was going to pop in as he was prone to transient visitors too, and I would be intrigued by their status and connections. I loved the characters and the whole underground vibe.

By now Mitch had a bedsit in town and I stayed there a lot. There was a group of us, all into pot and tripping. I had heroin in the back of my mind and had the odd dabble, but I had to keep that very quiet. My concerted effort to use everything else instead was beginning to fail. Heroin was quite scarce but this only heightened its elusive appeal. It was about this time that I met Edward, a memorable character who hailed from the Welsh valleys. He'd also lived in India for a time and was a Hare Krishna by trade. Sometimes he sported the bright orange robes, other times he was head-to-toe in hippy shit and sandals. He'd spent a lot of time in prayer and meditation and as a result he emitted an amazingly spiritual vibe. He was also very partial to the weed and speed, which suited me fine. He started bringing me weed to sell and I'd sell it for him easily, then he'd disappear again for a week or so, before floating back in to collect his cash. At the time he was the answer to all my prayers.

One day he turned up with a big bag of the best speed I'd ever seen or smelt. It had an amazing aroma, like strong super-concentrated cat's piss. It made my heart sing. Someone was knocking up high class speed in the Welsh valleys and Edward soon became my regular supplier of this pungent product. It sold incredibly well and the quality of it earned me the street cred I'd so often yearned for. It was still before the days of mobile phones and his appearances were always unannounced and sporadic, but I was always happy to see him. I took pride in the fact that it was the best speed in town. My status was rising, his speed was earning me respect.

He was such an unlikely dealer; he was a deeply spiritual pacifist, but it soon became clear that he was consuming a lot of his own product, and eventually he ended up with what I now know to be serious speed psychosis. The last we heard of him, he had wandered into a Welsh mountain in the snow in his bare feet and had lost his toes to frostbite. We never saw him again after that. I sometimes wonder what became of Edward. He was one of the good guys.

Bently and Robins were kept busy as the town started to flood with amphetamine and dexies. Uppers were thick on the ground. I was becoming lax at upholding my personal rule to avoid the needle and was now injecting speed habitually. The buzz was unparalleled and I couldn't stop myself. I was always quick to justify my dangerous habit by comparing myself to those I deemed far worse, a staple defence for any self-respecting addict. It wasn't long before I started taking heroin more often. I'd hooked up with a dealer and had ready cash, due to my own dealing activities. I was flying high. Bizarrely, Sniff now also had a girlfriend called Mitch, but we didn't see as much of each other any more although we did share nights out and time as couples occasionally. I gave Sniff some smack once, but after a few days, he decided it wasn't for him. Before long, it started to become a block within our friendship. I managed short stretches of snorting or bombing speed but the needle was always calling my name.

Chinky Novello lived just down the road and he'd really been around the block, being a whole generation ahead of me and having lived through the seventies. To my mind he was a serious junkie, but quite remarkably he had a stunningly beautiful girlfriend who only smoked dope, which in our world made her straight. He had something else that I coveted. He was the proud owner of an antique glass syringe, complete with its own custom-made metal box, known as 'Novello's needle'. Works were hard to come by and I used to borrow it from him frequently. I've no idea what it was intended for, elephants judging by the size of the needle. I had to screw its fat spike onto the barrel and it was so big and blunt I used to sharpen it on a match box. The fact I coveted such a device speaks volumes for the desperation.

I was already in the grip of an insidious needle fixation. I was still learning to inject myself and this was far from an ideal starter kit. I did have the sense to wash it out before stabbing around in my arm, if you can call that sense. Sometimes I'd bleed profusely, yet I remained staunchly undeterred. I used to have a kit (spoon, shoelace and works) stashed under the floorboards in the bathroom. Sometimes I'd be in there for ages stabbing around unsuccessfully, and it started to cause problems between me and Mitch, as she did not share the same fixation. Strangely, I found this secretive, shady, dark side of drugs enormously appealing. The duality of using is now starkly apparent to me; the higher the stakes, the bigger the high. I was beginning to step into a new subculture, one darker and far murkier than that of pot and mushrooms. I was being drawn down, my needle and smack fixations deepening, I was entering Junkie Ville, a dog eat dog world. I spent many years going back and forth to the needle, thinking the needle was the problem. It never once occurred to me that *I* was the problem.

My mother had moved back to Hereford by now. Teddy was with her but Alan had stayed in Chester with a girlfriend. I didn't see much of them, I was busy doing my own thing. Sniff had a soft spot for my brother Teddy. He liked getting stoned with him on cannabis, as it kept him away from the glue for a while. My mum loved Sniff too. Sometimes we'd both go over and have a good smoke with Teddy. Teddy would have been about fifteen. Sniff was a talented artist and he'd painted a mural on Teddy's wall of some cannabis leaves and Pink Floyd's *The Wall* album cover. It was a small thing but it made Teddy really happy.

Once I was staying over the night in the spare room, when I heard my mother shouting and screaming from the kitchen. I rushed down the stairs to find her crying and covered in blood. Teddy was just standing there. I'd taken a baseball bat with me, assuming he'd hit our mother, and without thinking I swung the bat and hit him hard over the head. The noise it made haunts me to this day; a loud, hollow sickening, echoing thud of the wood. Teddy didn't go down, he stood there staring at me. He was very tough and he scared me. Suddenly he grabbed a knife and chased me upstairs, where I barricaded myself into the bedroom. I was scared for my life and I couldn't understand how he had withstood that blow. We were in a Mexican stand-off for a while. Finally, he went away and I emerged from the bedroom.

It turned out that the 'blood' was in fact tomato ketchup. He hadn't stabbed Mum or hit her, he'd thrown ketchup at her. With the sound of the bat still ringing in my ears, I regretted my unwarranted attack. I felt eternally guilty about that night. Teddy was already suffering with his mental health and a severe blow to the head would not have helped. Teddy's story does not end well, and I shall forever feel a deep sadness about the impulsive blow that I'd struck. He disappeared for a couple of days. He had a very pretty girlfriend at that time and there were rumours of a pregnancy and possible child. Despite his weak mental disposition, Teddy was physically tough as fuck. He was also handsome, wild and popular with girls; he had a lot going for him really. The tragedy of his story will stay with me forever.

Sometimes I'd go up into the Welsh mountains to visit The Convoy, a brigade of unruly travellers who lived in an array of vans and buses and took a lot of drugs. I was captivated by their wildness and debauchery, and I also knew they sold every drug going. These people were on the outside of society, they lived an utterly lawless lifestyle out in the wilderness, even taming and bareback riding the wild Hay Bluff horses. The landscape up there was hauntingly powerful. These marginalised people somehow managed to harness its power and even its horses, and they captured my imagination. It was so evocative, and their existence appeared to be almost post-apocalyptic. I was transfixed; yet again I was being drawn to the other side of society. My personal descent was gathering momentum.

My compulsion to embrace the warm, inside the womb haven of heroin, was in freefall. My limited willpower was failing. Later, heroin was to tear some of these alternative societies apart. It took no prisoners and had the power to destroy lives, families and even whole communities. It would drive a wedge between its devotees and its adversaries. I was yet to realise that it would destroy me too. I'd seen the warning signs but I'd chosen to ignore them. I'd picked my idols and they all teetered on the very edge.

Before long, things started to get more desperate for me. I'd moved in properly with Mitch. Through some connection of her parents, we were staying in a lovely house in the very affluent area of Broomy Hill. Mitch had a job in a giant chicken processing factory, whereas I'd decided that I was destined to become a poet. I was beginning to have more than just a dabble with the gear, only hindered by my poor finances and the patchy and paltry supply of heroin into Hereford. She had a moped that I would borrow to go out hunting for my drugs, sometimes not returning for days. It was a full-time job hunting out the gear. I threw myself into this new career wholeheartedly.

Because of its scarcity it was a life of lengthy chases, devastating disappointments, ruthless rip-offs and only the occasional good score. I was not deterred and having been ripped off myself, I started reciprocating in kind. Many a time someone would go off to Bristol to score and return ten hours later with a very long story and no gear. So I simply followed suit. It was a way to make easy money and the morality didn't concern me, now that desperation had started to sail my ship. My efforts to stay away from the needle were failing miserably. I was having to lie to Mitch about it, wearing long sleeves or claiming they were old marks. I was hooked on the intense ritual that the needle demanded. The mushroom of blood blooming in the barrel, the pushing of the plunger, the spreading warmth. Then the waiting, for all of life's menial problems to melt away.

Heroin being so scarce only served to fuel my growing obsession. Any that did come into Hereford was gone all too quickly. Most of it was coming in from Bristol, but I didn't know anyone there. I was a sitting duck for being ripped off, having to rely on others further down the junkie path than me. People who I had long held up as indicators of how not to be. Still I was oblivious to the fact that I was on that same path, just a generation behind. These people had serious habits to support, but I had to trust them to score for me. It was painful, often they would return high as kites, without my money or gear, carrying only a story of how they had been ripped off or pulled by the police. Sometimes it would be my whole week's giro money. Friendship counted for nothing in Junkie Ville.

By the second time I went to Glastonbury in 1986, my life had become far darker. I got in free by hiding under a pile of blankets in the back of someone's van. I had little money and I took a load of speed from a guy in a neighbouring tent. I was drinking heavily on it and ended up blacking out. My memory of that festival is patchy, but I do remember dropping acid and watching The Cure, while a thunder and lightning storm raged in the distance moving slowly towards the stage. The Cure was one of my favourites at that time, along with The Beatles, Pink Floyd, U2 and Simple Minds. Music has always been important to me and my taste has always remained eclectic.

My new-found friend heroin would rob me of all these passions.

I was up to my new tricks too. The lads who had given me the lift were in a different tent and I went around for a smoke with them, carrying only ulterior motives. One lad had all his money in a silver tin, which I managed to slip into my pocket in between smiles and banter. My priority was buying more drugs – honesty or loyalty was on the back burner. The coke I bought was shit and I was left with a gnawing feeling of guilt and disappointment. Junkie desperation had started to get a grip of me and my second Glastonbury was tainted by it. I was no longer a wide-eyed innocent. I was a user, a thief and a liar.

By now I was well known to the police. I'd been charged with a few minor possessions and maybe a couple of criminal damages too. I was selling a bit of pot, but my heydays of selling Edward's excellent speed were long gone. I had my first 'script' around this time too. It was before the days of drug services, but I'd managed to persuade a doctor to provide me with a DF118 prescription to help me stay off the heroin. The initial relief was huge, half a dozen a day would keep me happy. Before long I was taking them in handfuls, and it wasn't long before the doctor ended my script. I'd been back too many times with countless stories of either losing it or having it stolen. I couldn't understand it, how dare they? I couldn't maintain or regulate my use at all. I didn't realise it had been of my own doing.

Typically, that thought simply didn't cross my mind.

Due to my growing habit and the patchy supply, I'd started to get into codeine linctus, which could be bought from a chemist shop for the bargain price of one pound. The hit wasn't as intense, but it was a good substitute all the same. It took longer to work than a needle full of gear but within half an hour I'd feel indestructible once more and not dope sick. Of course, I consumed it a bottle at a time. Before long, I became known by the various pharmacists of Hereford and I couldn't get served anywhere. My initial plan was to flag old people down in the streets and ask them to buy some for me. I'd concocted a story about having a poorly nan who needed it urgently. Sometimes it would take all day to find a willing victim. Worse than that, sometimes they'd come back with Pholcodine instead, having been persuaded by the pharmacist that it was adequate. Pholcodine contained far less opiate and was a long way from adequate for me. So I started asking them to get Gee's linctus if they didn't have codeine linctus. Gee's was an opiate squill, and while it would take the edge off, it would also make me sick as a dog. A whole bottle of that stuff was a big ask, even for me. It tasted like death in a bottle but I still drank it, holding my nose as I swallowed it down.

In utter desperation I started making exotic day trips to acquire stocks of my linctus of choice. I'd catch a cheap coach as far afield as Birmingham, so I could do tours of the chemist shops. I'd dress well, shine my shoes and carry a leather briefcase, posing as some kind of young businessman. I'd always make my purchase on behalf of my elderly grandmother. Pharmacists were starting to get wise to the junkie's linctus lies and I felt like I was on stage. My success rate was roughly fifty-fifty. If I was lucky, I'd return to Hereford with a few bottles of my precious supplies. The jangling of the bottles was music to my ears.

Some hippies I knew rented a flat in the city centre, above a dental practice. I discovered that I could get into the dentist's via the internal stairs and I became partial to having a nosey. Dentists carry drug supplies and I'd often find Valium or Lignocaine. Once I found a batch of Cocaine Hydrochloride, which caused me huge excitement but it turned out to be highly anti-climactic. The rush was disappointing – but then it was dated 1982, so was years old

On one memorable occasion I pinched some Adrenaline ampoules, small vials purpose-made for injecting. Without considering any potential dangers, I injected myself as soon as opportunity allowed. As the cold rush crept up my arm, my heart started pounding powerfully and uncontrollably. I felt convinced I was about to die. It was an intensely unpleasant and traumatic experience, lasting for about fifteen minutes. It was like a panic attack in a bottle. After the terrifying storm had passed, I swore to myself that I would never inject anything ever again. That resolution lasted for at least two weeks.

Another phenomenon every junkie lives in fear of is the dreaded dirty hit. Any foreign body in the syringe can cause atrocious headaches, chills and vomiting. I had my fair share of them, but even these could not dampen my ever-deepening needle fixation. I took to eating six paracetamols prior to every hit. I knew that this pre-emptive painkilling dose would take the edge off a dirty hit. The paralysing painful headaches that would bring me to my knees, quite literally, might edge down one tiny notch. However, this precaution offered little protection from the devastating accompanying nausea. I frequently found myself crippled and paralysed by these, and for hours at a time. Every hit was akin to Russian roulette from this, a dirty hit or overdose.

It could be heavenly, or it could be pure hell. All in a day's work for any self-respecting junkie. I even had a bad hit from injecting LSD once. I'd got hold of some strong White Lightning blotters. Every intolerable sensation was amplified until I felt like I was about to die. It speaks volumes as to the utter madness of this hedonistic career I had decided to pursue. I never injected acid again; I did occasionally learn my lesson.

It was around this time that the first Drug Services opened in Hereford. Before this specialised service emerged, there was little help available for people with addiction issues. It was called DASH (Drug and Alcohol Services Hereford) and I'd heard that they could prescribe a magical heroin substitute called Methadone. I was prescribed thirty millilitres a day. I'd heard rumours of Methadone from Birkenhead, but it was now deemed that even leafy Hereford had a significant enough heroin problem to warrant a specialised service. I was one of DASH's first clients and I maintained a relationship with them for many years. Initially the methadone provided me with an incredible sense of relief, I could function on my prescription, topping it up with weed and alcohol. I expected this to be the end of all my problems. I had a lot to learn.

This brand-new service gave me a break from the constant stress of scoring, and also stalking down fresh needles, which were akin to hen's teeth back then. Before the days of needle exchanges, finding pins was a pursuit in and of itself. They were frequently re-used many times and sometimes shared. Whispers of Aids and Hep C had just started to circulate, but any concerns paled into insignificance in the face of opiate addiction and needle fixation. I was spinning bullets, dicing with death, again akin to Russian roulette.

Madness when I look back, but hindsight is a wonderful thing.

After several arrests for small amounts of cannabis possession, I found myself in Pucklechurch Remand Centre, near Bristol. Back then there was no choice but do a bare-back withdrawal whenever you got banged up. Druggies like me were often sent to the hospital wing and if you were very lucky you might get a couple of paracetamols. Elva, my probation officer, came to see me for what proved to be a fortuitous visit. She suggested that I make a plea to enter a rehabilitation centre, in order to avoid a prison sentence. I was lucky to secure a place at a rehab in Weston-Super-Mare. I had no idea what to expect, but I was keen to avoid prison. It was here, in Weston, that my eyes began to open. Could I turn my life around and head in a new direction?

It was to be a more treacherous journey than I ever imagined.

Chapter Six

Weston and Beyond.

I had a day out of prison for my assessment at W Counselling Services, a 12-Step Rehabilitation Centre. Having no idea about the 12-Step concept, I persuaded Elva to buy me a drink at a pub. She placated me with a measly half-pint. It was a day out, a few fags and a beer. I had no idea about the journey that lay ahead, or the abstinence-based programme I was about to enter. They offered me a place and my prison sentence was deferred for three months while I attended rehabilitation. Weston is a small, quiet coastal town, not far from Bristol, unknown territory for me. Elva drove me there early one morning, a smile on my face, jubilant that I was not going to be physically locked up. I was nervous and intrigued. There were about twenty-five clients and the group rooms were based above a bank in the town centre. We were housed in a couple of different properties. I falsely claimed I was withdrawing and was given Methadone tablets for the first week or so. I was chuffed. Stunts like that had become second nature.

The place was a real eye-opener for me, as I very quickly realised that addiction did not discriminate. There were people from all walks of life. There was a ballerina pill-head, who sadly later went on to hang herself. There was a Brazilian singer coke-head.

There was another singer who was an over-eater and a pot-head. Another chap was a member of the aristocracy, who, like me, was a smack-head. He was contrasted by another man from London, who had lived on the streets for years, another, but very different, kind of smack-head. There was the son of a Greek shipping magnate and someone else from Portugal. All addictions and classes were represented; I was fascinated. I was surprised by how strict rehab was and the group sessions were plain old brutal and honest. I had given it little prior thought and I was shocked and bewildered. I expected to get clean and that would be me sorted. Unbeknown to me, I was about to embark on a deep and painful journey.

The first thing every client had to do was to write their life story and read it out to the group. The next day we would re-group and everyone would give honest feedback on the story they had been told. The aim of this feedback was to be as harsh as possible, to shock the addict into realising the error of their ways. I was given soul-searing feedback about the way I had treated my mother and grandparents. One lad shouted "you're a fucking cunt". I had to sit and take it, while inwardly screaming and squirming. It wasn't terribly strategic, but it certainly smashed my denial and shocked me into facing certain realities. My drug problem and behaviours had hurt those that I loved the most. I felt raw and I was without the emotional protection that opiates had offered me. We were encouraged to attend 12-Step support meetings in town, in the evenings. This was my first experience of 12-Step Recovery Fellowships. It all went over my head at first; it was a whole new world.

For some reason Weston was, and still is, a recovery and rehab hotspot. It was still early days for my particular fellowship, but Weston already had several weekly meetings, due to the number of rehabs around the town. London had a good scattering of meetings but they were still very thin on the ground in other areas. Since these early days, the growth of meetings throughout the UK has been exponential. I didn't know what to make of all this new information at first. The idea of total abstinence was alien and terrifying, but Elva had convinced me that it could help. Initially I didn't take it seriously enough and started buying bottles of codeine linctus as soon as I was allowed out, once my detox had finished. I had access to new chemists where I would not be recognised and it was too much for me to resist. My roommate also managed to get hold of some weed one night and we got totally stoned. Abstinence was a difficult concept to grasp.

Then one day soon after, I started to feel guilty about my using; it was contrary to the rules. I was baffled, as rules had never been any concern of mine before. They were normally there to be broken. The linctus also started to make me feel down and sickly, as opposed to high and warm. Its iridescent shine had started to fade as it was mixed in with a dose of truth about my condition. This was a magical and surprising turnaround for me. Suddenly, I felt a deep shame and I made myself sick, to expel the last of the linctus from my system. With this new-found conscience, I also owned up to smoking the dope too. This involved grassing on my roommate and now friend, Cockney Mo. It went against the grain but I knew I wanted to stay clean, and that total honesty was required if I was to preserve my brand-new desire for sobriety. Something was shifting within me. I could see others who were months or even years clean, showing it could be done. A seed of hope was beginning to germinate.

It began to register that my problem was far bigger than just the substances I'd been taking. I had a condition that meant I suffered from an uncontrollable compulsion to change the way I felt – by any means possible, whatever the cost. I needed to reverse this pattern, hence the total abstinence. Otherwise, I could quite easily spend my life substituting one substance for another. I needed to avoid all mind-altering substances; the very last thing any addict wants to hear. I was shocked to hear that this included alcohol, but it is a mind-altering substance, after all. I attended my very first 12-Step Fellowship Convention. It was held on the end of the pier in Weston and there were hundreds of clean addicts there. They looked happy, had nice clothes and good jobs. Who knew that was even possible? My seed of hope was nourished and began to grow.

I started communicating with my grandparents again. My feelings were coming back, and I missed them and felt guilty for what I had put them through. I was attending regular meetings and after my three-month stay was over, I was allowed back to live with them. I was clean and back in my sanctuary once again. I felt optimistic about the future for the first time. They welcomed me back because they could see a real change in me. They had faith in me, even though I'd stolen from them and treated them badly. I'd also kept hold of my girlfriend Mitch. Although she had used drugs too, she could put them down easily and wasn't like me in this respect. I felt I'd been given a fresh start; life seemed exciting.

I was going back monthly for aftercare at the rehab, and before long I landed a job. It was hardly glamorous, just folding and packing bin bags in a huge bin bag factory, eight-hour mixed shifts at a time, but I stuck to it, I liked having some honest, hard-earned money coming in. My life was starting to straighten out quite quickly. Initially I saved up and bought myself a push-bike. Then I got a 125cc motorbike, which looked like something left over from Germany in the Second World War. Mitch had moved in with me and my grandparents, but we started to argue more and more. She was keen to move on, get our own place, and start a family. That all seemed a bit drastic and scary to me. She eventually got her own place and we were still seeing each other on and off. Then she met a lad from the army at Hereford's infamous nightclub The Crystal Rooms. Our relationship ended once and for all; we'd become very different people. I found the break-up difficult and very nearly went off the rails, but I bought a better motorbike instead, a much more powerful Honda CX500, a real gem. I still loved my motorbikes. I invested in a different kind of buzz.

I started going fishing again, with Stan the Man, who was one of my straighter friends, as he was as keen on fishing as I was. He got me into CB radios, a huge craze at that time, as we were still before the mobile phone era. We both got good rigs and the distance we could communicate over increased from local to further afield. Stan was a bit of lady's man by now and his CB name or 'handle' was The Shafter, mine was Spaceman. A handle could speak a thousand words.

He always had the very best of rigs, with all the bells and whistles, even echo and reverb facilities. It turned out the Italians were mad for CBs too, and we spoke to many of them. Sometimes we spoke to people as far away as North Africa. It opened up my world a little bit more. I was seeing less of Sniff, due to my new clean-living lifestyle. I couldn't afford to hang around with him any more. He'd always managed to use drugs far more successfully than me and was still happily living his bohemian lifestyle.   By necessity, we drifted apart.

Stan by now had bought himself a lovely Ford Cortina, a cool car and very much of that era. I realised that I could drive a Reliant Robin three-wheeler on my motorbike licence and managed to buy one cheap. These were marginally less cool, but I didn't care. It was freedom, free from the weather conditions that are the blight of every biker. I applied for a job as a steel erector, without even knowing what the job entailed. I got the job and ended up working for a guy who lived about fourteen miles outside of Hereford. Then we'd go out as a team, erecting steel framed building, usually huge agricultural barns or factories. I loved it, it challenged me. It was a whole new buzz working at height.

It was hard and dangerous work too. Back then health and safety was in its infancy and we'd be walking about on beams, without harnesses, at great heights. We only ever wore the harnesses during site visits from officials, so the job was a daily thrill.   It required confidence and bravery and some madness; I got very good at it. It was a rush and also a real sense of achievement when a build was completed. We had to rely on each other while carrying roof beaming together in the air. It felt a bit like a circus act to me sometimes. I soon moved to a similar company closer to Hereford, where we often worked away, sleeping in a caravan. The wages were far better but it was extremely hard work. I was clean and I was fit as a fiddle.

My second Reliant Robin was purple, then I graduated to a proper car, a polar white Vauxhall Cavalier. I was starting to feel like an actual grown up; job, driving licence and now a car too. That car looked mint and was my pride and joy. I'd also learnt to weld and was becoming quite a skilled metal worker. I knew several other men who'd fallen and hurt themselves. Luckily, I only ever had one relatively minor accident. I learned never to look at the floor, just to focus on the beam and my next step. That job required real steel and focus and nerve; I loved it.

My love of fishing had returned and I was spending many hours on the riverbanks of Hereford. It was my version of meditation, in all weathers and conditions. I almost always put the fish back into the river, but I believe it also re-awakened a primal hunter-gatherer instinct in me. It was one such fishing trip that lead to me experiencing a different kind of catch. The river was difficult to fish, but I'd found a small inlet in which to hang my rod. I was sitting quietly when an elderly woman came by on the riverbank. I was baffled as to where she had come from and where she was going. She was headed down towards an unpassable river, but she seemed to be calling something, so I assumed she was maybe looking for a missing pet. I said nothing, and she made her way past me. I assumed she would come back soon, after discovering the flooded footpath. I paid it no more mind. I was lost in my own concentration.

I was cold, but happily fishing, when I heard her calling again. Then I thought I heard the word "Help!" I headed off to investigate and was shocked to see the woman had fallen into the swollen river. She was clutching onto a tree that had grown outwards over the water. She was a fair way off the bank and in a deadly predicament. All I could think was "it's fucking freezing, how the hell has she ended up in there?" A bloke on the pathway above was shouting at me, "Go on then, go get her." I was thinking, "You come down here and fucking go get her!"   It was far easier said than done.

Despite my fears, I took my wellies off and started wading in. I let the current take me until I too was clutching onto the tree. It was beyond bitterly cold and I was struggling to catch my breath. Finally, I managed to get hold of her. The bloke from above had called the police and was fetching a lifebuoy from further back along the path. My eyes were only a few inches above the water level, with the wild river churning towards me. The view upstream was terrifying – angry swirling waters, and a huge tree stump heading in our direction. I felt very fearful and briefly wondered how my life might come to end in this surreal fashion. Finally, the man managed to throw the life ring and it drifted towards me, I looped it over the woman and sent her back to the bank, to safety. Now it was just me, the freezing river and the approaching tree trunk. In a panic I managed to hurl myself towards the shore before scrambling up the bank, freezing and bedraggled. Two police officers had now arrived and I knew them both quite well. Thinking only about getting warm and dry, I made my way back to my grandparents, a half-mile walk away. I got in, told them briefly about what had happened, before running a hot bath and eating a meal. I had to soak the cold out of my bones.

The next day I'd forgotten about the whole escapade and went about my day. Then I received a call from the *Hereford Times*, wanting to know my story and to arrange a photoshoot with me. The next day I was splashed across the front of the paper, a "local hero". The picture featured me holding a lifebuoy, wearing one of my Nan's hand-knitted cardigans. The story also prompted an award. Who would have thought it?

I'd underestimated the peril I had put myself into, but this had not gone unnoticed by the local bobbies. I'd thrown myself into a freezing, raging river, a river that had claimed a lot of lives. I had ignored my own safety to save an unknown elderly lady. Later on, I was invited to attend a ceremony at the Town Hall, where I was awarded a testimonial on parchment – a Royal Humane Society Award for bravery, on a fancy scroll, endorsed by the Queen and signed by a member of the aristocracy. It starkly contrasted with the last time I'd featured in the local papers, as a reckless and ungodly criminal making off with the cathedral donation chest. It felt good to be famous as opposed to infamous, but also a little embarrassing.

I was clean and still very young. I saw Mitch a few times after my fifteen minutes of fame. Owing to my new status as a local hero, she was tempted to take me back. Again, it didn't really work out between us. I started going out to clubs to find a new girlfriend, succeeding with numerous short flings but mothing serious. I was with people my own age, all of whom were drinking or taking recreational drugs, and to some extent I felt like an outsider once again. Slowly I stopped going to recovery meetings and started going out to more and more pubs and clubs instead. I was on a slippery slope without even realising it. I thought I was having a good time, oblivious to what lay ahead.

I found being clean quite lonely. I was the only one of my age in recovery, and even though the older alcoholics in a different fellowship had welcomed me, I didn't really fully fit in. I tried to start up 12-Step fellowship meetings for people with the same drug problems as me. On a couple of occasions, we had a bunch of visitors up from London and a few that attended at times, but no-one stuck with it very consistently. Abstinence is a giant leap for youngsters to make. In the end I reluctantly folded the meeting. I'd had a gold necklace made by a jeweller, designed in the logo of my fellowship. It was a beautiful thing. I wouldn't keep hold of it for very long.

I started working the taxis at the weekends as well, with Stan and his brothers. I was earning good money, plus tips, with the added bonus of meeting plenty of women. I had it made, surely? I started seeing more of Sniff too. He was now a proper tattoo artist and he set about covering up some of his earlier very novice work. I gave him free rein and he covered me in intricate bird tattoos. This meant we were spending a lot of time together, and he was still a heavy pot smoker. One day, temptation prevailed and I persuaded him that I would be fine to have a smoke with him. He was wary, keen that I maintain my new lifestyle. Having convinced myself, I managed to win him round and I got stoned out of my mind. I'd not had a drug in my system for three years. It felt fucking amazing.

I was fearful that I would immediately be hooked back into addiction, but nothing much seemed to happen at first. What a relief! I made what I thought was a rational decision; I would smoke a little pot in the evenings, to help me relax. It felt so good to have a release, something to look forward to at the end of each day. Now I really did have it sorted.

Before long, I was buying my own supplies. Very quickly, it seemed to make perfect sense for me to buy weights instead, so that I could sell some on to cover my own costs, like any sensible person would. I'd be an idiot not to. Within a few weeks I was smoking on my way to work as well. Then it seemed foolish not to have a few pints to wash the pot down with, but only in the evenings of course. I had enough money, after all. The slippery slope had begun to steepen. Before long, heroin started to sing to me. My defences were down and I was in freefall yet again. I was abseiling off the edge of a cliff without a harness.

I didn't know how far I would fall.

Chapter Seven

A Lesson in History

My days were revolving around using more and more, and little else seemed of importance. I was still working, but my performance was suffering, and my using was slowly but surely progressing. I was still steel erecting and doing a bit of taxi work on the side at the weekends. My ears pricked up as people started talking about new party drugs like ecstasy. I wanted to give using another go, to see if I could learn from my old mistakes and use more successfully this time. However exciting these new drugs sounded, however keen I was to experiment, heroin was still my master. Eventually, I started to treat myself to the odd bag of brown powder. What was the worst that could happen? This time I would handle it.

I didn't want to be seen associating with the known addicts of Hereford, and this meant going to great lengths to keep my using private. It was easier to buy methadone under-the-radar, so I started buying big bottles of the stuff. It still wasn't easy and sometimes I had to go all the way to Liverpool for it – a six-hour round trip that would sometimes end in me crashing a car. Of course, I'd treat myself to a bit of heroin while I was there.

I was desperate to keep my clandestine love affair a closely guarded secret. Sometimes I'd head back to

Chester, to score from junkies I knew from my past. I was still just about managing to keep my job, but I'd started to eat into an overdraft and began cashing cheques too. All of these scoring journeys, dealing with addicts who I hardly knew, resulted in some dangerous situations. But these were minor details to any self-respecting junkie and all part of the thrill of the chase.

Once, I'd gone up to see Jazza, an old junkie pal I knew from my old estate in Chester. The estate that had by now been ravaged by heroin addiction. We had a system. He'd go and score for me, I'd give him a 'sorter' and then I'd head home. On one occasion there was a girl round at his. She was a really big girl, on the fat side for an addict. Unbeknown to me I had a target on my head yet again. Out of nowhere she whacked me round the back of the head with a hefty fire poker. She meant it and nearly took my head off, but I didn't go down. She knew I had money, but I managed to get out of the house. In a panic, I buried my money in a nearby graveyard while I considered my options. Eventually I managed to score, and I sighed a big relief; that was all that mattered after all. But it shook me up, I'd never been mugged like that, especially in a place where I felt I was among friends. Later I heard from Alan that my pal had been in on it too. This was the world I was entering, nowhere and no-one was safe. I found there to be little honour among junkies.

Early on in this relapse, I made the unusual decision to get away from it all. I could think of nowhere more exotic to venture than sunny Barbados. I'd only been abroad once before, and I set off on my exciting escapade. I landed in paradise with no idea of where I was going to stay or what I was going to do. I stumbled across a beachside residence owned by two elderly sisters. They let me stay for a very reasonable fee, cooking me traditional Caribbean food on occasion and generally looking after me. They tended to retreat to their beds early; I could then watch the TV and relax. I'd found my sanctuary, a home from home.

I scored some weed of course, but then I realised that there was no heroin on the entire island – which was strange as I had partly gone there to get away from it! It just wasn't part of the scene, it was all weed, cocaine and crack. I hadn't thought this through very well. I decided to visit a doctor. Surely he could prescribe me some methadone? I was informed that methadone was not available on the island either. Why would there be when they didn't have a heroin problem? My heart sank, my holiday in paradise was looking more like purgatory. I'd already been dabbling with the local crack, and coming down off that stuff was bad, it was pretty pokey. I needed some opiates to go with it and also come down on as I was getting fuckin' paranoid too. Luckily the good doctor wrote me out a nice fat script for Diamorphine. My heart began to sing. Those tablets were like heaven on this earth, a very pure opiate. Suddenly my holiday was looking up, big stylee. I had the best weed in the world, cocaine, crack and morphine. I travelled around pretending I was a guitarist in a rock band. I was hoping to pick up women, but it didn't work and I didn't care. I was with my first true love, drugs.

Even paradise wasn't enough, though. I rapidly ran out of money and had to claim my travellers' cheques had been stolen. Fortunately, they were instantly replaced with cash by a company rep who delivered it by hand. Of course, it would have been rude not to hit the doctor up for another script, using the classic line of "I've lost them". It worked a treat – happy days. I'd also been venturing into the shanty towns at night, scoring crack and weed. It was a buzz, a rush, a hit. Ducking and diving down the back alleys in the dark and the unlit streets, I was used to that after all, but this time guns were part of the danger. I talked my way out of a few hairy situations too. I always had the gift of the gab and an aptitude for manipulation. It saved my skin on too many occasions to count.

As a result of this dream holiday, I returned home with a worse habit than I had left with. I'd also acquired a taste for crack and cocaine. Rather than sorting me out, my trip to paradise had kicked my addiction up a big fat notch. I came back a different person, a desperate one. It was my fault, I'd added fuel to the fire.

I was still trying to keep my prestige of being clean alive, all the while having a secret affair. I succeeded in living a double life, for a while at least. I was still looking healthy too, compared to the average junkie anyway. I felt I was a cut above, confident I would never sink to their depths. The fact I had access to money and was slightly apart from the rest, also made me vulnerable. I was a trifle naive about the harsh reality of true addiction. It still hadn't taken me to its darkest depths.

Another time, I was up in Liverpool, scoring a weight with my pal Jazza, who had denied any previous involvement in the attempted mugging. We succeeded and went back to Chester for a use-up. I'm not sure what we'd scored that day, it was gear but maybe it was cut with something else. I ended up going over in a major way. I'm told they couldn't bring me round at all. The usual junkie protocol back then was to drag the unconscious body out onto the street and call an ambulance. Jazza didn't do this though, probably worried that my much-feared brother Alan would hear about it. So they decided to carry me up the stairs to a bed and wait for me to come around. They left me up there until the next day, but I still showed no signs of reviving. They'd been shaking me, slapping me, and of course robbing me, for over twenty-four hours. Eventually, fuelled by sheer panic, they called an ambulance. I was rushed into the Countess Hospital and eventually regained consciousness. I was wracked with pain and my legs refused to work. I was bewildered, confused and devastated; how had this happened?

The only thing I could think to do was to call my father. I felt utterly helpless. He was surprisingly caring, despite knowing that I had overdosed. I'd had no choice but to be honest with him. He took me back to the home he lived in with his new wife. I was still very ill and they put me to bed. I didn't know what was happening to me, I couldn't keep down any food or fluids. After a few days I was no better, and my father drove me back to my grandparents', hoping they could nurse me back to health. They must have been shocked by the state I was in. They had noticed a change in me but had held on to their hopes that I was still clean and in recovery. Seeing me a shadow of my former self was a blow to them.

I continued to get weaker and weaker. I could keep nothing down, everything was coming straight back up. It was now nearly a week since the overdose and I was showing no sign of improvement. In fact, I was going downhill. Eventually my grandmother called the doctor, who luckily came out to the house. After checking me over he called an ambulance immediately. I was rushed into intensive care for extensive blood tests. These revealed I required urgent dialysis – I was in renal failure. I later learned that they had called my family in that evening to make them aware that I may not make it through the night. I was hooked up to endless tubes as they attempted to flush my kidneys through. It was a critical twenty-four hours and death was precariously close.

It seems that being left in a comatose state for many hours had led to muscle death in my left leg. The death of those muscle fibres had released toxins into my bloodstream, which in turn leads to severe kidney overload and ultimately renal failure. If I had not been admitted to hospital that day, I would have died within a matter of hours. I stayed in ICU for nearly two weeks, as they continued to flush my kidneys through. Slowly I came around and I was alone in the ward. I saw a doctor in a white coat floating by, doing his rounds. I said to him "are you God?" He smiled and replied "no", before going about his business. I genuinely wasn't sure if I was alive or dead.

As I regained my faculties further, I became overwhelmed by the most incredible, unbearable thirst. Having not been able to keep anything down for nearly a week and now being on nil by mouth, I craved water desperately. I've never experienced a craving like it. It made any previous drug cravings seem like child's play. I was delirious and I couldn't understand why they wouldn't give me anything to drink. I was climbing the walls, begging them, harassing them, but all to no avail. All I could think about was the river. I fantasised about diving into its refreshing depths and drinking down my body weight in water. Dreaming of the heavenly River Wye, I ripped out the various tubes, needles and pipes and tried to stand up, planning to climb out of the window and run down to the river. I was naked, apart from a flimsy hospital gown, and I soon discovered that my legs were useless. I was way too weak and I folded into a heap on the floor, realising that I wouldn't be running anywhere for a long time. The monitor alarms began to resound all around me as I lay there, finally realising how very ill I was.

After that escapade they agreed to give me a solitary ice cube every four hours. Those magical cubes of joy were the best hit I've ever had. Simply pure frozen water. Aside from them, it was a tough time for me. Family came to visit, all distressed, looking at me like I might die at any moment. Mitch came to see me briefly and that gave me a real lift, as I still held onto the idea of getting her back. My sponsor, Polly, from the fellowship in Hereford, also visited several times. She'd been generously supporting me for the past three years even though we had little in common. She was a well-spoken middle-class lady who had a good job with Social Services. She was probably in her fifties back then, and a very active fellowship member. She knew that there was a 12-Step meeting held in the psych ward, which she arranged to take me to in a wheelchair. Of course, I snuck a quick roll-up cigarette on the way. It was a mad meeting and yet again I learnt that neither alcoholism nor addiction discriminates. There was a blind woman and a man with severe cerebral palsy, both suffering from acute alcoholism. It has been known for those with alcohol problems to look down on or shun junkies, but I have never experienced that. I have always received a warm and friendly welcome. I've never been turned away by any fellowship, ever.

Eventually I moved to a normal ward and was allowed to eat and drink. Finally I was sent home, to my grandparent's house. My journey back to full health was to be a long, frustrating and painful one. It was months before I could walk even as far as the corner shops. I'd also damaged my sciatic nerve, so I used a stick and was attending physiotherapy. I'd gone from being strong and fit, navigating steel beams at height, to hardly being able to shuffle to the bathroom. After many months I was able to stagger the whole one mile to the swimming baths, in order to accelerate my physical recovery. Polly was still driving me to meetings. She is probably in her seventies now, still sober to this day. I owe her a great deal and value her presence in my life during that period

It took me over six months to regain a semblance of reasonable health. I was also grieving the loss of

Mitch. It had become clear that she was seeing someone else and we had no future together. At some point I was able to return to work, steel erecting and taxi driving once again. My grandparents moved to a different house and I moved with them. I felt sad to leave the little tin house that had been my sanctuary for so many years, but the new place was modern. No longer did my grandparents have to cope with ice inside the windows, condensation and draughts. It was far more suitable for their declining health but it was the end of an era for me.

Slowly but surely, I was getting back on track. I started clubbing and dating a bit again too. My focus was on the external trappings; the girls, the cars, the trimmings. I paid not enough attention to how I felt on the inside. I was young and it was understandable, but I had a lot to learn. Most of it the hard way. I also started to spend a lot of time in the bookies, sometimes losing all my money in one go. Unbeknown to me, I had started yet another descent.

In a cruel twist of fate, my grandfather had been diagnosed with stomach cancer. It was difficult and upsetting for everyone. He'd been prescribed some little pink pills for the pain and again, my ears pricked up. They were called Diconal and I'd never tried them. Before long I'd helped myself to his entire prescription. I'd started injecting them too. My opiate receptors had yet again been opened, the switch had been flicked. Soon I'd slipped back into full-bore addiction, yet again going to great lengths to keep it all a dark little secret. Once, I travelled down to London for a big blow-out, away from the prying eyes of Hereford. Soon I'd run out of cheques to cash, sold my car, lost my job and was seriously struggling for money. I even sold my gold fellowship necklace for scrap. But the gear seemed to be getting better and better. It was strong and a little bit moreish. It had me by the balls. I was right where it wanted me, on a downward spiral.

Chapter Eight

Lessons to Learn

I didn't keep my job for much longer. If I was withdrawing, I'd be weak and sweaty and I'd be found lying down in the back of the van. My work ethic was in sharp decline. My secret little love affair was beginning to flourish and take over. My poor grandparents had their suspicions, although they clung to their denial for as long as they could. They so wanted me to stay clean and do well, but they had seen the warning signs before. My grandmother had also been diagnosed with cancer, so now they were both unwell. As I buried myself deeper into addiction, their serious health issues went straight over my head. I was rapidly returning to typical self-centred addict mode. I loved my grandparents deeply and could not allow myself to think about their declining health. It was easier, and less painful, to bury my head in my beloved light-brown powder. As they struggled to care for each other, they could no longer cope with me. I was asked to leave; I'd lost my sanctuary yet again.

Initially, I moved from one cheap bedsit to the next. Having now lost my job, I was relying solely on benefits. Eventually I found digs above a pub called The Golden Lion. I was on the top floor, and it had an open house feel with all the other occupants also being users. None of them were into opiates though, they stuck mainly to pot, speed and acid. Before long I was selling speed and pot again, and things were starting to feel a lot more social. I relished the powder power of dealing and I was very careful to keep my opiate use and methadone script a closely guarded secret. I remained faithful to my old friend, the needle, but always behind a firmly closed door. My arms were already becoming a mess, lined with track marks and unsightly sores. Long sleeves were essential, even in sweltering heat.

I binged on party drugs to the extreme, regularly embarking on three or four-day benders, relying on my opiates to see me through the deathly come downs. I was selling a lot of speed from a new contact in Liverpool. Edward was long gone, sadly. My weight was dropping rapidly, as I was never able to sell drugs without using them too. Whenever I went up to score in Liverpool, I always treated myself to a little weight of heroin. It would be rude not to. My compulsion to use heroin never went away, despite my script and party drug binges. Once it's got you, it never lets go.

I'd go back to my grandparents from time to time, normally to scrounge money which I seldom paid back. In the end I was turned away by my uncle. I'd fleeced them too many times, he told me. At the time I had no comprehension of what they must have been going through, both fighting for their lives. I'd drifted away from my entire family by now. Both brothers were living in Chester and I'd bump into my mother on occasion in town, but only by chance. We had little connection left; I was only interested in one thing.

The party scene had begun to take off around Hereford. I befriended the Jackson twins, who were both aspiring DJs. They put parties on out of town and I immersed myself in this new underground scene. Everyone was taking ecstasy – well everyone I knew, at least. I'll never forget my first E. It was at a rave in The Cavern in Liverpool. I recall an amazing feeling of love and energy, and the overwhelmingly deep connection to the music and everyone around me. I wanted to live this life, the party life! I didn't want to be in the rat trap of heroin addiction.

One day I had an urge to get away from it all. I fancied a day out, an adventure! I bought myself a cheap day-return to London, even though I had no idea what I wanted to do or where I wanted to go. I was walking through a London train station when I saw a very attractive Japanese girl. I said something funny and we struck up a connection. She was a university student called Yukiko, the daughter of a professor. I was instantly attracted to her, she was petite and very pretty, and for some unknown reason she was very keen on me too. My drug addled brain could barely compute what was happening. She ended up coming back to Hereford with me for the weekend soon after. She used to come up at weekends and we'd go out raving together. I kept my opiate affair hidden but we took party drugs together. She must have been attracted to my particular brand of insanity and bought right into my madness. I assume she had been confined by a strict academic upbringing and was looking to spread her wild little wings. She fell for me and I was never quite sure why.

Eventually, I convinced her to move up to Hereford with me, claiming that she would learn the English language better if she immersed herself in the culture. I borrowed money from her and bought a little van for us to run around in. It was a boxy little Suzuki which looked more like a toy car. I didn't care, it helped with my dealing pursuits. I'd got a beautiful girlfriend, I was dealing and I was mobile. Things were looking up for me, but how long would it last? I was oblivious at the time, but I treated her very badly. I fleeced her, I even slapped her a couple of times and I gave her a lot of drugs. I even gave her heroin once but it nearly killed her. In return, she naively gave me her virginity. I didn't sleep with her straight away, as I really did treasure her and didn't want to defile her. It's one of the ugly dualities of addiction; you can care deeply for someone but still hurt them, against your own will. Nothing and no-one can stand between the addict and his poison of choice. Years later, I tried to track her down to make amends but she was impossible to locate. I still carry deep regret and sadness around my treatment of Koki. There was no malevolence in my treatment of her but it was not my finest hour. I loved her but I also used her.

One day something strange happened. The police came around to the flat and arrested me. I was dragged into the station and kept there for about six hours, before being released without charge. When I returned, Koki ('Coke'-'Eeee' as I called her) was long gone and I never saw her again. I'm convinced the police arrested me in order to persuade her to leave. Maybe they had seen the unhealthy dynamic from afar, as I was well known to them. It was a bad day for me, but in the long run a good day for Koki. With hindsight, I'm glad she got away.

I felt very sorry for myself after that. My heart ached and my drug progression worsened. I'd been very careful to restore my reputation as a non-junkie. I wanted to mix in these new party circles without carrying the stigma of heroin addiction. Yet again I kept my methadone and opiate use to myself. No-one trusted a junkie, they had a reputation as thieves, liars and grasses. In other words, they'd sell their own grandmother for a box of Diconal. I worked hard to restore my already tarnished character; I'd been outcast from recreational drug circles before. I loved the feeling of belonging, for 6-8 hours at a time that this new party scene brought.

My kudos was high, as I could get hold of good speed. I went to a few illegal raves out on the airfield. They were mainly put on by the travellers and the police would be there in force, in cars, vans and helicopters. We put our hoods up and partied on, the police forming a surreal perimeter fence. It felt subversive and dark, and I wasn't sure if I liked that feeling or not. I feared the law, I didn't like rubbing shoulders with them, literally. I was used to the smack world, where I did everything in my power to avoid the police. They were my biggest foe for many years, real or imagined.

My beloved methadone script was also a troublesome burden to carry. It required turning up for appointments and providing clean urine samples, both of which are impossible for any self-respecting addict. An addict is neither famed for his reliability or his drug-free piss. As a result, my script was frequently stopped, or put on hold, for days or weeks at a time. Then I would have a big problem. It was a considerable stress – in fact, an opiate habit is one big constant stress. I'd be forced to scratch around, buying either meth or gear. Luckily, I was cut a lot of slack by the drug services. They'd known me when I was clean, and in many ways they were rooting for me. Because I had been abstinent for those years prior, they didn't know me as just a junkie. I'd been unique in Hereford at that time; no-one else had succeeded in remaining totally clean. I'd banked a healthy credit of care and respect.

One Christmas, I was late to pick up my script and missed it. Nobody wants to be withdrawing over Christmas, it was to be avoided at all cost. The shops were closed, criminal opportunities were more limited and supply could be patchy. I was destitute, scared and depressed. In desperation I presented myself at A&E, tearfully explaining my predicament to a sympathetic nurse. She went above and beyond, rousing the resentful pharmacist out of hours. He arrived at the hospital with an emergency pre-scription. His anger and disgust were palpable. Who can blame him? Understandably, junkies are no-one's favourite folk, in fact they tend to be resolute pains in the arse. Let's face it, we're a bunch of jokers! We seldom work, frequently steal, and are an abject drain on society. I didn't compute this at the time, but with hindsight it cannot be overlooked. However, I will never forget that kindly nurse, she helped me when most would have shunned me. She had spared me a Christmas of cold turkey.

Opiate addiction is a cruel and ruthless affliction. While the highs bring extreme pleasure and huge rewards, the lows bring untold pain and desperate misery. It's akin to balancing on the sharp blade of a double-edged sword. On one side ecstasy, on the other agony. The drive for the high depleting the rational mind, urging it to overlook the painful price that must always be paid in one form or another. It's the same with all addictions, they can never be rationally explained. While scripts are not the answer to treating addiction long-term, they play an important role in harm reduction and temporary stabilisation. They reduce desperation and therefore crime. They also reduce illness and disease. Of course, this is if they are taken as prescribed and only taken alone.

By now, the drug services in Hereford had started a needle exchange. Owing to diseases such as Hep C and HIV, it was possible to have a plentiful supply of clean pins. A life-saving resource, although I frequently forgot to attend when required and found myself re-using the same old blunt pins repeatedly. It's that chaotic junkie syndrome yet again, I'd have struggled to organise myself a wash in a bath house. Health and safety was a long way down my list of life's little priorities. I was aware of these diseases, but it didn't change the way I behaved. Once, I used a needle belonging to a woman in Liverpool, who'd told me she was HIV positive. I washed it through with tap water and carried on. I wanted a hit; life really was that simple.

Another dangerous habit I had was to drive while gouching out on heroin (nodding off to sleep). If I went to Liverpool to score, I'd take some before I headed back home, obviously. As a result, my driving style consisted of bouncing off the curbs, while 'resting my eyes'. The curbs acted as my hazard warning system. It's a miracle I didn't die or take anyone else out with me. I travelled miles and miles bouncing off the kerbs, my eyes too droopy to see. Something was watching over me yet again.

On one occasion, I was returning from Liverpool the worse for wear. Somehow, I'd manage to zone out, crossing the opposite carriageway, before descending a steep embankment. Suddenly I came to, realising with horror the error of my ways. I was carrying speed, heroin and acid, a sitting duck. Ominous blue lights came flashing towards me. Things were looking dire and I envisaged a lengthy sentence. My very best acting skills were mustered and I convinced the coppers that I'd swerved to avoid a dog. Without carrying out background checks, they towed me back up the bank and sent me merrily on my way. A minor miracle.

I negotiated the rest of the journey with droopy eyes and a nodding head, finally hitting the outskirts of Hereford, relieved and exhausted. Relaxing slightly, I must have nodded off again, hitting a curb with such force that the flimsy little van flipped over onto its roof. I was suspended upside down, travelling at speed, sparks flying past from either side of the van, before the windscreen shattered all over me. The van finally came to rest upside down, in the middle of the road. It was the dead of night and the roads were deserted. I crawled out, disorientated and panicking, I was carrying, remember? I needed to get away from the van but I wasn't sure which way to head. I wanted to get home, to refuge, yet I'd lost all sense of direction. The housing was sparse as I was right on the edge of the city but I found a door on which to knock. A sympathetic man answered my prayers and pointed me towards the city centre. I walked away with my life, and with my drugs.

The next day, I visited a recovery pound to look at my van, and I was shocked by the wreck that confronted me. It was bashed and caved in like a trampled sardine can. How I'd walked away without so much as a scratch was beyond me. I received no charges and I also managed to claim on my insurance for the van. A gruelling journey, but a ridiculously fortunate one. One of many blessed car crashes I'd walked away from unscathed. I'd had several incidents of losing the road and careering through hedges and fences, once ending up on a railway track. I was a dreadful driver, a dangerous, careless and reckless one who never seemed to learn from my mistakes. With hindsight, it was tremendously selfish. I had no more care for others than I did for myself. By grace and good fortune, no-one else was ever injured. Something I will be eternally grateful for.

By now, I was on my arse. I'd messed up with my dealing contacts because I repeatedly incurred debts. Very few addicts manage to deal drugs successfully for any length of time, so it was a common story. My habit had increased, as expected and I became worse and worse at maintaining my treasured, yet troublesome, meth script. I was little more than a sad and lonely giro junkie. Suicidal thoughts began to haunt me. I'd descended so far down, I was struggling to see a way out. Aged only about twenty-six, I was convinced I would be dead by the age of thirty-two and certain I would live out the rest of my days as a helpless drug addict. If only I could keep the drugs rolling in for the next six years, until I could rest my weary bones in peace. Death had already started to look like an appealing prospect. I would go out in a blaze of glory!

Amid all this chaos and desperation, both of my grandparents died. I was so detached from my feelings and my family that I only heard about their deaths through chance encounters. My grandmother, my eternal ally, passed away first, but I was so dishevelled and ashamed that I didn't even attend her funeral. Shortly afterwards my grandfather also died. Again, news travelled down the grapevine to me but again I felt too unworthy to show my face at the funeral. Numbed out by drugs, their deaths didn't really penetrate my consciousness. I wouldn't feel my grief for many years to come.

By now, my mother had remarried and became Mrs Taylor. Her new husband would not allow any of us brothers into the house, due to our drug taking. Unbeknown to us, he was a big drinker, prone to serious violence against our mother. They had a flat on Springfield Avenue, although they spent time away in his caravan, owing to his gypsy heritage and a job recovering cars from motorways. We were oblivious to her plight, all on our own individual slippery slopes. Fortunately, it was not a long marriage and my mother had happier times ahead. She deserved them! They divorced after a couple of years, but our whole family had become fragmented. Alan and Teddy both lived in Chester. Teddy's mental health was in further decline and Alan attempted to keep a brotherly eye on him, inviting him around for meals and baths. Teddy had never been any good at caring for himself. We all had tough times ahead of us.

For me, many arduous years of utterly miserable using were to follow. I existed, a haunted and unhappy shadow of my former self. I owned nothing, moved from one grim bedsit to the next, wearing the same stinking, stained clothes for weeks on end. Hygiene had become of little consequence. I was painfully thin and pale grey in colour. All of which mattered little. I was concerned only with heroin, my meth script, speed and my weekly giro cheque. I started shoplifting and committing other petty crimes. I was forever in and out of the courts on suspended sentences and was occasionally remanded in prison. I normally ended up on the hospital wing due to my drug dependency. I lived in fear of being arrested and locked up, where I would have no choice but to withdraw. I had slowly but surely become a stereotypical junkie. I'd been opiate dependent for a good stretch and the withdrawals were horrific by now. The worst time to be arrested was a Friday afternoon, because you knew you'd be in the cells until Monday morning. A fate worse than death for any heroin addict.

It was on one of these short stays in Gloucester prison, that I was padded up on the hospital wing with quite an impressive character. He was about my age, but unlike me, he really had his head screwed on. He'd been caught with over thirty kilos of weed in his garage (and that's a lot of weed to be busted with). He shouldn't have been on the hospital wing, but he'd told them he was suffering from panic attacks. He was well connected and managed to get hold of whole ounces of weed at a time. We devised a clever bucket bong contraption in our cell, always careful to climb up to the window to exhale the pungent fumes. When not in use, the bong would be dismantled back down into its individually innocuous parts.

Sometimes he would tell me to shout the guards, as he launched himself into a full-blown panic attack. He had the guards convinced by these Oscar-winning performances and ended up being shipped out to the Stone Bow Unit, aka the local nut ward. He was a clever fucker; life's a breeze in those places, compared to prison. He'd done a few months in the nut ward and had been declared unfit to stand trial. He'd successfully avoided a lengthy prison sentence and was already free as a fucking fairy. I liked and envied his style; he was a touch of class.

But my powers of persuasion were still intact. Once, I talked a pot acquaintance into giving me his chequebook and card. He was to wait three days before reporting it missing, I would share the spoils with him, and he would be compensated by the bank. It seemed like a sensible thing for him to do. However, within a matter of hours I had hatched new and more exciting plans that did not involve him. Not only was I kiting cheques anywhere and everywhere, but I also realised I had the raw materials to apply for a temporary passport in his name. I got busy buying tents and camping supplies. I was off to heaven – Amsterdam – travelling on his dime.

I pitched my swanky new tent in a field on the out-skirts of the city. I'd then go into the city to cash his cheques and buy my drugs. Before long I was nabbed by the Dutch police for using the dodgy card and hauled unceremoniously into the station. It was all foreign and very modern, they were even handing out Methadone to addicts in the cells, something I was not used to. Fortunately, when I'd been arrested, I only had my own passport with me, his was back in the tent. I knew if the police found the fake passport, I'd be in line for much more serious charges. I eventually managed to convince them that I'd found the card and couldn't remember where I'd pitched my tent. I knew I'd be in serious trouble if they found the false passport, stolen goods, or looked into the spending on the card. Luck was on my side and they gave up pursuing me further. I was at the station for a few days, gratefully swigging down their methadone. Although I wasn't rattling, smoking wasn't allowed, so I spent my time desperate for a fag instead. If it's not one craving, it's another.

I was also worried about what they would do with me. After a few days they finally plonked me on a ferry bound for England. They furnished me with thirty euros for food and drink. Foolishly I spent this on board, convinced I would be arrested at the British port. Now I had something else to worry about. There was a police warrant out for me in the UK for failure to appear in court and I assumed the Dutch would have notified the police back home. That was how I lived my life, a constant game of cat and mouse. But the police were not waiting for me, which threw up a whole new set of problems. I was now penniless, miles from Hereford and withdrawals were in the post. Life was a constant and soul crushing ballache.

I jumped the train across England. I usually pretended to be asleep over an opened newspaper, or I'd hide in the toilets. I was a seasoned pro when it came to free train journeys. I arrived home rattling and tired, my next little issue now being my government assistance giro cheque. I needed it urgently, yet it was common for the police to arrest people at the job centre as they collected their cheque. It was always a nasty surprise to be walking out, giro in hand, only to be grabbed by the police. I had no choice but to risk it, and again lady luck was shining down on me. I negotiated the back alleys of Hereford and cashed my precious giro without issue. My relief was palpable. I'd evaded arrest once again.

My fear of rattling in a cell constantly taunted me, it had happened too many times. Generously, I gave the guy who had given me the chequebook and card a bottle of whisky and forty fags. The warrant was still hanging over my head, but I was used to that. I was always evading court or genuinely forgetting to attend. I'd have to stick to the back streets and alleyways for a while longer. I was used to navigating the underbelly of the city.

Because I'd stayed clean in the past, had a bravery award, and had built up a good relationship with my brief, the courts tended to be lenient with me. My patient and kind-hearted brief always claimed that a "custodial sentence would serve my client no purpose at all". It usually worked, but it did tarnish me with a dubious reputation as being a possible grass. I didn't care, so long as I wasn't rattling in a cell.

I still managed to sell the speed from my contact in Liverpool, if I could get myself organised. Mobile phones and pagers were becoming more common, so this made organising long-distance scoring slightly easier. I didn't have a phone, but he did. The guy was solid and his speed was unsurpassed in quality. The same went for his coke and, unsurprisingly, I developed a taste for injecting the stuff. This came with two downsides – I could easily get through an awful lot of it, and it also made me paranoid as fuck. As a result of my prolonged speed and coke usage, I was trapped in the purgatory that is drug induced paranoid psychosis. I suffered with this for many years, long after my final last hit.

I owed money to some nasty dealers in Chester and for many years I was convinced they were still after me. I would see them lurking in the shadows and hear them talking behind my back, I would spend hours listening as they whispered taunts at me through walls or windows. It was a scratchy existence and because they never actually caught up with me, I convinced myself that they were playing with me for their own amusement, having some fun with me, before they shot me, or hacked my legs off with a rusty sword, as they had threatened to do if I did not pay them. I lived in morbid fear for my life, year after year. Once I even begged the police to bang me up in the cells, shoving an eighth of weed on the counter after they initially refused. I had to give them no choice; I needed to feel safe for just one night. But I could still hear them. They were whispering and taunting me through the cell walls. They knew every move I made, they communicated on walkie talkies, were clever strategists, and they were slowly but surely hunting me down. Sometimes I'd spend a whole night pleading with them to spare me; I knew they were hiding behind the chair in my room. The fact that it was self-created made it feel no less real – at the time I was under its spell. It was a torturous and unrelenting existence.

I went to the hospital to beg them for help, convinced I was about to be shot. In the end they put me in the local psych ward, and luckily they gave me some methadone as I was withdrawing badly. I wanted them to take the terrors away. Lowered from my relentless upper usage, a fragment of doubt crept in, was I really being hunted? Then I heard them outside, they were climbing up the drainpipes and whispering to me. I was right after all and they had found me. I checked myself out of the hospital in a blind panic. What I really needed was psychological help.

Whenever I ended up on remand in prison, I was convinced they were still after me. I believed they were in league with the prison officers and the plot to kill me was still in full flow. Only now I was trapped, I was a captive target. It was a living hell. One painful night I reached breaking point and I begged to see the prison doctor. I wanted him to knock me out, I couldn't cope for a second longer. I was told the doctor would see me in the morning. I started to break the table in my cell and smash it about, screaming for medical attention as I did so. Next came in the riot squad officers with batons and shields (well over the top) to pacify me.

I was stripped naked and dressed in a smock, before the door was slammed shut on the padded cell and loudly bolted. I should have felt safe but I didn't, I could still hear the whisperings. I started screaming,

"I'll cut myself to shreds if you don't help me." The guard opened the hatch, laughing, "Yeah right, what with? Go on then!" I knew they'd forgotten to remove my watch, so I smashed it to pieces and began slashing my arms with the broken glass. Now that I'd injured myself the doctor had to be called. I was given some kind of downer. It helped, but only by a fraction. I wanted help or else I wanted to die. After a couple of days, I was moved to a bare cell and given a mattress on the floor. I was withdrawing too. It wasn't like nowadays, there was no methadone or meds like that given in prison, it was tough turkey. I never told them about the voices, I didn't trust them. Before long I was released, and I was back out into the madness. Uppers, downers, needles, and the voices. The downers turned the volume down but never for very long.

I knew that injecting the speed and coke made this exhausting 'reality' worse, yet I couldn't stop doing it. The coke was so pure, it melted away in cold water, the rush so intense, the compulsion too strong. Neither the paranoia nor the dire state of my failing veins was enough to stop me. Nothing was. By now I'd lost all of my main veins; they were collapsed and as tough as leather. I now had to use a much finer half-millimetre syringe and I'd spend hours stabbing at myself. My feet, my legs, my palms, and even under my fingernails had all been targeted. I only had capillaries left, so it seemed. Nothing was easy any more, a living nightmare.

I'd also graduated into a prolific shoplifter. I'd pinch anything, from fur coats to fairy cakes. I'd walk miles and miles across town selling my wares, whatever they happened to be. Sometimes I'd nick to order; makeup, clothes, electricals. Or I'd resort back to my best sellers – joints of beef and bottles of spirits. Selling stuff was always possible but it required cheek, resilience and lots of leg work. My days of being a car owner were a long way behind me. It wasn't an easy career move for a paranoid psychotic who already felt like he was being watched and hunted. I'd weave through the back alleys, in fear of both the police and my relentless hunters. I was a frightened mouse, being pursued by some very big cats.

For a time, I was homeless, no fixed abode as it was called, or NFA. If I couldn't find a sofa to surf, I'd sleep in derelict buildings, unlocked cars or anywhere remotely sheltered. I knew of a block of bedsits with a communal bathroom, and I'd sneak in and sleep in the bath. That was until the landlord found me, and he was wielding a baseball bat and it hurt, so I didn't return to that particular safe haven. There was a caravan on a building site that I could get into sometimes. Occasionally I'd oversleep and they'd arrive for work and come into the caravan to make coffee. I'd lie stock still underneath the filthy tarpaulins at the back, trying not to even breathe. I'm surprised they never sniffed me out. I rarely washed, I had one set of clothes, I was infested with head lice, and I didn't even know it. I was painfully lonely and at an all-time low. I knew that I had inflicted this living hell upon myself, which only made it worse. I also knew that I didn't have to be living like this. I'd been clean before but I couldn't find my way back.

It was alleged, so the story goes, that there was a tiny bank in a small market town I knew well from my travels. It was said that one day I hatched a daring and foolhardy plan, fuelled by a few pints of Stella. Apparently I wrote a note, stole a mask, and nicked a cap gun from a toy store. The day was busy and the streets were bustling with happy shoppers. Apparently I entered the bank and by sheer luck it was devoid of any other customers. I approached the counter, my head and face covered by my new mask. As I wielded my fake gun at the bank teller, I slid my note across the counter. It read "fill a bag with money". I held the gun steady and stared him down. I glanced down at the cheap kids' toy and it glowed of purest plastic. The teller was convinced it was the real deal, it was pointing straight at him, after all. He desperately filled a money sack with notes and hurled it towards me. I left the bank at a hasty, yet casual, saunter. I did not look back.

The story goes that outside I was able to mingle among the bustling shoppers, removing my mask with a swift flick and dispatching it onto a bin along with the toy gun. The money under my jacket, I weaved my way out of the town centre, several thousand pounds the better off. They said I made my way out of town, heading towards Liverpool, that I had a debt that needed paying. It was further alleged that after a binge I finally made it back to Hereford.

I actually was arrested on suspicion of that armed robbery. I wasn't entirely surprised, my paranoia had expected as much. I was hauled into the station in a very serious fashion. Before long, I was dressed up in a scarf and mask and shoved into an identity line-up. Most of my line-up companions were mask toting policemen and a couple of locals who got paid something like £5 a time for the work. As luck would have it, I was ignored and one of the coppers was selected. My pounding heart sang relief for a short while at least. My shoes were taken for examination and my handwriting analysed. This was a serious business, I could be looking at a lengthy stretch. Half of the druggies' doors in Herefordshire had gone in, the police were determined to weed out the culprit. They'd put word out among the grasses and arrested a lot of other people, offering to let them go in exchange for any information.

My trusty brief was on my side though. He only knew me as a petty criminal and he must have known this was too far away from my usual MO. My mother was called in to persuade me to confess, a tactic that fell onto deaf ears. They were suffering from a serious lack of evidence. A dealer had grassed that I'd had an uncharacteristically fat wedge of cash, but that was literally all they had. My shoe prints came to nothing and there was no CCTV. They had nothing solid and had to release me. I've never been so relieved to walk out of a police station. Someone less paranoid than I may have gone around town bragging about something like this for kudos. Many acquaintances quizzed me with impressed curiosity. I said nothing to no-one, ever. For once my drug-induced paranoid psychosis was my friend, it kept me out of trouble and more accusations. It was said I was naively clever; so simple a plan had actually worked. After relatively limited planning and a few pints of Stella. So it was said.

My intrepid moment's aside, life went on in much the same way, one year more or less merging with the next. Drug highs, drug lows, blows, sickness, dirt, grime, selling, stealing, paranoia, ducking, dodging and diving. Memories are scant but I do remember one particular Christmas. I was at my mother's on Christmas Day. It was unusual because both Alan and Teddy had come down from Chester. I was stunned to discover that all three of us were suffering from heroin withdrawal. Alan had been so anti-heroin when we were younger, and I had no idea that it had also got the better of Teddy too. I was shocked and saddened. It was a miserable Christmas, we were all penniless. It must have been horrible for our mother, we were all trying to blag money from her, money that she didn't have. In the end she gave us her last few quid and we bought some pot between us. It didn't really help, but it was better than nothing and we were relieved. It was Christmas, we were all doing cold turkey and sleeping on mother's living room floor. On Boxing Day, we went our separate ways. We'd never see Teddy again.

Alan, now a full-blown addict himself, was on his own mission of self-destruction. He'd been stabbed back in Chester and had come into conflict with some very nasty characters. He'd done a fair bit of selling too and had at times done quite well for himself. For a while he was flying around in a sports car, until he nearly killed his girlfriend in an accident where she'd gone flying out of the plastic back window of a soft top at high speed and rolled down the road. It was rumoured that he was heavily into safe snatching up and down the country. He too had learnt that a heroin and coke habit could be a pricey little problem. It was also rumoured that once he happened across a box of gold treasure in the grounds of a monastery; it was clearly a monk's hoard, which I always found slightly ironic. Alan was a prolific sneak thief and I heard that this was a big find. Rumour has it that it kept him in drugs for over six months. Come to think of it, he did go through an abnormally generous patch for a while. He was also a real tough nut. If you were a drug dealer who was sitting on drugs or cash, your door would be going through and you would be handing over your stash. 'Taxing' was commonplace, a hazard of the dealer's job. It was also an unreportable crime, which gave it a unique appeal. I never had the balls for it, but our Alan did.

After several bouts of homelessness and living in empty-bedsit-land, I managed to acquire my own council flat. It was just another derelict dive though, complete with damp and mice. At least it was a base. I can't say it was warm and dry, because I could rarely afford heating. My mother didn't live far away. By now she had divorced the pikey and had met a Liverpudlian guitarist called Kirk. One day I went to her flat, probably in search of food or money. Alan was now living in a flat next to The Golden Lion, in Hereford, and he was doing a bit of dealing. As I walked up the stairs, Alan was waiting for me at the top. He announced, "Our Teddy's dead." It didn't register, I couldn't take the information in. How could he be? He was only twenty-four! He wasn't meant to die before me.

The police had been round earlier that day. They'd said Teddy had been found dead in his flat back in Chester. He'd been moved out of the tower block, where he used to take acid while climbing about on the roof. Due to his mental health problems, he was under the care of some agency or other. He was meant to have been safer in his new ground floor flat, that's what we'd all believed. Because he was so bad at taking care of himself, he would give his benefit book to a woman who ran a local café. She would then ensure that he had one good square meal a day and also look after his benefit book for him. When he'd not showed up for his meals, she'd raised the alarm. The police had found our Teddy dead. He'd been drinking and taking methadone, he'd passed out, but he never came back round. He'd choked to death on his own vomit. Our mother was inconsolable. She'd been running up and down the street screaming out "my son, my son." I've never seen a person in so much pain and distress. She's never fully recovered from losing Teddy, I don't think mothers do. I was numb. I couldn't help her, I didn't know how to, so I left her flat, and went and smoked a lot of dope. I didn't fully grieve his death; I was too numbed out by drugs. At the time I used it for sympathy, in the hope of getting a few free drugs. That's why I will never forget that miserable Christmas, the last time I saw Teddy alive. Our Teddy – kind, mad, sensitive, funny and tragically addicted.

I did attend this funeral. We were all on the front row. I had my arm around our mother, she was sobbing her heart out and I did my best to be there for her. She had three sons, all in the grips of ruthless addiction, and now one was dead. Our father was there too. I hadn't seen him since my overdose. The funeral was held in Hereford, but some of Teddy's friends had come down from Chester. I recall seeing a black girl. Later Alan said that he thought she'd had Teddy's child a few months after his death. Maybe there's a Little Teddy out there somewhere?

A while before his death, Alan had got wind that a lad was selling Teddy methadone. He'd paid this lad a visit and warned him off. After Teddy's death, Alan and our father hunted the lad down, planning to take revenge. They found him, bundled him into the back of a car and drove him out into the countryside. They proceeded to give the lad a good leathering. From what I can gather it was a horrible beating and I heard rumour of broken bones and all sorts. He took the brunt of two very frightening men's anger. It probably made them feel a bit better, and it was the way things worked back then. Some call it council housing estate mentality, but it wouldn't bring our Teddy back.

After Teddy's loss, our mother really struggled. She had her pleasant, clean and tidy flat on Springfield Road, but she wanted to move up to live with Kirk. I'm guessing she needed a change of scene. She asked me if I wanted her flat. I jumped at the chance of course. I'd be the best kept smack head in town. We managed to do an exchange with the council. I was home and dry, or so I hoped. I had big ideas. I'd stick to my script, smoke pot and drink a cheap bottle of sherry in the evening, to warm me through and help me sleep. I would be straight, that was my idea of living, of being normal.

I really had no idea of how to live an ordinary life. I actually did consider myself straight or clean for a while. Even though everything revolved around numbing myself out, that was as far as my aspirations stretched. I stuck to my new plan for a while. The highlight of my week would be watching *The X-Files* and maybe a morbid documentary or two. My mother had left her little dog, Fly, with me. A little whippet cross who I tried my best to look after, but my efforts frequently fell well short. It was around this time that I remember vividly the death of Princess Diana. Despite my downer usage, it hit me pretty hard. It was all over the news and I was mesmerised by how an entire nation was unified in grief. I even made a black armband and wore it on the day of the funeral. Even though I was clean, the state of the flat deteriorated, regardless of my best intentions. I didn't sleep in the bed, preferring the couch, I had painted the bedroom walls in gaudy tie-die colours. My mildly more manageable sherry days were to be short lived.

I reconnected with a DJ contact from the past, who had now been dragged down by the smack himself. He was a more affluent junkie than me, and he sold the stuff. I'd helped him with some good drug contacts in the past, so we had a bit of a bond. This relinquished connection enabled me to start selling again. Before long the flat had evolved into a full-bore shooting gallery. There was a lot of traffic through the place, the buzzer buzzed, the stairs heaved and I had a way of supporting my habit. God knows what the elderly lady downstairs thought. At the time, I didn't care. I was back in the game; I was the man.

I had a system in place. I'd bury most of my stash in the garden and only bring in a gram or so at a time. Once it was bagged up, I'd stash the bags within the rubber seal of a window. I hoped it was too high up for sniffer dogs to locate. I always pretended I was getting it from somewhere else when I had customers round. The flat may have been busy, but I was still lonely and I trusted no-one. My door came in a couple of times, but the police never found anything except paraphernalia. My cunning and paranoia stood me in good stead once again. I really thought I had it going on; I could afford to use, I had a flat, and I'd regained a bit of powder power. In reality, I was a walking, talking car crash. I was lonely, depressed and out of my mind with paranoia. My body was little more than a skeletal pincushion. By now I was collecting boxes of a hundred needles from the drug services. I thought nothing of it. My cocktails of choice at that time was the faithful speed-ball, a potentially fatal mixture of heroin and cocaine or amphetamine. Death is not un-common, owing to the antagonistic nature of the two drugs. I knew this, but I never gave it much thought.

One night I felt in a very dark mood. The voices were haunting me and a deep-down darkness bubbled within me. Sometimes when that happened, I'd see the stark grimness of my life, yet I couldn't envisage a way out. I started to feel a strong, dark presence. The flat still had a lot of my mother's things in it, as she'd left it fully stocked. One of the windows had a shelf above it, and on that shelf stood a big chunky wooden crucifix. Suddenly the crucifix fell from the shelf with a loud thud. It had landed facing me, upright in a chair. The thing was, the chair wasn't directly under the window. Somehow the cross had managed to travel several feet sideways, before lodging in its unlikely final posture. I felt it staring straight at me. I had no idea how it had landed in the chair and I still don't. I wasn't hallucinating, it was all very real. If anything, it shocked me back into reality. I felt I could sense Teddy in the room and I didn't like it – as a rule I tried not to think about him. It hurt, and I was in enough pain already.

Even though I didn't really want it to, my life went on. I had the security of the flat and continued to deal heroin and anything else I could get hold of. The status of being a dealer gave me a certain kudos with junkies and drug users of the opposite sex. I made a very unlikely hook-up with a girl called Chloe. She was only dabbling in heroin when we first met, but she was attracted to my status as a hard-drug user and dealer. She was tall, dark, attractive and from a wealthy local business family. I couldn't understand what on earth she saw in me, I was a lost-it junkie after all, but as ever had the gift of the gab and some charm. Of course, it's obvious now, she would have gained a certain type of status herself, as the girlfriend of a heroin dealer. Bizarrely, heroin carries with some a certain elite status within some drug circles, being both feared and revered simultaneously. So our relationship had a weirdly twisted symbiotic pay-off. Her parents lived in a self-build out in the countryside, it had a huge sweeping driveway, a lake, extensive grounds and a purpose-built annex for Chloe. She was young, attractive and wealthy; I had landed, finally. A date night would consist of a big session on the heroin, coke and speed. To me she was posh and straight; I was her dream bad boy.

She ended up moving in with me and I was managing to stay on top of the dealing and could support our habits, just about. I tried to cut down my use of the needle to fit in with Chloe. My hands were riddled with track-marks and I was paying Razor, by now a biker-junkie, to cover them up with tattoos. I'd known him from The Saracen's Head pub years before. He'd been so anti-smack back then, but was by now ruined by it. I came across a surprising number of such people over the years. Heroin had a unique power and did not discriminate. I was paying Razor in smack; in return he had free rein with his tattoo gun. He covered my hand in a tribal Maori tattoo; big thick deep ones that I lived to regret in later years. Yet another stupid drug-induced decision.

As our relationship had brought Chloe down a level, it had likewise brought me up a notch. She brought a pinch of order to my life of chaos and bedlam. She had not sunk to my depths and I raised my game to accommodate her. I didn't want to lose her. This is not to say that my paranoia and madness had left the building. Chloe went through hell with me. I was now convinced the flat was bugged by the police and they were filming me from up in the attic. I felt like I was under constant surveillance and frequently acted for the cameras. Ironically, I still continued to take and sell drugs; I didn't have a choice about that. At times I became convinced that Chloe was a part of this plot, believing she had befriended me purely to report back to the police. I'd think I could hear her whispering and plotting against me. It was a sticky foundation for any relationship, but somehow she stuck by me. We'd visit her parents and I would feel naked, crippled by shame and worthlessness. In their presence my bravado and status would evaporate. I couldn't even smile as I was vaguely aware that my teeth had seen better days. The blight of every junkie; oral hygiene being but a distant memory. I had long resembled an anti-drug poster boy. Life was simple; just avoid all mirrors.

I had some crippling bouts of paranoia, so severe that I actually wanted to get clean. I knew my relentless drug use was making matters worse. I was running out of balls, and rapidly. Once I fled to my mother's place on the Wirral, to withdraw and sort my life out. I was in a total mess. My arms were swollen and bruised from injecting, I was emaciated and in severe emotional and mental distress. I lay on the sofa in Kirk and my mother's flat, wracked by horrendous withdrawals. Kirk tolerated the situation out of love for my mother; she had finally found a very decent and gentle man. He'd been a guitar player in a band but had been forced to give it up due to a degenerative eye disease. A small man with strawberry blond hair who was warm and kind. My mother had finally found some happiness in him.

A curious fact about Kirk is that he had a genuine, but illegitimate, bloodline lineage to the King of Spain. Strange but true, for a man living in a two-bedroomed flat on the Wirral. After the first day there, I became convinced that cars parked up in the car park were my persecutors, yet again in pursuit of me. I watched the street relentlessly, twitching with acute anxiety. Then my twisted and deluded mind constructed a different scenario. I imaged they were hounding me in order to encourage me to sort my life out and get clean. They had now become almost benevolent pursuers; my mind was shot. This same psychosis had been haunting me for years. I was mentally very unwell and part of me knew it too. I turned to drinking spirits in an attempt to ease the torture of withdrawal. I managed to see it through for about five days – I was determined to cast my old life aside, Chloe included. However, as the days passed, my willpower and determination dwindled. Chloe came to visit and before I knew it, we were out scoring as always. I was right back to where I had started, yet again. I had gone through five days of hell for nothing.

I was with Chloe for a few years all told, using, dealing, rattling, and desperately trying to stay clean. The drugs didn't work any longer and staying clean wasn't working either. Nothing worked any more. The state of the flat slowly but surely declined. We never slept in the bed, it was like a sacred untouched hPim grail. We gouched out on the sofa, one day running into the next; depressing at best. At some point we became conscious enough to finally realise that the dog was infested with fleas and we were infested with lice. It had been that way for months, but we hadn't noticed. We were like the living dead.

Alan was incarcerated around this time. He'd got wind that someone was trying to set him up, so he went to visit the bloke, carrying an iron bar. He did a lot of damage and got a good few years. He was initially charged with attempted murder, but this was eventually lessened to GBH. It was during this stretch in Gloucester Prison that he decided to get married. The lucky lady was called Nicky. Chloe and I received an invite to the wedding and, with our mother, we made four guests in total. He'd been allowed out for the wedding, with two guards in tow. The cuffs were removed for the ceremony, after which he was allowed an hour for a mini-celebration. Half the reason he had organised this wedding was so that he could get his hands on a sorter and I'd taken a couple of grams of smack and some coke in, as a wedding present. I handed it over and he 'plugged' it; he was good to go. I'm sure he strutted back into that prison on top of the world. Married and an arse full of drugs, what more could an inmate want? With a stash like that he would have been king of the wing.

I'd taken a video camera along to record this most bizarre and decidedly unromantic occasion. I watched it back and it merely provided me with a deeply shaming reality check. With horror, I watched myself smiling. I had very few teeth left, and the ones that remained were either rotten or stained. I rarely looked in a mirror and was oblivious to what I actually looked like; a toothless emaciated ghoul. I was disturbed and riddled with a deep shame. Chloe still had all her teeth; what on earth was she doing with me? That recording which was supposed to be funny was ironically a shaming and painful dose of reality.

One night in a haze of drug fuelled depression and fearful paranoia, I concluded that it was for the best to take a paracetamol overdose. I ended up in A&E a good few hours later, I have no idea how. They told me that it was too late to pump by stomach and I would have to wait a few days to find out if I'd done myself serious damage. I was admitted and tubed up to the hilt, withrawing too, of course. My paranoid delusions escalated as I waited to see if I would die. I began to believe that everyone who visited the ward had really come to look at me. To see me – a circus freak, a total fuck-up, a lost cause.

I started to repeatedly make the sign of the cross with my eyes, as an antidote to the evil that coursed through my veins. My aunt brought her son Jeremy to see me. I was viewed as some kind of exhibit, an example of how not to live your life. I became convinced that I was evil and begged to see a priest. I wanted to be exorcised. Eventually they found a willing member of the clergy and he came to talk to me. The curtains were drawn around my bed, as I explained that I was born on the sixth month, of 1966. He looked me straight in the eyes and smiled. He said, "you don't need an exorcism, son." I spent some time trying to convince him but he quietly left. I lay there, unsure of whether to believe him or not. Such thoughts had haunted me since childhood.

I lasted about four days before my drug cravings became unbearable and I unhooked myself and walked back out into the madness. I was lucky never to be psyched-off and drugged up for the rest of my life. Those were still the days of electric shock treatment, but luckily I evaded it. I was in and out of psych wards for years, so severe were my delusions, but by luck or grace I was never in for long. All the time, in the back of my mind, I knew I didn't have to be living this life. I'd been clean before, surely I could do it again? That's all I wanted, to be free of my crippling drug dependency. In a rare lucid moment, I had the idea to move back to Weston. I could clean-up, attend 12-Step meetings and sort my shit out.

Chloe and I packed our bags and drove to Weston Super Mare. Thankfully Chloe had a car, courtesy of her parents. It was on a whim – we had made no plans and didn't know where we were going to stay. We abandoned the flat in Hereford. The bills hadn't been paid for months, the bathroom was sprayed with blood from cleaning out syringes and the place was heaving with grime. I was glad to be out of there. We were driving towards a new life, full of fear about the withdrawals and excitement about what lay ahead. We attended a 12-Step meeting that night and I bumped into a guy I knew from before, called Steve. He let us stay and we were up most of the night chatting about recovery and life in general. I was worried my persecutors had followed me, but Steve was a big burly guy and he made me feel safe. I was now convinced that they believed me to be a police informer and wanted to kill me. I was trapped in an endlessly changing plot.

Steve reassured me that I would be all right. He spent most of the night talking about his girlfriend, who had just left him. He was heartbroken and probably glad of the company. He was a staunch 12-Step member, with fifteen years of sobriety under his belt. He was later to start drinking again, due to this break-up, and sadly died of his alcoholism after a fairly short time. The guy was a good soul and yet another sad loss.

We soon found a bedsit and I managed to score. This was to be our very last hit, as the junkie said to the nun. Needless to say, as soon as the withdrawals started, I was out looking for ways and means to buy more. Weston was not the new chapter we had hoped for. In fact, it was even more miserable. I didn't have the contacts, so making ends meet was far tougher. I was terrified of shoplifting and getting locked up. We were both scratching round, spending more time rattling than high. It was utter misery. Sometimes Chloe's parents would send us lump sums, due to our desperate manipulations, but other than that we were mainly skint. I had the very best intentions but they always came to nothing. Ironically, we'd ended up in a bedsit that was right next door to a drug rehabilitation unit. I would see the clients coming and going, looking healthier, cleaner and happier each day. It made me feel worse about my own situation, but it also gave me back a tiny glimmer of hope. I felt like I hadn't smiled in months, or years even.

To make matters worse, I couldn't get a methadone script in Weston. I tried, but they wouldn't script me. Those were desperate times. Meth had always been my safety net, now I was out on the raw, ragged and frequently rattling edge. We still had Chloe's car and we were often back and forward to Hereford, scoring and swapping stuff. That car did a lot of scoring miles. Sporadically we tried in vain to stop, but we couldn't do it. The most we ever got to was day three, then we'd buckle and Chloe would be on the phone begging her mum for money. She got a job in a care home, though god knows how she kept it, she was rattling half the time. Her monthly pay cheques would be gone within a few days. I did land a couple of jobs, but they didn't last very long. One was in a mushroom factory, out in the countryside, amid a sea of poly-tunnels and sheds. It wasn't the type of mushroom picking I was accustomed to, but I suppose I had genuine experience. I got fired from that one for punching someone. I believed him to be spying on me for my persecutors. The other job was in a catalogue sorting factory. I lost that job because an expensive penknife had gone missing. In addition to these misdemeanours I was terribly unreliable; I couldn't work if I was sick, which was most of time. I certainly wasn't going to win any employee of the month awards.

I had one pair of shoes. A pair of smart looking brown brogues. They looked great, but they were split down the back, so they were loose and difficult to walk in. I didn't even steal a new pair of shoes; I'd lost my mojo for shoplifting. The only thing I used to nick was a tub of Ben & Jerry's ice cream on a Sunday night. Don't ask me why, it was a weird little habit, a rare Sunday treat. I was still tormented by my paranoid delusions and by now I'd decided that I was a government experiment. I was suspected to have both HIV and Hep C and I believed I was being monitored and studied by the powers that be. From our bedroom window I could see a radio mast, and whenever I got hot sweats I believed that they were cooking me alive with radio waves. My mind wasn't my own.

The dog, Fly, was now in failing health due to old age. She was a loyal and loving dog and we'd done our best to care for her. However, our best often wasn't nearly good enough. Sadly, she wasn't always taken for walks when we were sick. She was always fed at least, but very cheaply, and it wasn't a stable environment. We eventually took her to be put to sleep; it was the kindest thing to do. I still wish I'd taken better care of her, although I did the best I could. She came everywhere with me, like a shadow. Again, I had hurt something that I loved.

I hooked up with a Cockney guy who had a smart method of breaking into BT phone-boxes. It involved making a couple of clever holes in the right places, and then removing the coin box. It took him a few minutes and he needed a lookout and view-blocker at the door. We travelled far and wide in search of new phone-boxes to hit. Sometimes they were full of money, sometimes they only yielded a few meagre coins. I wasn't given a fifty-fifty split, I'd get a sorter. From my sorter I was meant to sort Chloe too, but sometimes I didn't. Never ever trust a rattling junkie, even if they're your best friend.

In a way, not getting a meth script was a blessing in disguise. If I'd had one, I wouldn't have felt so desperate for change. I could have chugged along in the misery for much longer. I didn't see it at the time, but it is true. I'd started drinking a lot, out of sheer desperation. Chloe had gone to work one day, and I'd necked a bottle of vodka. I decided to take her beloved Ford Escort for a spin. I ended up wrapping it into the back of brand-new Mercedes. I was filled with remorse over that, not the fact that I lost my licence, but that I'd let Chloe down and destroyed her beloved car. In the end her father replaced it, but he didn't like me by this stage. They were getting wise and were not happy about the direction their much-loved daughter's life was heading. Who could blame them? For my part, I am sure my relationship with Chloe saved my life. She was a great leveller, and she just about kept my head above water. She wouldn't let me sink too far below the surface.

Spending more time rattling than using was grinding me down. I was on cheap strong cider when I could afford it. It was rotten stuff that had certainly never seen an apple. I'd nick a quid out of Chloe's purse first thing in the morning and stumble to the corner shop for a can. I had to have something. I had to hold my nose to drink the rancid poison, because I hated the taste of it so much. I just wanted to sleep, to slip away, to not be. The doctor had given me some pills for my head. They didn't work, but they did mong me out and make me dribble. I'd applied for every Social Services crisis loan going and I was clean out of scams; I was running out of options. I was getting sick and tired of feeling sick and tired. All the time I was watching the clients in the next-door rehab getting better, healthier and smiling. The lucky fuckers. I wanted to smile again, or die, either option would do. I'd tried another detox in a local hospital but left after seven days.

In my desperation, I knocked on the door of the rehab I had attended over ten years previously. I begged them to take me in. Of course, they couldn't, I'd need some funding. I begged the drug services for help. They suggested that I apply for a rehab out of Weston; I'd stand a better chance in a town that I hadn't used in. To get a place I needed to keep up appointments and show willing. After years of failing to keep any appointment, I was sufficiently desperate to give it my best shot. I specifically asked for a 12-Step rehab and I was eventually offered a place at one, many miles away in Lancashire. After a couple of phone assessments, my place was confirmed and a date was set. I was nervous and anxious and I knew I had to leave Chloe behind. I felt very sad and failed to make the set date, out of sheer fear. Luckily, they offered me a second date – a rare occurrence, so I was told, as places were funded by strict Social Services' criteria. Normally you only get one chance, as places are expensive and much sought after but I had always been a good blagger. A second date was set. I'd promised that I was clean and did not require a detox. I lied; I knew I was going to be very ill indeed.

Chloe was to drive me up there and we stopped by at my mother's on the Wirral. Alan, now a free man, had moved up there too and was living on the infamous Woodchurch estate in Birkenhead. We went around to see him; he was with his new wife and they had a child now too. He was up to no good and doing a bit of dealing. I was beginning to go into withdrawal and he was smoking gear right under my nose. He offered me some. For the first time in my entire life I said "No." I'd made a decision; The Decision. I left his flat feeling rough, but different. I don't know what had come over me, but I was going to rehab. Something had changed. Chloe drove me the rest of the way to the rehab. It was a huge old Victorian house that had seen better days, on the edge of a coastal town called St. Annes. We said our goodbyes and I walked in through the grand old doorway. I didn't look back; I daren't. I was desperate to start a brand-new chapter.

Chapter Nine

Rehab Revisited

It was 5 December, 2000 and I was literally shaking with fear. I stood in the hallway, feeling like a little lost lamb. The grand old house, which now functioned as a rehab, had seen better days. I could smell a pungent mixture of detergent and cigarette smoke and I could hear a plethora of voices coming from the room on my right. I was quickly ushered up the huge sweeping staircase to the nurse's station. I was strip-searched by a stern breezeblock of a woman called Maud. She snapped on her rubber gloves with relish, but thankfully my cavity remained unsearched. I suppose it was her idea of a little joke. Half of my few possessions were confiscated; I was not allowed any books or music and certain toiletries were prohibited. Any aerosols or perfumery were taken, to prevent inhalation or consumption. My vital signs were taken and I was matter-of-factly informed that if I didn't get clean, I would not have long left to live. All I could think about were the dreaded withdrawals ahead of me. I'd told them I didn't require a detox; a lie. I knew I was going to feel very rough, very soon.

I was allocated a bedroom and then introduced into the group sitting room. The air was thick with cigarette smoke as about twenty-five residents stared at me, weighing me up. All ages, sexes, shapes and sizes were represented. I was overwhelmed and couldn't take it all in. All I knew was that some looked well and some looked sick, like me. I could already feel the first icy tingles of withdrawal. There were some big personalities, balanced out by some extremely meek ones. I kept myself to myself and smoked a roll-up in the corner. I tried to look cool but I didn't feel it.   My insides were churning and my brain was racing.

I had a rough night and it became obvious that I was not as clean as I had claimed to be. They called the doctor out and I was prescribed Clonidine, a medication that is rumoured to reduce the severity of cold turkey by lowering blood-pressure and reducing the mental instability. I can vouch for the fact that it does very little. I didn't sleep for weeks, I poured with sweat constantly and I couldn't keep my restless legs still. I do think it took the edge off the anxiety, stomach cramps and acute temperature fluctuations that accompany any withdrawal. I was still in hell though, but I had committed to this place. In a way, I suppose I had already surrendered.

It was a very strict institution, more austere than the one in Weston. It was to be weeks before I would be allowed any freedom at all, and even then, it was heavily restricted. We were in dreaded groups all day long and most evenings too. These groups were brutal, revealing and frequently shaming or enlightening. Several residents were on what were called jail swerves. They would need to complete the nine-month programme to avoid lengthy prison sentences. Some left, finding the idea of five years in prison a more palatable prospect. Groups were well structured but ruthless. This place wanted its clients to go deep. Some couldn't handle it but I was ready. Regardless of how ill those on detox were, we were required to go into groups, morning to night, explosive stomach issues being the only chance of being excused. There was no rest for the wicked, so they say.

The nights were long and a prospect I feared. I was allowed downstairs twice each night, for a timed cigarette break. Sometimes a member of the night staff would sit with me while I smoked, as I sat huddled over the electric fire. Other than those brief respites, they were endlessly long, very lonely nights of racing brain, sweating, kicking legs, cravings, dark haunting thoughts and utter desperation. For anyone who has not had the pleasure of heroin withdrawal, I cannot emphasise enough how grotesque an experience it is. The body malfunctions in every way possible, coupled with the rawest and most melancholy of emotional states. I possessed not a shred of happiness or positivity; it's a very hard thing to see through. This darkness reached a peak during those long, interminable nights.

Their bloody sleepy tea did absolutely nothing to alleviate this particular brand of torture. I'd taken a lot of drugs for a long time and a chamomile tea was not about to combat my chronic withdrawal insomnia. In the end, they gave me a Walkman and an Enya tape. It took the edge away from the deafening silence and the booming volume of my own torturous thoughts. I found some of the more obscure tracks powerful, and in the dead of night I shed my first tears for many a year. Something was shifting and it wasn't pretty.

I'd been buying and taking a lot of meth too, and methadone withdrawals are a far lengthier affair. I'd mutter the odd prayer during those ceaseless nights. Who I was praying to was unclear, but I prayed all the same. They call it the gift of desperation. It was the same desperation that stopped me walking out, finding a local junkie and scoring a big fat bag of heroin. I'd look at the blackboard, on which clean-time was recorded next to all our names, in ranked order. I was at the very bottom. I wanted to hit the milestones of 30 days, 60 days and 90 days, but they felt like a lifetime away. One day of rattling equates to a several weeks of normal time.

I'd only been there about a week when I learned that I had become an uncle. Alan's partner had had a second child, who they named Leah. The happy news actually landed; I felt it and it hit home! I was happy to be an uncle. I was looking forward to my new role and could picture a future ahead of me for the first time in a long while. Because the veil of drugs was slowly evaporating, not only could I feel, but I could also remember. I remember my days in that rehab more vividly than any of the proceeding years. It's an experience that will stay with me forever. It was tough but it was also tremendously powerful.

I sat in those groups, ill as hell and not wanting to be there. I was soaked with sweat, as was the back of my chair. This unsightly sweating phenomenon continued for months. It transpired (or perspired) that it wasn't merely the withdrawals, but a symptom of my pent-up emotional state. I was so full of fear and shame and so emotionally shut down, that my only outlet seemed to be via my sweat glands – and out my feelings poured, quite literally. Groups were intense and could be confrontational and often brutal, with the aim of breaking down the walls of resilient denial and defence that every addict has spent years fortifying. They were also endlessly fascinating and informative, which had the spin-off effect of keeping my busy brain occupied. The basic programme consisted of a life story, so that the group and counsellors could get to know you, followed by consequence letters from family and Step-One groups. Even if it wasn't your group, it was constantly triggering. Another person's story would resonate and trigger off painful feelings, whether you liked it or not. Many days were gruelling and emotionally strenuous.

Step-One groups involved forcing the addict to face up to the powerlessness and unmanageability of their drug and alcohol use. Everyone would wade in with hurtful insights and sometimes abuse. One working girl was hit with "you're nothing more than a human spunk bucket", but it was all right because it was prefaced with the phrase "with care and respect". That's how groups went down. After a while I started to enjoy them, so long as I wasn't the target. There were also powerful moments of genuine and loving concern. It was harsh, but often with good reason and the structure and discipline had been carefully planned. In many ways I admire the way that place functioned, though these days the ethics would be questionable. It was like a well-oiled psychological transformation machine.

As soon as the worst of the rattle was over, everyone with few exceptions, gained a ravenous appetite. Meals were highlights and in particular the supper trolley. Every night at about 9pm it would be wheeled in, piled with cheap sandwiches and biscuits. Even our behaviour around this was monitored carefully. You would be challenged if you ate too little or if you ate too much. It was not uncommon for female addicts to also harbour dormant eating disorders, which would often resurface once the drugs had been removed. If they did not eat enough this would be a concern. They would then be monitored and a fellow peer would be put on vomit watch. If a resident ate too much, then this would also be challenged, as they were deemed to be fixing their feelings with food. Swearing and even farting were heavily fined and money would be taken out of our weekly pocket money. You could be challenged for isolating, but also for being too friendly. If you were over-conscious of how you dressed, you'd be dressed in rags from the dreaded cupboard under the stairs. This was called a scruffy assignment. But not being smart enough was also a crime. Sometimes it felt like a no-win, but the aim was to eliminate all means by which an addict might fix themselves. There was usually a member of staff around, watching and listening. No stone went unturned in their efforts to break down the addict. Our every move was monitored and analysed. The cunning and defensive addict was left with nowhere to hide.

We were all made to do therapeutic duties, which included cleaning and other household chores. We were force-marched around the block twice daily on the walk of shame and had little, if any, free time. There were no free lunches in that gaff. The therapists ruled with iron rods, honed carefully from power and fear. I was tempted to do a runner many times, but I had nowhere else to go and I knew I'd use again if I did. After the first month or so I started to get more sleep and began engaging in the group process. It may have been a seven-day-a-week boot camp, Big Brother on Steroids type affair, but I witnessed some amazing transformations in there. I saw addicts and alcoholics waking up to the damage of their addictions and having spiritual awakenings. I also saw people walk out the door, only to be dead within a couple of days. Countless people didn't make it; a rare few are still clean to this day. It literally was a matter of life or death.

My psychosis had followed me up to Lancashire of course, but I felt safer than I had done in a long time. I was tucked away in a remote location, which helped a lot, but additionally my mind was kept busy which helped to keep my demons at bay. One of the few times I reconnected with my old life was when my mother came up for my Family Conference. The idea was for the family to confront the addict with the harshest realities and truth of their using. They were asked to write a letter detailing the damage and hurt that they had caused, and then to read that letter out to the addict. These conferences were much feared and had taken on an almost mythical status within the house. I was expecting a half hour catalogue of resentments and horror stories from my mother. All she had written was *"My son needs to believe in himself again, forgive himself and realise his worth"*. That simple insight hit me like a steam train on speed. My mother was not full of resentment and hatred. Her enduring love and ability to forgive shook me to my core. Despite everything, she still saw the best in me and wished me well. I could also feel her deep pain and vulnerability. Even the counsellors did not press her for gory specifics; they felt the power of her carefully chosen words. It was a powerful and transformative moment for me.

The counsellors could be formidable, most notably the infamous head counsellor, Sal. A powerfully built blonde woman in her fifties, she always wore a power suit and heels. She was brutal and blunt but she also helped me. She told me how it was and didn't mince her words, but I also felt genuine care from her too. Some residents bore a deep hatred for her but I surprised myself and held her in high regard. She had noticed that I was paralysed by a racing over-analytical brain. She encouraged me to feel as opposed to think. Something easier said than done.

Slowly I crept up the leader board and eventually hit the significant milestone of 60 days! I remember sitting at my dark bedroom window and watching the sun rising above the horizon. I was waking up to the beauty as well as the pain. There was a dim and distant world out there and I wanted to be a part of it. I hadn't ever watched the sun rising in real life, free from a heavy shroud of substances. I could hear the birds singing, smell the crisp winter air through the cracks of the draughty sash window, and I could feel a wave of excitement and optimism. My senses were coming back to life – I was coming back to life.

I was a bit of loner in many ways. I was so deter-mined and focused on making a go of it this time and I was also aware that I had been given a free detox, something that normally costs a lot of money. They could have sent me home, but they didn't and I was very grateful to them. My luck of the devil had saved the day once again. I'd also been here before and was terrified of not making it this time. I was fearful, angry, analytical and deeply perceptive. I made a few good friends over the months, some of whom I've remained in contact with ever since. Deep bonds are formed in such an intense environment.

There were some incredibly funny people too. Addicts, on the whole, are a very funny bunch. I have enduring memories of proper belly laughing until my sides and face hurt. I'd not used my laughing muscles in a long time. I was actually alive, no longer one of the walking dead. I was beginning to feel the good and the bad. Larry and Bean were the resident comedians, both so quick-witted it was almost painful. Both were talented impressionists, who unleashed their talents mainly at the expense of the counsellors. They both eventually went back out there and I've no idea what became of them, sadly. As was the case for countless others.

The house was heaving at the seams with indescribably rich characters. Bean and Larry will always stay with me, they brought immeasurable comedic value. There was a Scouse alcoholic called Paul, who used to work on the fishing trawlers. He'd regale us with tales of how he used to "fuck a cod" on quiet lonely nights at sea. He didn't even say if the poor things were dead but I'm sure they were when he'd finished with them. There was a Chorley girl called Beth, who bounced around like some kind of gangster's moll, fresh out of prison. Sandy was a right royal mess, she had no teeth at all, until one day the dentist fitted her with the biggest set of false gnashers I've ever seen. Of course, we weren't the kind of folk to mock the afflicted, but it was often impossible not to. She looked vaguely like a cross between a chimp and a horse. Lucy came in looking a trifle on the rough side. Unusually, she was overweight, with punk clothes, fishnet stockings and bright badly dyed orange and blue hair. I could never have predicted what the future would hold.

I had a crush on a very posh alcoholic from Cheltenham, called Katherine. There were several very posh people, who tended to affect an air of superiority as they were 'only' alcoholics. In reality, they were often in a worse physical state than us junkies, suffering horrors such as wet brain and liver sclerosis. Sal was always quick to point this out to them, however posh they might be. Their letters from home revealed that they were so posh, they'd been drinking nail polish remover or paint thinner.

Then there were a couple of imposters who turned out not to be addicts at all. One was a taxi driver who claimed that crack tasted like bubblegum. He was wrong, and he was out the door, quick sharp. I was hoping they would say the same to me, but that never happened. Who was I kidding? It's what they call denial. I barely had a vein or a tooth left. We had a Cockney gangster who, upon deeper scrutiny, was not interested in recovery but needed somewhere to lie low for a couple of months. He too was rapidly discharged.

There was a fairly even split of addicts and alcoholics. The alcoholics tended to be grandiose while the addicts would be looking down at their hubris and grandiosity, labelling them as either posh tossers or lightweights. It was like the best *Generation Game* conveyer belt I'd ever seen; every few days another spectacularly fucked-up human specimen would appear before my eyes. It was a rich and highly amusing tapestry and tragic in the same breath. Like I said, Big Brother on Steroids.

We were so ensconced in that bizarre and unique environment that the outside world seemed distant, yet a bustling high street was a few yards down the road. It was such a hard-core regime and totally structured – and it worked. It almost shocked clients back to life. Because my mind was occupied from 7am until 10pm, there was little time to feel loneliness or self-pity, although we all did at times. I still found some time to wallow in misery and self-pity; why break the habit of a lifetime? This was challenged by Sal, who simply would not tolerate anyone sitting on their pity pot. Slowly, those times decreased and I began to thrive for the first time in a long time. Even on a Sunday we partook in group activities, either rounders on the beach or games in the local church hall. Once a week we did line dancing, which was surreal. I'd heard rumour of it shortly after I'd arrived but assumed it was another wind-up. It wasn't. I'd never seen the toothless masses, myself included, doing a kick-ball-change to Dolly Parton. We were also encouraged to meditate and pray. A couple of evenings a week we walked in crocodile fashion to local 12-Step fellowship meetings. Again, I was inspired to see people who were managing to stay clean and live rich lives on the out – and I'm not referring to financial riches. Each week that passed, my hope and optimism increased.

There really was never a dull moment. There was always some drama or other unravelling. Part of me loved it – it was endlessly fascinating. The dynamics of the group were intriguing. Someone was usually up to something they shouldn't be, but the counsellors would invariably sniff it out. They had amazing noses, powerful sixth senses, and I was starting to discover that I had one too. I started to realise that my instincts were important and could often be relied upon more than my other faculties. I began to tune myself in and gained significant wisdom. You couldn't sit in three laborious groups every day, week after week, and not brim with new insights. I could tell when people were telling the truth and being real and when they were not. My gut would start to twitch at the first sign of bullshit. This ability strengthened, the more I connected with my own feelings. At first, I could relate more to other's feelings than my own. I had been so totally shut down. Everyone was so exposed, it was a steep learning curve for us all. Because we went through this intense journey together, strong and powerful bonds began to form.

Sexual relationships were forbidden and getting away with anything on that front was very rare. The counsellors had noses like bloodhounds for any kind of special relationship. I managed to steer clear of becoming entangled with anyone. I was too scared of being evicted and I had nowhere else to go. It was called fixing, with good reason. Take the substances away and it is the first port of call for most with addiction issues. I had a couple of crushes but I kept myself safe. Several people were removed from the house for having illicit relations. We'd usually hear a couple of weeks later that one, or both of them, were using again, or even dead.

Two addicts in early recovery staying clean together is beyond rare.

After about three months of primary treatment, I was told that I would benefit significantly from secondary treatment. It had started to emerge that I'd had a tumultuous childhood; everyone started to emotionally leak after a while. I wanted and needed it, as I knew it was what I'd lacked the first time around. It all rested on me getting funding and after a couple weeks news came through that I'd got it. It involved moving to a different house and peeling back a lot more layers of the onion. I had to wait for a bed to become available first, which took several weeks and was a testing time. I nearly got into a fight with Larry, an offence that would have seen us both removed from the house instantly. My temper was coming to life too.

Lilly Lodge was a smaller, cosier type of house at the other end of town. It was nicknamed the house of love and it housed about fifteen, as opposed to thirty. Residents were allowed a lot more freedom and could even go into town at lunchtime, unaccompanied. It was still wall-to-wall groups though, morning till evening, five and half days a week.

I'd expected it to be easier. I was so very wrong.

Chapter Ten

Lily Lodge

We were deliberately told little about secondary treatment prior to arrival and it always sounded strangely elusive. While we were allowed slightly more freedom, the intensity did not diminish. I sat in my first group fearful of what lay ahead, pouring in my own, by now familiar, sweat. The head counsellor was a big burly Australian guy called Mark, who was in recovery himself and whom I came to greatly respect. He had developed the 'Beyond Addiction' programme at Lily Lodge, perfecting it over the years. At the time I was simply struck by his size and sheer presence. I sweated a little bit more, oblivious to the fact that he was actually a warm and caring man. The other counsellor was a female called Jacqui. She had a friendly and gentle energy, with oodles of dark curly hair and a kind wry smile. I already knew some of the other residents, as they had either moved on ahead of me, or I'd met them during activities or at 12-Step meetings. We were a motley looking crew.

The aim of secondary treatment was to tackle the addict's underlying issues and get right down to the real nitty gritty of a person, untangling their pains, fears, triggers, motivations and more importantly their trauma – thereby enabling them to feel happier and more complete, hopefully decreasing their inclination to numb themselves out with chemicals. It is well known that lots of individuals with addiction issues have suffered great traumas in their lives. Lily Lodge required residents to dig up this buried pain, stare it straight in the face, relive the emotions this evoked, and then begin their unique healing process. While primary treatment was concerned with breaking down the addict defence mechanisms, Lily Lodge was about engaging with the human and building them back up with nurturing care. Groups tended to be less confrontational and more support-ive. This didn't mean they were easier, they were very heavy indeed, as people were dealing with painful issues such as child abuse, sexual abuse, rape, abandonment and rejection, along with the guilt created by their own addiction. Many had had torturous childhoods, and many had lost or mistreated their own children during their addiction. Everyone was strongly encouraged to connect with these painful emotional memories. This wasn't always as easy as it might seem; many addicts have spent a lifetime supressing such feelings. After years of perfected repression, emotions can rarely be conjured at will. This was a struggle we all faced on a daily basis.

Once a week or so there would be a beef group, where anger and resentments within the house would be aired and hopefully resolved. With a house full of people all working on their deepest pains, dynamics can get tricky and heated. Often, feelings are transferred onto fellow residents and troubles can quickly spiral. There was a punch-bag room where everyone was encouraged to work off their anger. The tools consisted of a punch-bag, a baseball bat and a pair of boxing gloves. The pummelling and screams that came from that room would reverberate around the entire house. I practically lived in there at times.

New people came in, while others moved on into supported living, walked out, or were asked to leave. The latter normally happened if it was felt that they were not engaging in the process, got into some kind of intimate relationship, or of course relapsed on drink or drugs. Through all these comings and goings I made strong bonds with my fellow long-haul travellers. Sandy was still an entertaining inmate, with her notable new teeth and her stories of a smuggled in vibrator. Her shiny new gnashers had a habit of dropping down and clacking together while she spoke. Her long-term husband was still out there using and she would sneak off and see him. Then she did a lot of work to let him go, as he couldn't get clean and was due to serve a long prison sentence. Years later he found 12-Step recovery too and they got back together. They both now have substantial clean time and are still very happily married after forty-odd years. It's a happy little story within a sea of sad ones.

Stu was a big gentle guy from down south. We called him the Changeless Man. He was one of the few who survived the full duration without worrying about those bothersome little things called feelings. I think it's just the way he was, more well-balanced than the rest of us and a beautiful soul. Somehow, he didn't get kicked out for not engaging and he was a rock of kindness and support for many. Paul was from way up north and we called him Upside-Down Head, because he had no hair and a big black beard. The only way you could tell if he was having a feeling was when his big hairy toes wiggled around inside his Jesus sandals. Bean and Larry were still hanging in by the skin of their teeth, funny as fuck but not exactly mentally well. They eventually got kicked out after being caught watching porn videos on the TV. I don't know what became of Larry, but I saw Bean years later – ashen-grey, skinny and in full blown scoring mode. He was such a ruthlessly funny man, it was sad to see.

There was posh Brian, the alki with a gentleman's relish fixation, and Christine, the banshee, a tall, loud, mad woman from Warrington. Beth was still there. Very mouthy with a broad Lancashire accent, she fancied herself something rotten. Then again so did most of the men, but some people will shag anything in early recovery. Sex drives come back to life with a vengeance once the drugs are removed. People got up to all sorts but I'll spare you the gory details. Then there was a very young Asian lad nicknamed Bobby Damage, who really connected with his deep pain and cried an awful lot. Sometimes he'd be reduced to primal screams and sobbing. Dez fancied himself as Manchester's answer to Del Boy, a wheeler dealer whose dad would pick him up in a Bentley. He was trying so hard to connect with his feelings that in the end he settled for forcing or faking them. Once he claimed to be experiencing toxic shame; he wasn't. Ten out of ten for effort, but the shame was as phoney as the clothes he used to deal in. He got called out on it – Mark didn't miss much. That's not to say Dez is not a nice guy, he's a good friend to this day, a professional at his chosen career and besides, we were all full of shit at times. Lucy was also a fellow long hauler, the big punk girl with an unusual Yorkshire/Welsh hybrid accent. Now allowed to purchase hair dye in Lily Lodge, her hair was never the same colour two weeks in a row. My crush Katherine was still with us too, although she was engaged so she was off-limits, regrettably. There were many others who sadly didn't make the course, some of whom have since died. All of them great characters with heaps of unfulfilled potential.

In time, it was established what kind of issues I needed to address. Mark had included a lot of inner child work within the programme, so I was encouraged to focus on how I felt during my disempowering and tempestuous childhood. I had carried a lot of pain, fear, shame and anger for a long time. The instability of my early years had left me deeply insecure. I may have hidden it well, but it always lurked just below the surface. I believe that in a way my addiction was also my friend; it had attempted to self-medicate this pain away. Of course, it was a tactic that had royally backfired and had nearly cost me my life on many occasions. I also needed to deal with the guilt of my addiction and grieve for my brother and grandparents, feelings I'd spent recent years supressing and medicating. It was a time to start unpacking my skeletons.

Some groups could last for upwards of three hours and were so powerful they are utterly indescribable. Clients would frequently regress and be wracked by the pain emanating from their deepest wounds. Some would lie in a foetal position on the floor and sob their broken hearts out. Others would boil with a violent rage. Some would roar with pain and emit primal screams. I've never witnessed anything so raw, it was simply phenomenal in its power. It was awe-inspiring to witness such naked courage and healing. Sometimes we were sent out onto the huge deserted beach at night to release our feelings by screaming and shouting – until on one occasion, the coastguard was scrambled. We were never sent down there again. The process was emotionally taxing. Most residents had started sleeping well by now, owing to the fact that they were exhausted at the end of each day. We may not have been running marathons, but each day we participated in an emotional pentathlon. I'd started to learn that feelings can have a significant physical impact too; hence the word, feelings. They had been locked within my physical body since childhood.

We were in those groups all day, for five and half days a week most weeks. It was no less gruelling than primary treatment, more so in many ways. If you couldn't connect to your own issues, it was still draining to witness the pain in others. For many weeks I couldn't connect to the feelings I needed to. This meant that I was getting triggered constantly, without letting anything out. My pressure cooker was primed, ready to explode but I still couldn't release any pain. Jacqui provided me with a sketch pad and coloured pencils, in a last-ditch effort to find me an outlet for my traumas. It turned out to be the key that opened me up and I began channelling and expressing my feelings through art. The chasm had started to widen and I was teetering on the edge.

The real shift happened one night at about 1am. I was deeply immersed in a vivid dream, whereby I floated out of my body and rose up to the ceiling. Then I flipped over and was staring down at myself, peacefully sleeping. I hung there, weightless, staring. Then out of nowhere my whole body was slapped sideways and spun into a very small room that I didn't recognise. It was gloomy and dingy and I could make out a toilet and sink. I could feel a density behind me, a heavy, lingering, invisible presence. It wasn't a bad energy, but it was a weighty and powerful force. I have often felt this presence and it always make me think of Teddy. I'm sure he visits me from time to time, standing by my side like an invisible shadow. I was trying to look around but everything was in slow motion. Gradually I came to and I was again lying in my bed. It wasn't just another dream though; I knew it was different. I felt a strong intuitive urge and pull to go downstairs and start writing.

So I did just that. I crept down the stairs and began to write. The first issue that surfaced was the guilt around my grandparents. I'd not been there when they were ill and dying. I hadn't even attended their funerals. I felt a heavy weight of grief, guilt and shame. As I wrote, the tears poured out of me and this went on for about two solid hours. I wrote and wrote. My floodgates had opened. When the tears finally began to subside, I felt transformed. I felt embraced and soothed, my mind felt calm and crystal clear. I could feel a resonant clarity and two unfamiliar feelings – peace and serenity. I had never experienced such a release before. I could feel a warm, loving presence surrounding me. I was sitting in a circle of empty chairs, yet each one seemed to contain a palpable peaceful presence. I was not alone. I'd had my first clean, conscious, spiritual experience. The energy surrounding me was utterly angelic; kind, light and loving. I went back to bed a changed man, at the start of a brand-new journey.

The next morning, I told Mark about the dream and the presence I had felt. He understood, and he even believed me! I was encouraged to read out my journal to the group, to consolidate my progress. So this is how my treatment continued. I was granted special permission to go downstairs to write in the night if I felt the need. So I did, whenever the dreams propelled me to do so. This was frequently during the early hours of the morning, or the witching hours, a time when supernatural events, ghosts and apparitions are most likely to occur, so I'm told. I found I could connect so much better when I was alone; free from the fear of prying eyes and judgement. I was starting my journey of emotional recovery, as well as my recovery from drug addiction. I believe the two go hand in hand. The full healing process involves releasing pain, fear and suffering.

I went on to process the pain around my father (or stepfather). His brutality and cruelty, and how I'd felt when I'd learnt that he wasn't even my real father. My feelings around possibly never knowing who my real father was. My mother, her temper and her bad decisions around men. The loss of my brother, whom I had never properly grieved. I felt so guilty that I had not been able to help him, as I'd been trapped in my own hopeless addiction. Teddy had been a kind and innocent soul who suffered tremendously with his mental health and the sadness I carried for his tragic demise ran deep. I continued to use the art materials to focus and release my emotions. It almost became like a language for me. Sometimes they contained symbols that I did not understand, but they did look vaguely familiar and strangely hieroglyphic in nature. I felt I was connecting to something, I just didn't know what.

The bonds and connections formed in such an environment are immeasurably deep. It was the first time I had felt the beauty of raw, real, unveiled human connection. I started to develop a sixth sense for what others were feeling. The more I felt my own feelings, the better I could read and help others. I was develop-ing true human empathy, or the ability to be an empath. Mark had this ability in abundance and we ended up becoming almost friends. It was like I had a truth monitor installed, I could tell when people were being real. Often, I even had the ability to take them to the real heart of the matter; I could lead them to their root by asking the right questions. I intuitively knew where they needed to go, even if they didn't.

We were also given one-to-one counselling for anything too sensitive to take into group. I had many of these sessions and I was determined to make the most of this unique and powerful opportunity. Mark and Jacqui provided a perfect balance, and not just in the sense of female and male energies. Mark was more pragmatic and practical, while Jacqui was filled with warmth and empathy. I respected them both equally, for very different reasons.

We partook in other life experiences together too. We'd be crammed into the nutty bus (a clapped-out beige mini-van) and shipped off to 12-Step meetings around Lancashire. There were fun times as well. Once Stu, whose teeth were in better nick than most, had a big front tooth smashed out ice-skating. At least he now matched the rest of us. The irony of him losing a tooth was not lost on us. It's a comical sight to see fifteen addicts on an ice rink, sliding about like Bambi on speed, laughing so hard they end up doing the splits. Sometimes it would be other sporting activities or even the cinema. Once Jacqui took us all to the Lakes camping for a long weekend. One night we all lay out on the grass, looking up at the stars. We could see the Milky Way, the moon, shooting stars and watch satellites passing over. The size and scope of it all was almost overwhelming as Pink Floyd profoundly resonated from a boom box. Some of those people are still clean today. Some of them are no longer with us.

There were a couple of Unit Assistants who would drive us around in the bus and also worked nights at the house. John and Cee were both in recovery themselves and were good guys. Cee in particular worked a lot of hours and I became fond of him. He was calm, kind and intelligent. However, he stopped attending 12-Step meetings and several years later relapsed and died of his heroin addiction. He had untreated sex addiction that eventually led him back to his drug of choice; he did not survive it for long. Another decent human being lost to the grim reaper of addiction.

Home leave weekends were also a thing now. I went to stay with my mother at Kirk's in Liverpool, but I found it very hard work. I was wide open and full of feelings and I felt like a fish out of water when faced with ordinary life and ordinary people. However, I had rediscovered the soothing power of nature and I would spend time in the nearby woods whenever possible. I was still harbouring some resentments around my mother, and spending time with her could be more gruelling than wall-to-wall groups. I opted to stay an inmate more often than not. I had come to feel at home in this most extreme of institutions. I cannot emphasise enough the intensity of the whole experience. Lily Lodge consisted of about seven hours of groups a day for six months, excluding weekends, apart from some Saturday mornings. Just one week of which is more therapy than an average person does in their entire lifetime. I have never heard of anywhere else that's as intense and powerfully transformative. No-one can escape such an experience unchanged, unless of course your name is Stu. It was a finely tuned regime, tweaked to an extremely high level of therapeutic intensity.

Mark the counsellor ended up going back to Australia and relapsing on drink and drugs. In the end his liver gave up the ghost and he died from his addiction. It was a sad loss for the recovery community. He had helped hundreds of people over the years, but in the end he had failed himself. Like Cee, he had drifted away from 12-Step recovery meetings. He'd had a huge impact on my recovery and my life and I shall never forget him. He had done so much work on himself emotionally, yet he had stopped treating his own addiction issues. I imagine he must have been in quite an isolated place, a lone wolf fighting everyone else's addictions while disregarding his own. 12-Step recovery groups may not be perfect and are not for everyone, but they provide an invaluable support network and unique connection. I know many counsellors who have maintained their own sanity by continuing to attend meetings. I often wonder if things could have been different for Mark, Cee and countless others. So many have been lost. It is in part why I felt compelled to write this book, their memory in mind.

This level of emotional exposure in such an intense environment comes at a heavy price. It took me at least a year to detox from treatment. You can never unknow what you have come to know, never again live in dumbed-down denial, once your mind has been blown wide open. You cannot unknow your wounds, your pain and your triggers. Sometimes I think of my brother Alan. He'd had a similar childhood to me, used drugs in a similar way, yet he has never done this type of recovery. He'd come off the hard drugs after being sectioned for six months. He has never attended a rehab or entered into any form of emotional recovery. He is still comfortably numb, having never looked deep within.

He still smokes pot and necks the odd tablet, but he is no longer in the grips of a crippling addiction. Sometimes I look at him and envy his ignorance; he rarely looks back and, in some ways, seems so accepting. His life is so simple, it seems, and mine so complex. But I garnered a precious gift from the work I have done. I have learnt that you cannot just muffle out the bad feelings. So, as I have released the bad, I have also allowed and made space for the good; the joy, the love and the peace. On a good day, I wouldn't have it any other way. It took courage to see my process through and sometimes I wanted to run. The price I paid was the loss of any blissful ignorance, but I gained a far more deep and unique freedom.

Long term, I am certainly the happier and more emotionally free, something I think Alan is jealous of at times. His issues leak out sideways in the form of panic attacks and low-level depression. Both paths have their benefits and their costs. On a bad day I resent the pain of my journey; on a good day I am grateful beyond measure. Not everyone gets such a chance, many others are not ready to make the most of opportunities that are offered. This time I was ready, and I lasted the course.

After about six months of the relentless Lily regime, I felt I'd had enough. I started acting out and kicking off. I punched a hole in my bedroom wall; I'd begun to feel like a caged animal. I craved freedom. I received a warning, and it was agreed that it was time for me to move on. It was time for me to fly the nest; to leave the safe and cosy structured confines of full-time treatment. It was a welcome, yet ominous, prospect. I thought I was at the end of a journey, but it was just beginning.

Chapter Eleven

Detox from Rehab.

Luckily, the rehab provided a supported living third stage. It was situated in another big old Victorian house by the sea, which we were encouraged to run by ourselves. I had my own room on the top floor. Groups were facilitated a couple of times a week but the rest of the time the house was unstaffed. The focus was now on learning life skills and integrating ourselves back into the community. Groups were mainly about house dynamics or practical living skills. We were helped to sort out our benefits, open bank accounts etc, and take up voluntary work. Most of us had never really lived a normal life and found even simple everyday tasks surprisingly challenging. Stunted by our drink and drug use, we had never really grown up. Shell shocked by the treatment process, it took time to readjust.

We were allowed almost total freedom now and I was out and about exploring the big wide world. It was both exciting and daunting. We would get lifts to out of town meetings, which felt remarkably liberating. We ventured as far afield as Manchester, Lancaster and Blackburn! I wangled myself a little voluntary job in the Age Concern café. They left me to run the place two afternoons a week and I loved the feeling of having responsibility and being trusted.

I enjoyed some of the characters that were regular visitors and built up friendships with them. Some of them were miserable, moaning old gits, but I enjoyed them all the same. I'd not had non-junkie public relations in nearly twenty years. I was delighted to be trusted, however meagre the takings were – no-one had trusted me with anything for a very long time. It felt so good to be contributing positively to society and it made a refreshing change. I did a basic computer course at Age Concern too. They let me join in for free, as I was by now a trusted volunteer. I could go home at the end of each day and sleep soundly, knowing that I had done no harm that day. Living with a clear conscience was a whole new experience for me.

I also continued with my Inner Child work, making my way through a book of emotionally demanding exercises and occasionally popping back to Lily Lodge for a one-to-one with Mark. I now started to explore meditation more deeply and practised it daily. I did mainly guided meditations back then, but I struggled with visualisations. I'd get random macabre images intercepting my efforts and spoiling my flow. Then I began to understand that different sound frequencies and vibrations could assist in going deeper during meditation. I began a deeper investigation into this and made it a daily practise. I was willing to try just about anything to find some peace.

I was spiritually well but this didn't prevent one of my worst nightmares from materialising. Due to my willingness to engage in the recovery process, I had taken all of myself into the groups. I had willingly and foolishly disclosed a childhood incident around which

I carried a very deep shame. There had been method in my madness – I had decided to expose this shame to the light, in order to disperse it. I wanted to unburden myself of the issues that regularly reduced me to a sweating wreck, due to supressed shame. We were encouraged to take these brave steps, with support. However, this ethos and my bravery proved to be detrimental as time went by. Not everyone was on the same page and my confidentiality was broken by other Lily residents. As I was at my most vulnerable, back out in the big wide world I became aware that rumours were circulating and things were being said about me. It was such a shameful incident that I wanted to use, run and kill myself, all at the same time. There were at least two weeks when I wanted to die, literally. I was crippled with a toxic, suffocating shame, a sense of betrayal and rejection.

It left me with a deep sense of mistrust, isolation and alienation. I was too vulnerable to move away, plus I had nowhere to go. I didn't particularly want to use or die either. I was forced to work through this shame, dig deep and attempt to rise above the gossip and cruelty. It pushed me to my limit and was my worst nightmare. It is a fact that a lot of people in recovery are not well individuals and with hindsight I should have realised this. All of us were messed up, trying to get emotionally and spiritually well, and everyone was at different stages in this process. I had a strong sense that this was my last chance, which meant I was in a different place to many others. To some it is all a big joke; to me it was life and death.

I had put my heart and soul into emotional recovery and now this shaming exposure was a bitter pill to swallow. I had to weather the storm, simply because I had no other choice. I have always tried to choose my friends more wisely since then but it's always a tricky balancing act. This incident has come back to bite me over and over again throughout the years, even from people I hardly know. I've sometimes wondered if I will ever shake the stigma. I suspect I triggered others around similar issues, but I will never know for sure. I've since learnt that it's not overly uncommon, it's just that I was foolish enough to disclose my demons naively to some with the maturity of a foetus. A lesson learnt. I haven't mentioned the actual incident in this book for that very reason, although I did consider it. If there is any upside at all, I suppose it made me stronger in the long run. I'd weathered my worst nightmare and survived an extreme dose of toxic shame. I stood in the stillness of my spiritual, emotional and mental strength while the storm and wild winds blew past me. I now knew that this shame alone could not kill me but I knew it had taken others.

It contaminated and tainted my fresh start, but I still believed fully in the concept that it's crucial to expose your darkest demons in order to fully recover. Since then I've seen many old-timers go back out into the junkie wilderness. Many of these readily admit it was because they had left their most painful stones unturned. I became far more discerning about who I shared my inner world with, but I continued to engage in the process. I had so many synchronicities and coincidences occurring at that time that I knew I was on the right path. The Steps had led me to start unpicking my life, which in turn had led onto inner child work. This extreme level of healing was forced upon me, and although I wanted to die at the time, in the long run it helped to heal me. Demons dissolve away when exposed to the light.

I also gained a new respect for the sanctity of trust. Because my own trust had been abused so painfully, I knew I would never do the same to others. Paradoxically, it reinforced my recovery too. It had punctured my dignity and caused me untold pain, but it also gave a level of strength and determination that I would previously have never thought possible. I'd survived the trenches and I now approached recovery with even more courage and insight. I'm always humbled when I see this courage in others. Emotional recovery requires bravery; it's a very powerful thing.

I will never be proud of this incident but I have reached a place where I can bear it. It was very difficult to find a good enough reason to forgive myself and it will always be a work in progress. I have seen others share deeply personal issues at conventions in front of hundreds of people and it's a powerful and transformative sight to behold. One member, from Eastern Europe, shared in detail how she had been systematically sexually abused by both her brother and her father as a child. Another member disclosed that he had fucked his own prostitute mother while in the grips of his addiction. This level of exposure can prove to be either deeply healing or highly damaging, I've seen it work both ways. I believe that if these disclosures are made within a safe space, they can be healing and unburdening. As a result, I can look at myself in the mirror and have found I can walk with a lightness of spirit, previously unknown to me. I've left no skeleton unturned, or stones in my closet.

There were about ten other residents in this house but for a number of reasons I was still a bit of a loner. I'd met a few new people who had already moved on and even had their own flats. Some of them were at college or had proper jobs. I struck up a few new friendships but still felt I was on a different page to most. I wasn't interested in bouncing about, pumping myself up at the gym and turning myself orange at the sunbed shop. I had a sense of purpose and a deeper journey to undertake. I was far more interested in staying clean and healing emotionally. After my profound spiritual experiences, I'd started attending a local group called New Horizons. These people were into everything: UFOs, conspiracy theories, alternative therapies, healing and spiritual teachings. There was once even a healer who could exude a curative oil from the palms of his hands. I was sceptical at first, even considering that maybe he had injected it under his skin himself. However, after witnessing his healing abilities, I concluded that I had no reason to doubt the man. My mind and spirit were both wide open.

Be it coincidence or not, my Hep C cleared up on its own within a year of me being diagnosed. It is a common illness among those who have been friends with the needle. It usually requires many months of unpleasant Interferon or some other treatment in order to be sent packing and that treatment is not always successful. I was relieved that I did not need to suffer this ordeal and was given a clean bill of health. There is about a ten per cent chance of this happening for anyone, but I can't help wondering if my healing journey had a part to play.

I began to have some profound experiences during meditations; sometimes I could feel a pure healing energy entering me. Once it came to me in the form of a white dove during a group meditation at New Horizons. On another occasion it plunged deep inside my chest and coursed through my body, filling me with euphoric vibrations. I remember one time the candles in my room flickered violently but there was no breeze. I then felt a penetrating energy entering my chest and filling me up. I can only describe it as a sacred spirit, a pure holy energy. I am not a fan of conventional religion, but I can only imagine it to be both sacred and holy. I have no idea what these experiences meant, I just know that they happened. They strengthened my faith and helped me significantly in my recovery. I couldn't forget them and I could always refer back to them. I knew that forces greater than myself existed. Sometimes I questioned my own sanity, although I knew I wasn't mad. Mark always listened and even validated me. It was important that I felt understood. These experiences were not insane, or unique to me.

The 12-Steps were developed by several individuals who also shared a faith. There is a strong spiritual basis to the 12-Steps, the same thread of spirituality that than can be found in most religions. They are based on a foundation of kindness, positivity, honesty, humility, gratitude, faith and redemption. A spiritual awakening is deemed to be an important cornerstone of this recovery process. I felt that this is what I was experiencing. Everyone experiences these awakenings of spirit in different ways and to varying degrees. Some are far more practical and educational, while others turn to more conventional religious notions. I can only speak of my own experience.

Towards the end of my time in this halfway house I had begun to strike up a friendship with Lucy. She was in the room next door and was beginning to look a lot better than a few months previously. She had started to flirt with me and I was flattered. We did get along well. We ended up sleeping together one night, which went against the rules of the house. The next day I was wracked with guilt, feeling dishonest and I eventually told Mark about it. He was fairly tolerant, but it was agreed that it was time for me to move on, yet again. It was time to fly the nest and get my own accommodation. An important next step in becoming a valuable member of society.

I found a flat a few doors up from where I was already living. It felt close enough to still feel safe and I was grateful for this proximity. The owner knew I was in early recovery and was happy to have me as a tenant. Within a couple of weeks, I'd moved in. It was a lovely top floor flat and I was happy. Everything had slotted into place. Somehow, I was eligible for back pay with my benefits, which enabled me to buy what I needed to turn the flat into a home. Even though life was very basic, I was grateful for every little thing. I wanted for nothing; even Kwik Save no frills beans on toast seemed perfect. I was happy to live a simple life, free from any excessive frills. Anything was more than I had had in recent years. I'd buy cheap short-dated food from the supermarket and smoke my roll ups. I was warm, dry, comfortable, clean and following a spiritual path. What a difference a year can make!

To add to this amazing new life, I got my first ever mobile phone. They'd been out for years but I'd never had one. It was a nice big Nokia brick, state of the art, and I loved it. I even learnt how to text! A phone is an important means of connection in recovery – the fellowship encourages everyone to find a sponsor and ring that person regularly, sometimes daily. A sponsor is also someone who will take you through the 12 steps; a process that involves finding the reality of your past, growing spiritually, making amends for wrongdoings and improving yourself as you grow. It is also recommended to reach out to friends if ever you feel like using or are simply having a bad day. Another fundamental is to reach out to new people and help them on their journey. With the help of my shiny new Nokia I could do all of this. I was connected, but not with dealers or punters.

Chloe came up to stay with me for a weekend. It was lovely to see her, but she was still on a prescription and I knew I couldn't get involved with her again. I still felt warmly towards her but I wasn't heartbroken by the prospect of letting her go. We slept together a couple of times, but when she left, I knew I couldn't see her again romantically. I knew instinctively that letting her go was the right thing to do. I had to follow my gut and protect my recovery. We'd grown into very different people. I had changed beyond measure, while she had remained much the same. It could never have worked. I knew as I waved her off that we had different paths to tread.

I also remember receiving a strange letter from an anonymous source. She claimed to be a psychic medium who had things to tell me. The return address was a PO Box, so I couldn't even begin to trace this mystery person. I was intrigued. They were typed letters with a black and white photograph of an old lady in the top corner. The writer claimed to know me, and things about me, urging me to reply with £20 if I wanted to know more. I was so curious I replied with the £20. The reply arrived and I was blown away by the accuracy of the information it contained. I was also suspicious that it was someone I knew, playing a devious trick. All the same, we corresponded for a short while and I was impressed with the perceptively accurate and mysterious letters I received in return. I was then asked to carry out an incantation at a set time, the instructions vaguely resembling that of a spell but worded in a kindly and loving way. I was unsure what to do.

I agonised over it for a few days, filled with curiosity and fear. In the end I carried out the incantation on the stated day, at the required time. I was relieved when nothing bad happened, but nothing good happened either. I went to bed relieved and curious all the same. I was drifting off when I felt an incredibly strong and pleasant presence enter through the top of my head. The next day I felt effervescent with love and joy. I attributed it to the incantation I had performed but I'll never know for sure. In the end I replied that I did not wish to correspond any further and the letters stopped. I have never found out where they came from. Just another minor mystery which I have never forgotten.

I continued to take solace and refuge in nature. I still had the same old negative tapes playing in my head, voices that told me I was worthless, and worse. At such times I would turn to nature for comfort. I could feel its vibrations and this helped to ease away my kinks. I'd been working on myself in an intense manner for over a year by now and I was beginning to feel the benefits. For the first time in many years I was no longer ruled by my paranoid psychosis; it had significantly retreated during treatment. I no longer felt like I was being chased and that my life was in constant danger. It was amazing to finally put these demons to rest, because they had ruled my life for so long. Treatment had been such a safe environment. Even though they were physically ordinary old houses, inside they felt like fortresses. I've never felt safer. I had needed such an experience and I shall always be grateful for it.

My connection with nature strengthened further as time passed, and on bad days I needed this solace. There's a local park that has a hidden rose garden, surrounded by tall trees. I used to sit there often, especially when I was wrestling with my negative demons and ugly shame. I'd sit there in silence, and the trees would converse with me, silently. The more silent I was, the louder this quiet communication became. I often feel a very old wisdom coming from trees. Some of them have been around for hundreds of years. They have witnessed a lot and possess a timelessness. There is a hill in Hereford that looks down over the city and is home to many ancient trees. I used to sit on that hill and think about what those trees have witnessed, how they must have seen the city grow and evolve. I always wonder what unspoken wisdom those trees hold.

I also used to get a craving to drink in the colours of nature, I felt they could nourish my soul. This same rose garden was packed with vibrantly colourful flowers for much of the year. I particularly craved violet and indigo shades. I spent hours in that garden meditating. Or I'd sit on a favourite rock that protruded into the middle of a nearby stream. I didn't care what passers-by thought, I needed to do it.

There was an amazing psychic medium at New Horizons who had tangible abilities. I took Black Bob along, as he was always curious about what I was up to. He was one of the lads, a joker and a DJ with a cynical sense of humour. The psychic was an elderly lady, with long grey locks and piercing eyes. I suppose she looked how you'd expect a witchy type to look. She had this amazing ability to connect to spirits through physical means. Once they had made contact with her, she would take a sip of water. However, she wouldn't taste water, she would taste whatever that person's favourite drink was, be it sweet tea, strong coffee, beer or whisky. I never saw her get it wrong. She wasn't a showman or a charlatan, she had a genuine ability. On this occasion she took Bob's breath away with her accuracy and insight. She nailed him. I watched his jaw slowly drop until it was practically resting on the floor. He came back with me several times. Seeing is believing, or so the saying goes.

I went into the bowels of Blackpool for a one-to-one with this lady. Her house was dark and cluttered but I liked her, she felt genuine and warm. The house smelt of sage; she'd clearly been busy smudging. We sat down and she settled herself. Immediately she said she was getting "a male" coming through. The hairs on the back of my neck stood up. We sat in silence as she slowly reached for her glass of water. As she took a sip her face wrinkled with acute distaste, she almost spat the water across the room. She described an acrid, sweet and sickly medicinal taste. Then said she was feeling a bit woozy. I knew she was experiencing the chemically engineered bitter-sweet taste of methadone. My blood ran cold. Then she described that she was struggling to breathe and her throat felt blocked. She was re-living Teddy's death right before my eyes. He had choked on his own vomit while in a methadone and alcohol gouch. I was fascinated and speechless.

When she asked if this person had overdosed on drugs, I broke down in unrelenting tears. I had tried to grieve for Teddy in Lily Lodge, but I'd never quite managed to get there. Feelings take their own time and their own course and cannot be forced. But watching this lady struggling for breath and choking had catapulted me directly into grief. I couldn't stop crying and felt broken. She continued to floor me with accurate detail after accurate detail. She even knew my childhood nickname had been Stargazer. I could feel his presence too. The room was filled with his light but dark, dense energy. He'd been relatively cheery as a young child but had developed severe mental health issues very young, and as a result he'd undergone harsh treatment and had been prescribed heavy medications. He may have even had ECT. The fact that he was severely punished for his bedwetting as a child will forever haunt me. I often wonder if things might have been different. Then, of course, he had sunk into the grips of addiction.

I had one question for him, "are you all right Teddy?" I was instantly struck by a powerful image. I could see a bright constellation of stars, a nebula, a cloud of brilliantly bright swirling dust; a star nursery. A bright new star emerged, newly born. I knew that he was OK, that he had returned to the universe as energy and was not gone completely. I took great comfort from this powerful image and insight.

This experience had propelled me into full blown grief for Teddy and I had to work through this pain for several weeks. It hurt, but it needed to happen. Teddy's brightness and darkness, pain and trauma, will never be forgotten by me. I have been to his grave many times since. I always wish that I'd been a better brother, that I could have looked after him more. He was an acutely sensitive lad and this sensitivity caused him great pain. For me he will always shine bright. This psychic experience proved to be a profound moment for me and reconfirmed what I already knew. There are energies around us that we can never fully understand.

I had also found a sponsor who was to be with me for many years to come. He was an older, well-educated man from another fellowship, who became rather like a surrogate father at times. I also became like a son to him, as his own son had disowned him, unable to forgive his father for his drinking days. Most people regain their families in recovery but it is not always the case. This man has seen me through many difficult times. He keeps thing simple, is very pragmatic and has acted as a mentor to me as well.

He is well into his twenties now, in recovery terms. He's been a big part of my recovery journey and I owe him a lot.

That period of my life was a time of huge readjustments, both emotionally and spiritually. I had started my journey into emotional/spiritual recovery, not realising that I'd embarked upon a lifelong voyage. Spiritually my eyes had opened wide, and I was left reeling from the shock of it. Early recovery is a testing time for all who encounter it. We can no longer revert to our default setting, using drugs to evade our feelings. The vicissitudes in our emotions are often extreme. I experienced times of great joy and times of deep pain and turmoil. Staying clean while riding those waves is a tall order. It's a storm all recovering addicts must one day or another weather.

Chapter Twelve

New Horizons, Art and India.

There came a time when I had to consider what I wanted to do with my life, now that I actually had one. I had zero qualifications; I'd spent my school days and exams glue sniffing, a pastime not renowned for bringing high achievements and favourable prospects. I started off by doing a City and Guilds in decorative art. It involved designing and decorating furniture, was creative and I loved it; I learnt a lot. For my finished piece I spent weeks decorating and stencilling a coffee table. I gifted this back to the rehab as a thank you gift.

I did a bit of a cash-in-hand removal work for a chap I'd met, but I knew I wanted to make some kind of career for myself. I signed up to do a diploma in Fine Art. I had no qualifications but I did have the artwork I'd produced since leaving Lily Lodge. They let me in on the strength of that alone. I'd also managed to put a few pieces of my art into a local gallery and some of them had sold. I was always delighted that my work actually had a value and was going to hang on someone's wall and have its own life journey which was mysterious to me. I felt I was leaving a legacy in some small way.

There were only two mature students on the course so it felt a bit odd, but I loved becoming educated at long last. I learnt a lot about artists and I became transfixed by the story of Van Gogh. His unique mixture of insanity and creative talent was something I could connect with. I loved his artistic bravery and the equally brave brush strokes in some of his work. He was proof that there is a thin line between madness and genius. I began to create pointillist pieces, which would take me weeks to produce. It became like a meditative process, I would go on real journeys in my mind as I made the thousands of tiny marks required to create a complete picture. I found that the artwork was running in parallel to my recovery. Each painting would take me on a journey that echoed the inner work I was doing. Memories and tears would form as each creation came to life.

The more I learnt, the more I realised how many artists had suffered from their own addiction issues. It's a very common combination. Likewise for musicians, writers and other creatives. I began to look into Outsider Art – created by the self-taught, especially those on the margins of society, such as prisoners, the mentally ill and the outcasts. I identified with many of them and felt that my Inner Child work had given me back my long-lost innocence and allowed to me look at the world through fresh eyes. This helped with my artwork, the two processes worked in tandem.

I returned to my youth in other ways at college. Once I received a warning for climbing on a roof to impress people; some things never change. Some of the teachers were incredibly inspiring, they were real individuals and were following their own paths, unconfined by the restraints of society. They taught me valuable lessons about perspective and dimension.

I was good at expressing myself through art, but less talented at sticking to the tedious constraints of exams. I produced great pieces of work, often among the best in the class, but often failed to accurately document the thought processes behind them. I'd decided that the work itself was more important and often neglected the accompanying disciplines of describing the process academically. I preferred abstract expression. I passed, but I let myself down, mark-wise. It seemed ironic to me that such a purely creative subject should be restricted by rigid rules. Both of my final exam pieces were centred on trees – yet again, they proved to be important to me. My most memorable piece was of a pencil sketched tree, contrasted by vibrant, colourful countryside. My mother still has that picture hanging on her wall. I gave it to her for her 60th birthday.

At some point I moved to a new flat on Lightburn Avenue and decided to do an art degree at the University in Preston. I also signed up for a part-time counselling course which I planned to juggle alongside the art. Luckily, I'd got my licence back and was able to drive again. I was now the proud owner of a £350 metallic blue Rover Mini-Metro. I was as free as a bird, not just in terms of transport, but also emotionally and spiritually! I was so free that within a couple of weeks I'd earned myself two speeding tickets. I was so unfettered and happy, I was rendered oblivious to the limits and constraints of the open road. Well that's my excuse anyway. I learnt very quickly that freedom can be pricey, so I slowed down.

Addiction had robbed me of my old passions, music and fishing. I began listening to music through fresh ears and it again became a vital aspect of my life. I rekindled many of my old favourites and picked up on new music too. I remained faithful to Pink Floyd, the Beatles, U2 and Simple Minds. I hated most of the new manufactured and artificial bands and music. I started going to live shows, the first being China Crisis in Liverpool's The Cavern. I even met the band afterwards. It blew my mind; I'd never pictured myself emerging from junkiedom and having such positive things in my life. My esteem was so low, and I'd been so far removed from society, that I couldn't believe I was worthy of shaking hands with stars. I was stars truck. Music became my therapy. I went to see China Crisis again; I was hooked. I've since been to some awe-inspiring concerts.

In contrast to this, I was also learning to embrace and enjoy silence. In very early recovery it had been almost unbearable for me – my head was too loud and my self-critical tape was relentless. Meditation had helped me to evolve through this painful process. Initially, I tried so hard to meditate that my head would physically hurt. This is far removed from the true goal of meditation, but slowly I learned to relax and with my eyes closed tune into the subtle sounds of my environment. The more I relaxed, the more I gained from it. From focusing outside of myself, it enabled me to observe my own thoughts – however crazy and random – for what they were. I could step outside of myself and was finally able to connect to the now. Again, the trees helped with this process as the sound of the wind moving through the leaves really spoke to me and sounded almost symphonic. The sound resonated within me, like something was blowing through my soul. I'm convinced that trees communicate with me without using language or voice. If humans possess genetic memory and wisdom, imagine the wisdom that ancient trees hold. They are still, wise and constantly witnessing. For me, they are a symbol of a Higher Power.

With the constant noise of modern life, we are seldom subjected to the power and wisdom of silence. I believe everyone has psychic abilities, but it's not developed or valued within our society. I felt drawn to it and took the time to pursue it, even though I didn't know exactly what I was pursuing. I was on a deep journey of self-discovery.

I'd sold all my fishing gear at the beginning of my last relapse. It was one of the first things to go, it had rapidly become a luxury item. I began to build up my kit again and started fishing around Lancashire, in the rivers in Wyre and Preston and at several local fisheries. I'd also take my kit whenever I went back to Hereford. The River Wye will always remain close to my heart. I mainly fished alone but made a few pals over the years. I was fishing with fresh eyes and ears and was taken back to the hours, days and nights I'd spent on the banks of rivers as a youngster. I remembered a time as a teenager when I'd spent a night on the riverbank and had witnessed literally hundreds of shooting stars. I must have witnessed some kind of cosmic phenomenon, but I was too young to fully appreciate and understand it at the time. I hoped for a repeat performance but I never got one. With my new-found knowledge I realised that fishing is akin to meditation. A fisherman spends hours immersed in the sights, sounds and peace of nature. Observing, reacting, focusing and being at one with it all.

I'd been seeing Lucy on and off, too. She now had her own flat near the centre of town and was fighting to get her two daughters back. They were living with their father in Scarborough, but sadly he remained in the grips of full-blown heroin addiction. Lucy and I just 'got' each other. Her hair was a bit all-over-the-place and she looked a bit different, but we had a genuine connection. She had a real power, and incredible eyes that could mobilise an army, and frequently did. Eyes that spoke a thousand words; eyes that I understood. We were both a tad bonkers but we had a real soul connection.

For no apparent reason I decided that I wanted to travel, and Goa was to be my destination. My decision was made. Lucy didn't want me to go, but I was determined to spread my wings. I booked a flight and headed off alone. This was my first big journey clean. The flight in itself blew my mind. The mere sight of the planet from above inspired awe within me; its scale, form, shape, beauty and endless natural patterns created by mountains, rivers and coastlines. The depth of the skyscapes tinged with colour from the setting and then rising sun. The flight path took the plane over the Middle East at night and I could see hundreds of fires burning out in the desert. It looked magical. I now believe they may have been flares from oil pump sites, which is slightly less magical than I had imagined, but quite a sight all the same. I had pictured tribal people gathered around open fires. I hardly read my book for the duration of the flight. The view from the window was enough for me and in awe I shed a tear at times.

Eventually we touched down in India and I was instantly struck by the dry dusty heat. The second thing to hit me square in the face was the poverty. During the bus journey through Goa I was saddened by the extreme divide between rich and poor. Next to luxury homes stood tin shacks, caked in dirt and flies; it was a jarring juxtaposition. After arriving at my reasonably posh hotel, I was dazed by the culture shock that awaited me out on the streets. I ventured out for basic supplies but found myself endlessly harassed by vendors of every kind. I'd been told to brush them aside, so I did just that, avoiding eye contact, or at least I tried. Among the shops, stalls and street hawkers were some terribly poor people.

There was one man who I will never forget. He was elderly and clearly had severe mental health issues. He was hunched down on a pathway, rocking back and forth and he'd wet himself, his urine ran down the dusty street in a thin trickle. Untold people passed him by without a second glance. He was sitting, quietly rocking, in his own mess. A shop keeper had provided him with a bowl of rice, but he seemed to be at the mercy of the streets. I'd never witnessed such a pitiful plight on English shores. The helplessness of his situation was profound. This helpless hopelessness triggered something within me; I'd felt out on the raw and ragged edge for so long myself. This sight, along with the many other beggars, the poverty, and the smell, shook me to my core. The deafening racket of beeping scooters, the crowds and the chaos, left me shell-shocked and feeling vulnerable. I'd never seen poverty to that extreme. I felt like I'd been hit by a juggernaut.

I hired a scooter and this provided me with some small comfort as I plucked up the courage to go exploring. Swooping along the small country roads, I spotted a father fishing with his son. I pulled over, my passion for fishing still burning bright. I clambered down to see them, they were smiling big wide smiles at me, yet they were suspicious of what I wanted and perhaps just being carefully polite. I joined them on the banks of the filthy looking trickle of a river, amazed by the primitive nature of their fishing tackle. They had only a bamboo cane, a piece of string and a bent pin. Skewered onto this pin was a tiny speck of batter or bread. It reminded me of something I'd used as a toddler when first trying to fish. I was struck by how little they had, and how basic their supplies were. I had hundreds of pounds worth of kit at home and I felt that now familiar pang of guilt. They spoke no English but were friendly and seemed happy. I gave them a few rupees and left them in peace. They didn't understand why I was giving them money, but they smiled and accepted it anyway. No aspect of India failed to provide some degree of cultural shock, even the fishermen with their bamboo sticks. I felt disproportionality wealthy compared to them.

The next day I made my way down to Anjuna Beach on my hired scooter. I'd heard through the grapevine that Sniff was living and working there. I'd not seen him for about thirteen years as he'd been living abroad for many of them. I was determined to find him but had no idea how I would. After wrestling my way through markets that reminded me of

Glastonbury, rag tag areas filled with huts and tents heaving with drug pushers of all varieties, I made it into a more civilised space. Eventually I tracked down his tattoo parlour. I was a complete surprise for him. I'd not seen him in ages, and I was clean too. Sniff had been there for a good few years and was well established on the scene. People came from all over the world to have a Sniff tattoo. The jammy sod was still managing to live an idealistic bohemian lifestyle. He'd never fallen prey to addiction like me and had remained a decent and well-respected member of the alternative lifestyle community. Seldom without a spliff hanging out of his mouth, Sniff was always just good old Sniff, he seemed like he had never changed. His basic but clean two-roomed tattoo parlour appeared to be thriving. He had customers waiting on the street outside, so I had lunch on the beach. It was amazing. The setting, the buzz of the place, and the best tuna I'd ever tasted.

Later we went back to his bungalow, where he lived with his German wife. It was a spacious home, complete with a housekeeper and a dog. His wife was out so I didn't meet her; I never did. He gave me a new pair of trousers because I'd had Delhi Belly pretty badly and my current pants had a couple of unpleasant stains. He was off out to a party in the jungle that night but I passed; I knew it would be a drug fest. I'd got a few years' clean time under my belt, but I felt a little vulnerable over there and I wasn't going to jeopardise my clean time for all the tea in India. Sniff was no longer a punk, as he was now a DJ on the rave scene. His style was as unique as ever.

A hybrid raver, punk, hippy, he's a thoroughly cool cat. He's always been well liked and trusted, mainly because he's solid and not an arsehole. I have immense respect for him for managing to maintain that lifestyle with such panache. He still leads the life that I would have loved to live but failed miserably at due to my issues with addiction. Sniff had spent years in Amsterdam prior to India. It turned out that his Michelle had also fallen prey to heroin addiction and had ended up living a life of begging and crime over there. Sniff had tried to help her out but to no avail. Sadly, she eventually died of an addiction-related illness. She had been so anti-smack when I had known her. A tragic irony and yet another unhappy loss.

Ever grateful for the fellowship, I managed to attend a couple of 12-Step meetings and hooked up with others in recovery. I met a core member who invited me to his house. He was older than me, well-to-do and well spoken, but he also loved to skate. He was big in the international skateboard scene, it appeared. So much so, that he'd had a skate park built in his backyard. He'd carved out a unique life for himself which was to be greatly admired. Maybe he's still over there, front-side heel-flipping in his own backyard. He made me very welcome and I found him a thoroughly interesting guy. That's another incredible perk of the fellowships; go anywhere in the world and you can find friendly like-minded folks. It's a perk I've relied on many times over globally.

I also did a lot of exploring on my own, hunting out the little nooks and crannies of Goa. I met some interesting and alternative people, many of them still caught up in the grips of addiction. I didn't spend too long around these people though. I simply couldn't afford to.

I decided to go back to see Sniff and have some work done, but I wasn't sure about a tattoo. I didn't want to be nursing a fresh tattoo in that blistering heat. Sniff was always an absolute wanker for encouraging people to do crazy shit, like tattooing a dead relative's ashes into their own skin. He was very keen for me to get my bell-end pierced. In the end we compromised and I had a nipple ring instead. Guess what? It hurt! I should have known better; I knew what he was like. He would openly admit he likes to inflict the pain – all in the best possible professional taste of course!

That night I made my way to a huge night market out in the countryside with a nomadic girl from Birmingham. She rode a new Enfield motorcycle that made my moped look childlike. The market was packed with every stall imaginable, buzzing with dancers and fire jugglers, heaving with locals and tourists, noisy with music and singing. Several Sadhus, daubed in orange and painted with ash, were up to weird and wonderful things but mainly sitting or standing on one leg. One had decided to spend his life standing on one leg and his beard was so long it touched the floor. It was amazing and I really loved it, but my nipple ring hurt and I was probably feeling a bit of shock from it. In the end I made my way back to the hotel on my scooter. The journey was magical. The roads were quiet and dark, the countryside sang and smelt wonderful, the heat had subsided, and the dust swirled. I was at one with the night and the scooter.

However, the next day I was still ill from the horrible malaria tablets I had been taking. I could still feel the effects of jetlag and I was starting to feel vulnerable and very tired. I craved home. The culture shock was taking its toll. Plus, I hate mosquitos and they love me. I was infested with weeping, itchy bites. By now I'd heard that I could pop into a chemist and buy a packet of Valium, probably for a few pence. I was feeling all-round vulnerable and I wasn't about to take any chances. The chemist shops had started to glint at me. I went to say goodbye to Sniff and brought my flight forward a week. I was craving safety and decided to come home early.

I'd had some amazing experiences, yet I also felt deeply disturbed. The poverty and suffering had got to me. Life was so cheap, and I felt unsafe in a place where death and disease were everywhere. I'd seen the old guy who kept messing himself many times and he was haunting me. The day before I flew home, I began to experience the true beauty of the place. Maybe I'd made too hasty a decision, but the flight had been changed. I'd already made the decision; I was going home. After arriving back it took a few days to reacclimatise but India lived on in my soul. I think it has that effect on everyone.

My most memorable souvenir was my new nipple ring, courtesy of Sniff. Lucy was shocked by it. I couldn't understand why, as I was already covered in bad tattoos. We went for a weekend away in Ross-on-Wye and stayed in a little hotel. I was up early one morning and decided to go out onto the balcony for a cigarette while Lucy slept in. The sliding door was a bit stiff, so I hadn't opened it fully. As I walked out, the nipple ring snagged on the door catch and virtually ripped my whole nipple off. The ring was no longer in place and there was blood everywhere. Lucy woke up to my blood, pain and panic. Guess what? It hurt! Thanks, Sniff!

I tried to settle back into normal life but I was struggling to juggle my two conflicting college disciplines of art and counselling. I felt something had to give. Having now gained qualifications in person-centred counselling, I decided to give up the art degree after the first year. I was sad to leave but needed to look into serious employment.

It was time to grow up and get a proper job, for the first time ever.

Chapter Thirteen

Working Life and The Early Years.

I needed to start thinking about becoming fully responsible for my own destiny and find work. I had a counselling qualification and I heard of a job for a trainee counsellor coming up at the rehab I'd been through. The fear I experienced around that interview was extreme. I'd developed stress-coping strategies which involved focusing on my immediate surroundings, in order to bring myself back into the present moment. Not only did that rehab hold significant emotional memories for me, but I was also aware that suitable local counselling positions were far from plentiful. I really wanted the job. The thought of graduating from client to counsellor was daunting but also exciting. It felt like a very big step up.

I got the job and was no longer in life's relegation zone. I was thrown straight in at the deep end, overseeing groups while desperately acclimatising myself to the new perspective. I'd always been fascinated by what went on behind the scenes, now I was about to find out. I knew that somewhere within their extensive filing system, would be a file on me. I was now party to behind the scenes and was on the inside of office meetings and politics. I was very keen and very green. My natural perceptiveness was an asset and I could give effective feedback from the outset. There was also a sense of power, which on the whole I tried to use responsibly. However, it would be an untruth to say that it didn't go to my head from time to time. I could be very challenging if I felt someone was not being honest. I could spot a fake at ten paces.

However, I was being triggered deeply and on a daily basis. I was like a sponge for feelings and this resulted in me taking too much on board. Emotionally I still was very raw and I lacked enough of the ability to separate my issues and feelings from other people's. Every night I went home carrying a heavy burden, full up and emotionally drowning. I was treading water in a huge, turbulent ocean. After a few weeks I began to feel suicidal. While I was strong with my perception, I was poor in terms of possessing a thick skin. Some people naturally have this self-shielding armour, I did not. I was still on the whole raw and vulnerable, I had after all continued with the intensive work on myself since leaving rehab. I started to wonder if I'd bitten off more than I could chew.

A good counsellor friend advised me to leave but stubbornly I stuck at it. I didn't want to let go of the job, the new career path and the status – and at the time it's all I believed I had going for me. With a criminal record and limited education, I felt I wasn't capable of gaining alternative employment easily. In the end my protective arrogance began to emerge, but I was so determined to hang in there, that my behaviour began to wobble. I'd lasted about ten weeks, but eventually I was asked to leave on very good terms and with one month's pay. A combination of my struggles and my resulting arrogant attitude had not gone unnoticed; I was working among highly perceptive people. My energy-absorbing personality had not been suited to such an emotive and pressured environment. My sensitivity was a gift but also a curse, especially unprotected.

I could probably have been diagnosed with some kind of mental health condition back then, but I chose to avoid the pills and embrace the recovery path instead. It later transpired that one of my closest colleagues had been in the middle of a relapse. I hadn't been that perceptive after all, however he hid it well with all the cunning a using addict has! I was devastated, but I also knew that it was the right decision for me, and for them too. I started to look for other work within the drug field, due to my experience and qualifications. I'd been volunteering at Drugline in Blackpool for a while and now also had a DANOS (substance misuse) qualification. Before long, a job came up at Drugline – and I got it. I became heavily involved with other services including the police, probation, social services and other outside agencies. It was a far more relaxed environment and I had my fair share of freedom and autonomy. Liaising with professionals, it really was living on the other side of life. No longer a client; I was now a colleague.

The focus of my job was harm reduction, as opposed to the total abstinence advocated by the 12-Steps. Several other workers were also in the fellowships and we tended to edge clients towards 12-Step recovery if we could. We knew it worked. The difficulty lies in persuading an addict that total abstinence is the best idea. Most addicts have to be utterly desperate to consider that as an option. It is a very long way from their default setting.

I didn't last very long at Drugline either; a few months at most, I believe. The staff dynamics were difficult and some of the 'favourites' appeared to have drug problems themselves. In the end, I crossed the wrong person and was asked to leave with a month's pay. It felt all too familiar. I accepted it and left, but I was worried and troubled about my future. I was back on benefits, signing on once again at the dreaded job centre. I had no idea what my future held and decided that one of the few options I had was to do odd jobs and call myself The Handy Man. I printed some very basic black and white leaflets and began pounding the streets, posting them into homes and businesses. I had hardly any experience except for two years as a steel erector and about six months labouring for a decorator in my early twenties. He'd barely let me lift a brush, so my experience was minimal at best. None of my recent qualifications equipped me for my latest career move, but amazingly I landed a couple of jobs and began to realise that the demand was there. I was desperate, clueless and skint.

After a few weeks of odd jobbing I had to admit to myself that I couldn't sign on and work as well. I made a pact with the universe; if I could gain a few weeks of consistent work, I would sign off. Within five days I had over a month's worth of bookings. I had to keep to my side of the deal, so I signed off, daunted by the lack of security that would follow. I set about rebranding my business with a more professional name, and again began leafleting the streets. My hand-printed leaflets seemed to be getting me a fair few jobs but, looking back, I was a bit of novice. I had no other choice but to learn as I went along, and it was a very steep learning curve. I knew a couple of other decorators who were kind enough to offer help and advice. I had to call on them a lot to begin within. It seemed I was a natural at the marketing and chat, though, as work kept coming in – but then I had to actually do the work. It was a stressful business to be in; I wasn't a businessman, or a decorator. I had to cash the cheques that my mouth had written.

Around this time, I had a remarkable yet terrifying experience. There was a local girl, well known to many, who walked the streets come rain or shine. She had mental health problems and used to calm herself down by walking, and she would cover vast distances along the coast. She was pretty, in her forties, and wore colourful designer clothes. She was one of those recognisable local characters and most people knew of her. She had been living in my Lightburn Avenue flat before me. One night, at around midnight, I was lying on the floor practising my meditation. I was quite deep into it when I felt the impression of a face swoop close to my mind's eye. Suddenly I went ice cold, opening my eyes with a frightening jolt. There was nothing to see but I knew I was in the presence of something. I felt frozen, not from the air, but from my core. Somehow, I realised it was this mysterious local girl. I couldn't see her, I just sensed it was her.

She wasn't someone I ever really thought about, I'd never even spoken to her, so that alone was strange. The whole situation was terrifying because the presence was so very strong. I can sense ley lines on country walks and other energies, but this energy was something else. It was very present and extremely powerful. I felt that she was dead but had no idea what to do. Out of sheer panic and fear, I rang an Indian spiritual healer and teacher I'd met at New Horizons. As it happened, he was sitting somewhere in Preston with three psychic mediums. They all felt the powerful energy coming through me and down the line to them. Fortuitously, I couldn't have rang a better person.

He instructed me that I needed to listen to what she wanted to say, advising that maybe I try to write it all down. After that he said I needed to persuade her to "go into the light". It may sound bizarre, but he said I needed to ask "the rescue team" to come and guide her into the light. I ended the call and grabbed a notebook. There was an awful lot going on in my head by this point. A lot of chatter – am I mad, what's going on, and this is very weird shit indeed. Additionally, I was scared to my very core. The difficulty with the writing was working out what was coming from her and what was coming from me. I began writing, regardless, and I wrote whatever came into my mind. I soon realised that as I wrote something from her, I would get an extreme rush of chilling energy from my core. I kept on writing, all the while doubting my own sanity.

Then came the really bonkers part; asking her to "go into the light". I had no better ideas, so I followed his instructions. I'd lost track of time, but it took a very long time of persuading until I had a sense that she was no longer present. I felt warmer and less scared and eventually I was confident that she had left the room. I was left alone, at about 3 am, with my mad scribblings. She had told me her ex-boyfriend had lured her to the place where he lived. He also had mental health issues and an alcohol problem too, in fact, they had met in a local mental health hospital. At the time, he didn't live in a house, but in an old abandoned farm shed on the edge of some local wasteland. Once he had got her there, he proceeded to hit her around the head before finally strangling her to death. She had been murdered, but because she had gone unwillingly, she hadn't passed over smoothly. I felt she wanted to tell someone the truth about what had happened; she was craving justice. Because she had died in such a brutal way, I had experienced some of the trauma she had felt in her final moments. Hence the unbearable fear that I had been gripped by.

The next morning I rang my Indian friend, as I was concerned about the information that I now held. He convinced me to call the police. I rang Blackpool Police Station and asked if they had anyone who was investigating the murder of a woman in St Annes. I was astonished when they put me through to an actual detective. I felt like a fool but I held my nerve. I explained "you're either going to come and lock me up, have me sectioned or hang up the phone, but I have something I have to tell you". I ran through the information I had about the presence, the luring to the abandoned building, the blow to the head and the strangling. The phone line went deadly quiet. After a very long pause he said, "well your sanity is all right, because all that information is correct, we have him in the cells now" I was speechless, my head felt like it was caving in with disbelief.

I'm a natural cynic and I'd always been sceptical about my sensitivity, but his words confirmed the cold hard factual reality of my gift. This wasn't out-there rubbish, this was fact. All the information I'd been given the previous night had been accurate. I was shaken and traumatised by the night's events. I left the flat and didn't go back for over a week, terrified that she would return or something else would happen. Eventually my fear receded, I moved back home and slowly forgot about the whole experience. For many years, that abandoned shed still stood on the desolate wasteland, visible from the main road. I couldn't understand why they didn't pull it down, it must have held some horrible residual energy. It's gone now, the land is crammed with expensive new housing. I still think of her whenever I drive that stretch of road.

I remember seeing a headline in the local paper about a year later. It said something like "Murder conviction and confirmation from beyond the grave". It mentioned a phone call that had come in shortly after the murder. I re-read it several times, realising that my call had been mentioned in court. I was no longer capable of doubting that there are other forces at work, not that I needed to by now. I already knew, but now 'I knew, I knew'. I'd always doubted my sanity, thinking I've taken a lot of drugs, maybe I'm just mad. My last shreds of doubt had finally evaporated.

I have been to several spiritualist churches and told that I could become a proper medium. However, I have no desire to be a showman, nor do I fancy making mistakes in front of audiences. I find this information can be patchy and unreliable from what I've witnessed. For me, it's more of a personal thing.

I've been visited by a few recovery friends who have passed away. One youngish lad in the fellowship was suffering from depression and eventually he committed suicide. I was so saddened by the tragic loss that I went to his funeral in Preston. It was a lovely service, but throughout I could sense his presence up near the coffin. He didn't feel sad though, he was finding the service and fuss quietly amusing. I was glad to see he was happy and no longer chronically depressed. I was also visited by Mary, a well-known figure within the fellowship, the daughter of a prominent politician in London. She too killed herself. She sent through a message of sorrow to a close friend. She felt like she had let this person down, by taking her own life instead of soldiering on. I tried, and failed, to track this person down to relay the message. Mary had helped me a lot over the years; she was much loved.

There was another man I knew well who died suddenly from a heart attack. He made his presence known and would not stop telling me something about a car. It wasn't making much sense and I struggled to decipher a clear enough message, so I kept it to myself. Many months later I bumped into his ex-partner and mentioned that he had communicated with me, "something about a car that I couldn't quite understand." She instantly knew what I was talking about. He had been in the process of buying a new car just before he passed away and he had wanted his partner's daughter to have his old car. His brother had come over and scooped up all of his possessions after his death, so the car had not gone to the young girl. He was unhappy about the situation and it was clearly bothering him. I was glad I'd mentioned it to her, it was comforting to her that he cared so much about her daughter. I often felt comforted by these passing visitors and reassured that there was more to life than meets the eye. It compounded my faith and helped my recovery in a sense, but I found it intrusive and scary at times.

Lucy and I were still living separately, and we were taking regular trips back and forth to Scarborough as she was trying to get her two daughters back. Social Services were involved, but it took time. We regularly visited their dad's house to collect them and sort things out. It was depressing to witness a using addict's home through fresh clean eyes. The place was a sight to behold in terms of hygiene and neglect, but it was probably no different to the way I had lived in the past. It was heartbreaking to leave the girls there, but the process could not be rushed. They had taught themselves to survive and were tough and fragile in equal measures. They had been dragged through their parent's addictions for their entire childhoods. It was a painful reminder of the reality of active addiction.

Lucy also worked at the rehab for a while and was then 'head-hunted' (as she modestly put it) by a local care company. She had a very humorous flair for the dramatic. We'd split up on occasion, but generally we were good together, considering literally everything is tricky in early recovery. If life is tricky, relationships can be agonising. They have an uncanny knack of exposing your deepest issues and insecurities and have proved to be the death of many an addict. It is a cliché of recovery to avoid them entirely for at least a year or two. Very few do and many either relapse or really struggle as a result. The advice is to get a plant – and if that plant survives for two years, it is time to consider a relationship. Firstly, they are dangerous in terms of relapse, one can easily drag the other back into a relapse. Secondly, they leave addicts prone to falling into the familiar trap of co-dependency, a painful trait common to many.   There are some however that make it and defy this logic.

It's also worth bearing in mind that freshly clean addicts do not have a clue who they actually are and these two years would at least give them a head start in the finding themselves process. However sound and well-based the theory, few manage to conform to the guideline, most know better, myself included. Not only does the sex drive return with a passion, but it is often too tempting to have someone else fill the love void many of us suffer from. Lucy and I did well to maintain the relationship at all, really. We were both trying to find ourselves and were on different paths. She always had a lot of friends, a great sense of humour and didn't take herself too seriously. Her main mission at that time was to become a mother to her daughters. She got her youngest daughter back first, but the older one chose to stay with her dad. They were teenagers and accustomed to the freedom and lack of boundaries provided by a parent in addiction. Eventually, after arduous negotiation and persuasion, they both returned to Lucy. They were both wild and damaged spirits.

They were all living in a flat on St Andrew's Road when the girls started complaining about seeing shadows and feeling a creepy presence. They were becoming hysterical with fear. Lucy too could feel a dark energy. Strange things kept happening with electrical items and the lights. They felt bone tired and drained the entire time too, as if it were sucking the energy out of them. With my recent experiences, Lucy called me in to perform a cleansing ritual. We looked into how to do it and set about clearing the 'badness' out. We'd purchased and amassed the required crystals and scents, used crystals and recited prayers to send the entity away, into the light. I never saw anything but I could feel it, and it was highly unpleasant. Midway through the ritual, Lucy said she felt it grab onto her leg before it whooshed out of the room. I also felt the energy lighten and we both hoped the problem had resolved. All was quiet for a couple of weeks, but then the darkness began to return. I had a strong sense it was the energy of a very depraved old man who had died at the property. This is possibly why he was making himself known to the teenage girls. The dark and perverse energy had returned.

Lucy moved out as quickly as possible; the girls were petrified. One of Lucy's friends went around to the flat to clean it after she had moved out. She was cynical about the stories and seemingly unbothered by them. Apparently, she was happily vacuuming when a tremendous howling emanated from the vacuum cleaner and reverberated within her gut. Seeking a valid explanation, she decided that the machine was faulty and continued on into the next room. Before long the same thing happened, but this time it was far louder and the feeling and vibration within her reached an unbearable intensity. She fled the flat and refused to return. The experience left her with panic attacks and sent her on her own quest for answers. I was certainly not alone with my sensitivity.

When considering relationships in early recovery, one occurrence will forever haunt me. It was a tragedy of terrible proportions few will ever forget and concerns the mysterious demise of Jay and Corey. Corey was a good friend of Lucy's and we both knew them quite well. Jay and Corey had completed treatment and had then entered into a relationship. They were both into 12-Step recovery and landed good jobs quite quickly. Slowly they started earning better money and drifted away from meetings; they had each other, after all. Within a few months rumour went out that they were using, so we didn't see much of them any more. Relapsed addicts tend to give fellowship folk a wide berth, as they feel ashamed. They were out using for a while; I'm not sure how long, but I believe Jay had got into some trouble and was looking at about eight years in prison. Then we heard word that they had both been found dead in a car.

The newspapers claimed it was a joint suicide. What led up to this tragic and irreversible decision, we will never know. I do know that I couldn't stop thinking about it for weeks. I've heard of many tragedies, but this will always stay with me. Corey had four children. It demonstrates the desolation, destruction and desperation and insanity of addiction. They were written up in the papers simply as "heroin addicts", but those of us who had known them in recovery knew them as much more than that. They had both shone bright when they had been clean. Neither would ever shine again. I still have a card they gave me for one of my clean time anniversaries. It reads:

"Don't forget to show hospitality to strangers, for some who have done this have entertained Angels without realising it" - Hebrews 13:2

It is signed to me with their love.

Fortunately, my relationship with Lucy didn't veer in the direction of relapse; we'd both been through the mill with addiction and we took recovery equally seriously. Lucy was as staunch as me. That's not to say we didn't have our turbulent times. Relationships have been known to bring out the worst in me, and in many others. My insecurities, my defences and my temper grow in stature.

I've been arrested a couple of times in recovery, due mainly to this explosive temper. I've even been to court a couple of times. Once, the police were called when I got into a serious scuffle with one of Lucy's male friends. I'm not even sure who started it and he got extremely angry and physical too, but he wasn't really the fighting type and in the end I got the better of him. I was arrested and taken down to the cells. There was a photo of him looking utterly dishevelled, and his specs had taken on a jaunty angle. On that same day, I'm deeply ashamed to say I had given Lucy a slap across the face while we were in a volatile argument. I had fines and compensation to pay. My temper has cost me dearly over the years.

Being in the cells clean was a rude awakening. I never thought that would happen to me now, it was something that only happened to junkies in my world.

The once familiar cell walls brought back floods of unhappy memories. I can't remember exactly what happened in court, but I got away fairly lightly, I believe, and avoided community service. After the dust had settled from both incidents, Lucy accepted my apologies and we moved into a large four-bedroomed house, where both of her daughters could live with us comfortably. We even got a dog, a tiny Jack Russell puppy called Marley. The place felt like a proper home; we even had a house-warming party. That year we enjoyed a couple of holidays abroad, visiting Italy and Spain. The future was beginning to look bright.

I've always suffered from a lightning quick temper, which has landed me in endless trouble. I think I supressed so much rage as a child, that if ever I feel humiliated or threatened, my instinctual reaction is to fight. One time I got into a confrontation with a man spoiling for a fight in the Argos car park. I pulled into the middle of the bay, but his car was lop-sided and therefore the cars were quite close. He instantly started shouting through his window. I was feeling quite sensitive and I started verbalising back. It got heated very quickly and I went around to his window. He was too mouthy for his own good and a scuffle began. I started to get a hammer and tools out of my van, I was seeing red by then. I managed to rein myself in and put the tools down, but he was offering me out down the nearby back alley. So we headed off away from the cameras, locked horns and I swung at him and cut his face, underneath his eye. Then he got me down and was choking the life out of me, asking if I'd had enough. Eventually I conceded and he let me go, but I went back at him and we began scuffling again. All in all, it was pretty ugly and playground stuff. Afterwards he went into Argos looking for his wife and I knew he was going to call the police, so I called them too, not wanting to look the villain. The police arrived and cuffed me. I was outraged and managed to persuade them that it had been six of one and half a dozen of the other. He admitted that he had offered me out which proved my point. They let me go, but I had to attend the police station at a later date. The police, yet again, were in possession of a photo. The man looked a real mess, his face bloody and his specs were on at that familiar jaunty angle. I'm sure they do that on purpose. Due to his own statement he'd basically shot himself in the foot and the CPS decided there was insufficient evidence to press charges and the matter was dropped. However, there were several weeks of stress and anxiety. If only I hadn't bought into the initial verbal exchange. It would have been far wiser to turn the other cheek and walk away.

I've never be one to learn easily and a while later I had a minor dispute with a traffic warden in Manchester. I felt he'd been hasty in writing me a ticket and I got verbally aggressive towards him. I shouted, "something really bad is going to happen to you within the next week." I'd meant it in an 'I'll put a curse on you' way, but he took it as a direct threat and I was hauled down to court in Manchester. He was Asian which was an added worry, as I didn't want to be charged with any kind of racist crime and I had been very verbal with him. The solicitor alone cost me £600, and yet again it had caused me months of stress and turmoil. I had another £600 in fines and compensation to pay. My anger had cost me dearly once more; £1200 in total. More consequences which I'd deserved. Learning to walk away is an on-going process for me.

My business had started to do quite well by now and one of the bedrooms became my office. I'd had my little Suzuki 'Noddy' van sign written by someone in the fellowship. My natural blagging ability and what I was learning was pulling in the work; the stress was in following it up with the practical skills required. By now I'd picked up a lot of the theory but my own decorating skills were never the best, although I was by then a graduate with a Fine Art Diploma. I was busy educating myself and learning from others. I also learnt a lot from my own mistakes – and in the early days there were many to learn from. I still felt like an imposter and a fraud.

My natural nous, street wisdom and recovery learning were growing the business at a rate of knots. I'd begun to get some bigger contracts on blocks of flats and other sizeable buildings. My learning curve inclined rapidly as these larger jobs began to trickle in. I had the edge on some of the larger companies, as I was still too small to be VAT registered. By now I employed a couple of other men and began doing less of the manual work myself. I was flying by the seat of my pants on these larger jobs. I knew little about scaffolding, cherry-pickers and access issues, and any mistakes suddenly became very expensive. It was an almost constant stress, from pricing to job completion. I found the pressure and challenge to be a real buzz.

I know many decorators who are happy doing a good honest day's work but don't want the stress and aggro of these bigger jobs. I, on the other hand, buzzed from the trials and risks involved. I started off inexperienced, but I had learned quickly and had good business instincts. I was now an accredited member of a professional trader's association and the profits were steadily increasing. Slowly, I was growing into my own skin. I felt less and less like a fraud.

My early management style left a lot to be desired. I was controlling, angry and constantly stressed. I could barely watch my employees stir a tin of paint without close supervision and constant guidance. I have improved a lot in this area over recent years, or at least I hope I have. The business constantly kept me on my toes. I'd asked the universe to show me a future and it had replied in style. I felt guided and directed by the successes bestowed upon me. At a time when I'd felt utterly hopeless and lost, a solution had been provided for me out of nowhere. It was reassuring. By hook, and a bit of crook, I had become a legitimate businessman.

Lucy's wild and troubled daughters brought with them their fair share of chaos and drama. I understood they were carrying damage and I empathised with them for that. However, my insight did not make it any easier to deal with. They were frequently absent from school and the police had been involved regard-ing their behaviour on numerous occasions. It was not an easy house to live in. I tried to maintain some order and authority, but I was painfully aware that I was not their father. It was a difficult path to tread. Neither was easy to reason with and they often lashed out with uncontrollable rage and angry behaviours. They were angry at the world and who could blame them?

Lucy had to deal with a lot of guilt about her addiction during their younger years. Anney, the eldest, started drinking very young; addiction tends to repeat in endless cycles. Once we went to Lucy's brother's wedding in Wales. Anney got totally hammered and we had to leave early as she was creating a scene. We were driving home and Anney was becoming increasingly impossible to handle. She kept grabbing at the steering wheel while Lucy was driving. We couldn't stop her and had to pull over. It was the middle of the night and we spent hours trying to persuade Anney to calm down. In the end, we were so at a loss with her, we called the police. We didn't know where else to turn. She was so angry and rebellious on occasion that she became frightening and dangerous. Even though I understood the reasons behind this rage, it didn't make it any easier to live with. I felt helpless in the face of her unrelenting anger and chaos

It was often hard for me to keep a lid on my temper during such times; never my strong suit to begin with. Once, Anney was being drunk and impossible yet again and I lost it. I grabbed her by her hair. I'd tried every other approach I could think of and it was a desperate reactive move. She stormed out of the house, slamming the door behind her (she was an accomplished door slammer). A few moments later I heard a worrying thud; it turned out she had put a brick through my van windscreen. She wasn't a pleasant drinker; it often brought out her very worst side. I regretted the fact that I'd lost it, but her behaviours continued, and we had no choice but to call the police again that night. I never thought I'd be calling on my old enemies so often.

The constant dramas and hostility were beginning to cause problems between Lucy and me. I couldn't cope with her children, even though I really had tried. Lucy couldn't cope with being torn between her children, and the fact that I couldn't cope with her children. There was no remedy and no solution, neither of us knew what to do. I was finding it intolerable. In the end Lucy left with the girls. I was sad she had gone, but I was also relieved to be free of the chaos and how it had affected me. I was not so young, but I was free and single. I brushed myself down and looked to the future.

Chapter Fourteen

Spreading My Wings and Learning to Fly

I was now rattling around in a big four-bedroomed house, contemplating my future. I missed Lucy but I knew it was the right decision. I knew it was for real this time too, it was over once and for all. We were both growing up in our recovery; I think we both harboured doubts about each other deep down but it was the intolerable situation that put the final nail in the coffin. I decided I was sick of paying rent and began looking into the possibility of getting a mortgage. There had been a time when I would never have pictured myself having anything so civilised, when I couldn't have even opened a bank account. I bought myself a nice two-bedroomed flat in a reasonable apartment complex not far from the house I had just moved out of. The flat needed a lot of work and Louis became my right-hand man. He was a very handy guy and his affable calmness was what I needed. Between the two of us we renovated the entire place, complete with new bathroom and kitchen. I was still missing Lucy but I threw myself into the business and the renovation. We still saw each other often, as we had shared custody of Marley the dog. I forced myself to focus on other things – my future, not my past.

Rather annoyingly, a partially blind, partially deaf and entirely senile elderly lady lived above my brand-new abode. Due to her numerous disabilities and mental fragility, she had an annoying habit of leaving her taps running, causing significant flooding. Really she should have been in a home and I got Social Services involved. Now I had completed my renovations I didn't want all my hard work to be literally washed away. One night I was woken by the sound of gushing water; it was pouring through the ceiling, everywhere. I ran upstairs but I couldn't get in, she was deaf, remember? In the end, I broke the door through and located the offending tap. She had slept through the entire saga. My flat was ruined, all my hard work down the drain. After that I began keeping a friendly eye on her, someone had to. I'd knock regularly and check she was all right and politely remind her about her taps, but she seemed to be deteriorating each day. Then I began to let myself in (using my shoulder) and check she was alive and that the taps were off each night. Sometimes I'd find the stove left on and cigarettes that had burnt down. She was a perilous neighbour. I lived with this constant anxiety for nearly a year. It was a crazy situation really, but I'd survived far worse.

I renovated the flat again with the insurance money and eventually the old lady popped her carpet slippers. I can't say I was overly upset; she was a pain to live below and she was very old. After she had died, I could feel her presence had gone from above, but I felt worried she might pay me the odd visit. I performed a ritual to keep her away, I didn't want her hanging around my flat. I was a little afraid of her and worried she might know I'd been sneaking into her flat for the past year. I'm relieved to say my rituals worked; she never did visit.

As well as building the business at a rapid rate, I began serving my 12-Step fellowship as an area representative, which involved travelling down to London and Leeds regularly. I enjoyed spreading my wings and meeting new people. I started doing a bit of solo travelling again too, always attending meetings abroad if I could. I made many new fellowship friends, and as I began to feel part of the fellowship on a global scale the world began to open up. My first significant and memorable trip was to Sarajevo. I was surprised to find it was in Bosnia, (I thought it sounded more South American), and I agreed to go. A few of us went along for that region's first convention. It was a fellowship in its infancy, with only two meetings a week in the entire region, one of which was solely attended by a dating couple.

Two New Yorkers, a Scot and a few from England went along to support these East European pioneers. The region consisted of three countries: Bosnia, Serbia and Croatia. The foreign contingent and I travelled in a car convoy on the twelve-hour journey from Croatia into Bosnia. I had no idea what to expect.

Suddenly, as we crossed the border into Bosnia, it became apparent that we were entering a country torn apart by war. I spotted a gable end peppered with hundreds of bullet holes, all at head and chest height, almost like it had been used by a firing squad. The whole place had an edgy and chilling feel; armed checkpoints and guards were in place frequently.

When we eventually arrived in Sarajevo, I was shocked to see entire sections of the city had been destroyed by the war. Every building in the city centre bore the scars of thousands of bullets.

I sat in that convention, realising that we were carrying the message of recovery into untouched and war-torn territories. The natives of that country, now sitting in a fellowship meeting, would have been living in fear for their lives, or out to kill each other, only a few years before. There was something about this powerful solution to addiction that transcended boundaries and borders, not just of land but of race, age and creed. It was a powerful realisation and one that speaks volumes about the power of the recovery fellowships. I realised how lucky we were to have a developed and well-structured fellowship where I lived. I've since heard that meetings were a rare oasis of peace during the troubles in Northern Ireland, a place where men from both sides could sit together in harmony.

I was often shocked by the primitive nature of the fellowship in these more remote places. Many of these countries have major drug problems, yet very little in terms of rehab, recovery or support. I later went to a convention in Macedonia, where we visited an amazing church. In a crypt within the church grounds, we discovered an abundance of needles, spoons and other drug paraphernalia. It was obvious that many of these eastern cities have major drug problems. I was pleased to be witnessing the birth of a fellowship that would help very many people in years to come. The UK and the USA are lucky to have a reliable and widespread network of fellowships and recovery; most people can access a meeting if they wish to. This luxury, that I had come to expect, is not a worldwide phenomenon. It was a privilege to help establish the fellowship further afield.

I purchased one of my very favourite souvenirs from a market in Bosnia – a carved and sculpted bullet casing that had been crafted into a pen. They had used the leftovers of war to create art, and the incongruity and duality of that hit me square in the chest. The art of war, quite literally turned on its head. Probably thirty people attended that Sarajevo convention in total, from a region of three entire countries. It was held in a very basic hostel, with rooms for working girls upstairs. It was poles apart from the Hilton conventions that I was used to, where hundreds gather. I'm happy to report that these East European fellowships are now thriving, with many meetings each week. I have returned to these areas quite a few times and was privileged to witness the fellowship over there flourishing. Each time I returned, recovery had blossomed further.

I later went on to represent the UK region at international level, a role that took me to many more places. It involved travelling to Los Angeles bi-annually for world service conferences. This new role also entailed travelling to conventions in Europe every year. As part of this duty I visited Egypt, Malta, Sweden, Moscow, Turkey, Spain, Germany, Slovakia and the Czech Republic. I came to realise that, throughout the world, the fellowship is at very different stages of evolution. Some countries do not even have the recovery literature translated into their own language. Not a textbook or even a leaflet to hand out to newcomers. The process of translation and approval through the official fellowship route takes months, if not years. Some of these fellowships exist on a diet of self-translated and photocopied books and documents.

It was an inspiration to see the ingenuity and resilience of these people. Members would visit hospitals and institutions with their own handmade literature. I was surprised to discover that even very modern countries, such as France, often have very few meetings outside of the major cities. Some of my work within the fellowship involved travelling to these countries to provide presentations and information. Different countries also have their own uniquely horrific drug epidemics. I heard horror stories in Russia about a drug called Crocodile, a homemade concoction of codeine, petrol and match heads that literally rots away the addict's flesh. Its nickname is 'dirty morphine'. I've never seen or heard of anything so horrible. Apparently, the addicts are so out of it that their already rotting flesh will then play host to maggots, until they are literally eaten alive.

I went to Russia twice and I was impressed by its vastness and architecture. The fellowship was reasonably well established, and they were highly organised, if a little officious. Most of my time was taken up in conferences, but I did visit Red Square and a couple of other well-known tourist haunts. Addiction is a worldwide phenomenon and as I see it now part of the human condition at varying degrees.

I began to do a lot of solo travelling at this time too, separate from my fellowship service duties. New

York became one of my favourite places and it was to become a regular haunt. I made a habit of flying out there every year on New Year's Day, spending a couple of weeks there at the start of every year. Business tended to be quiet at home and I loved the place. Again, I attended fellowship meetings and got to know many people, and as you would expect of New York, some real characters. I fell in love with the city the first time I went up The Empire State Building and watched the sun setting over the city. It was a mesmerising mixture of natural fading light and artificial illuminating light that I had never before witnessed; I could literally feel the buzz of the place. The city has an incredible raw energy about it, far less plastic and far more real than LA. There is so much to see. I could walk for miles soaking up the sights, characters and the people.

My first ever meeting in NY was in Queens and I felt welcome there from the very start. I instantly struck up a friendship with a guy who has made it his life mission to reach out to newcomers. Bluey, who is actually white and is known to many, is a big fellowship character. He is a recovering street junkie who has managed to survive for over twenty years with full-blown Aids. Bluey puts his longevity down to his spiritual well-being and ploughs most of his energy into helping others. He attends daily meetings and targets newcomers in order to carry the message of recovery. He was the first person in New York I connected with and I made a point of seeing him every year. Bluey is staunch and a passionate advocate of his fellowship and the recovery programme steps.

New York meetings are wall to wall characters; from guys who look like *The Blues Brothers*, to bikers, artists, extremists, bohemians and many more who have long ago lost their marbles. Each meeting tends to have its own unique personality and this is nowhere truer than in New York. I also came across a lot of people who were in recovery, yet also terminally ill, usually from either Hep C or Aids. It seemed relatively common over there, and it was not something I was used to. I knew people with Hep C and HIV back home, but they seemed to have their illnesses under control. I came to really like a guy with Irish heritage, who loved the Irish and especially their protest songs. He took the time to show me around New York, visiting museums and other interesting nooks and crannies. He introduced me to New York's tipping etiquette, giving me a very hard time when I initially refused to toe the line. He later died of Hep C, another one of those characters you never forget.

Overall the meetings were busier, bigger and louder than back home in little Lancashire. I went to a meeting in Brooklyn that seemed almost entirely populated with fully patched-up bikers. One guy, called Shotgun Steve, declared that he'd decided to come to a meeting instead of "fucking blowing some fucker's head off", and he meant it. When Americans heard my foreign accent, they were always keen to ask me to speak, so over the years I did a good quota of it. This 'telling your story' to a room full of strangers is both daunting and rewarding.

I was blown away by the rawness and honesty in some of the meetings, too. I'll never forget one guy who had stage-four stomach cancer. He stood in front of the meeting and loudly ranted about spirituality. He proclaimed, "I'm not one of those religious motherfuckers, down on their fucking knees all day long, fucking praying. I don't give a fuck about 'talk' and what you 'preach', I only give a fuck about what you fucking 'do' in your day to day lives, talk is cheap." I was initially shocked by his forceful nature but ended up respecting him immensely. He was dying, so he could say what he fucking wanted, he didn't care; he was also very real and very raw. Amazingly, he recovered from his cancer and is still alive today; yet another walking (and very much talking) miracle. Addiction generates many miracles; it is not all about death.

Bleecker Street was another meeting I came to love. Once I found myself anxiously standing in line to share, next to another chap from England. We chatted a bit and I kept thinking "I fucking know you"; it was really bugging me. Just as I was about to share, I realised I was standing beside the lead singer of a famous band. I was star struck and stage frightened all at the same time. I'd love to say who it was, but the fellowships demand anonymity, it's kind of important! It's all in the name 'anonymous'.

There were meetings in Harlem where I was literally the only white guy there. I'd venture into the depths of the neighbourhood in search of a meeting, ignoring warnings that it was a dangerous part of town. I knew if I made it to a meeting, it would be a safe haven; that's the amazing thing about the fellowship. One particular Harlem meeting spends most of its weekly takings on fried chicken and fries. This food is given out to newcomers and people from the streets. It was very much a front-line meeting. Homeless folk would wander in to enjoy the free food and friendly atmosphere, and the odd one would stay and end up recovering. Slowly over time it had become a very busy, thriving meeting. Wherever and whatever the meeting, I was always made to feel welcome; that's the other amazing thing about the fellowship. I also loved the attention of being English. I'm never one to turn away an extra dose of attention, however modest I may seem.

The street life of New York was endlessly fascinating to me. I loved riding the subway too. Carriage after carriage, crammed with a level of diversity that I had not witnessed before; mad buskers, cross-dressers, crazies and circle sleepers. Not to mention the graffiti on the way into Queens, which was an incredible sight to behold. I was sad to see so many injured ex-military men, reduced to begging from the confines of their wheelchairs. This wasn't something I was used to seeing in England.

I had a sponsor, for a number of years, who lived in Syracuse, a city tucked away in northern New York State. I'd fly up there and spend a few days with him whenever I was in New York. We also did a couple of trips together, once to a very frozen and wintery Niagara Falls. The fast-flowing water doesn't freeze, but the water all around was frozen into giant glistening peaks. The power and isolation of the place was awe inspiring. I imagined going back in time to when Native Americans roamed the planes of America. What a powerful sight that wilderness must have been!

We could not have been more different. He was a black guy who I'd taken a liking to because he laughed a lot, and loudly. I liked the fact he seemed happy and didn't take life too seriously. He was a Vietnam War veteran who was out of work due to an injured back, but on the quiet he did a roaring trade in copy designer gear. He was a genuine, pragmatic and sincere guy who I enjoyed spending time with. He'd been a Kung Fu champion in the past and was keen to help his daughter do well in the world of martial arts. Now a family man, who I'm sure had once been well connected.

We were chatting about guns one day after I'd seen a report on the news about a murdered policeman. It became clear that he was a gun owner and he showed me his weaponry. His collection consisted of a hefty handgun, a powerful shotgun and an AK47. I couldn't believe what I was seeing. Who would ever need to fire 750 rounds per minute? He calmly explained it was part of the culture and that if anyone broke into his house in the middle of the night, he would be reaching for his most powerful gun. Armed robberies were commonplace, and most households relied on the security that carrying weaponry provided. It was shocking, but I also understood in a way. I hadn't realised how serious the gun culture was and I had been oblivious of it until then. My sponsor worked a spiritual programme, and owned an AK47, now that is a paradoxical life lesson.

I became familiar with LA too, due to my service position. That service position blew my mind in terms of the fellowship's size, scale, organisation and global reach. There would be representatives from all over the world, sitting in a giant, sleek conference hall. It had the feel of a global summit, with delegates, facilitators and translators. It was not a free holiday but involved six very long days of often tedious negotiations. One of the big projects on the agenda back then was the process of approving and editing a new book to use within the official literature. An entire sub-committee had been compiling this book and it had to go through a complex and multi-layered process before it was sent to print. Other matters included money, policy and guideline decisions. It was an honour and a privilege to represent my country.

Outside of these long days we did venture out in the evenings, visiting places along the coast such as Venice Beach, Malibu and Fisherman's Cove. I loved Venice Beach. It was like Blackpool on acid, a rare melting pot frequented by down-and-outs and the extremely wealthy simultaneously. It had a carnival feel, a bit like 'Glastonbury by the sea'. The most notable thing about LA for me was its variety of meetings; there was such a huge chasm between rich areas and poor areas. The meetings in the rich areas can be populated by those who possess wealth and fame. The poorer areas have been seriously ravaged by crime, drugs and gangs. Yet again, recovery crosses borders, barriers and social divides.

The fellowship has enabled me to travel the world with a feeling of safety and security. I know that if I can find a meeting, I am guaranteed a warm welcome and a reassuring hug. I can go anywhere on my own and not feel alone. It's a unique phenomenon and I am fortunate to be a part of it. I probably wouldn't have done as much travelling without this invaluable safety net. A meeting is a great place to meet new people, feel safe and get the local know-how and lowdown. I've never had a bum steer from a meeting; I'd always find out the best places to eat and the hidden gems to visit. It's allowed me the freedom (and given me the balls) to travel alone, all over the world.

Occasionally I've sat in meetings where I've not understood a word due to the language barrier, but I've still been made to feel welcome and received warm hugs instead. I have rarely felt on my own, due to my fellowship connections. I have done the odd trip with others too; once I did a road trip along the west coast of America with Dez Y. We'd hired an open-topped Ford Mustang and set off up the coast in the glorious Californian sunshine. I was amazed by the murals in San Francisco and the thick sea mist rolling in over Alcatraz and the Golden Gate Bridge. Sights I never could have imagined seeing a few years before.

Now that's what I call recovery. A far cry from a prison cell, a police station or a tarpaulin in a filthy builder's caravan. Without the 12-Step fellowship I wouldn't have done any of this. The likelihood is I wouldn't even be alive. I try to keep this in mind and remain grateful.

Chapter Fifteen

Clean Toxicity and Death

I was happy in my flat, but I also felt lonely and began hanging around on dating sites hoping to fill the void; it's a common recovery behaviour. I've experienced some dreadful dates over the years, as a result of dabbling on such sites. I met up with a woman from South Shore in Blackpool who looked nothing like her profile pictures. As soon as she opened her mouth, I knew she was not for me. Her voice was rough and both of her teeth were discoloured. I escaped to the loo and after contemplating climbing out of the window, rang a friend to fake an emergency phone call in five minutes time. It worked and I couldn't get out of there quick enough. Such sites throw up some nasty surprises.

I also a met a beautiful Brazilian girl and we went on a date to Liverpool. It turned out she was already living with a lorry driver who had brought her over to this country, but she was getting a bit bored and looking to find a bigger pot of gold. I was looking for something a bit deeper than to be a dolly bird's sugar daddy so I didn't see her again either. Overall, I found dating sites could be useful if I'm spiritually well. On bad days, when my addiction is running riot, they can be used for a quick fix and one-night stands have occurred which have left me feeling empty and internally bankrupt.

About six months after we split up, Lucy was diagnosed with a very rare and difficult form of stomach cancer. She'd had symptoms for a couple of years but had merely been prescribed fibre drinks and IBS medication. By the time the cancer was recognised she had some sizeable tumours. I loved her but I knew I couldn't go back to her.

I was chasing success and wealth; automatically and naively equating the two. Having come from a working-class family and grown up on council housing estates where money was always tight, then having sunk down to the status of street junkie, it felt natural for me to want to better myself. Having had nothing, I wanted everything – and finally I could see a way of achieving it. It took years for me to realise that 'worth' and money are not the same. Money is not happiness. I've had times of having everything, but inside I've felt empty and alone. I have since learnt the very valuable distinction.

Within a short time, I was able to take on a second property and became a landlord. It was a time of much chasing. I was also chasing a partner, until one day I met someone by chance. I was operating a cherry picker machine up on a posh block of flats on the very affluent part of the seafront, overlooking the green and a windmill. It's a road that commands some of this area's highest property prices. I spotted an attractive blond woman coming in and out of the flats and one day I chanced my luck and asked if she fancied making me a brew and a bacon butty. I can only assume she found this cheeky approach charming and endearing, because before long Kristin and I were an item. She mixed in very posh circles locally.

Early on, I felt I needed to tell her about my past and the fact that I was in recovery. Reassured by my confession and emotional maturity, she confided in me that she had health issues which left her with long-term problems. Having suffered with colitis, she'd had some of her bowel removed and had been left with a colostomy bag, or pouch, as she called it. She was bothered it would be an issue for me. It wasn't, in my mind she was still a real catch. She was beautiful, classy and intelligent. I still felt I was punching well above my weight, as they say. She was deeply affected and hung up about her pouch and her health issues. She was often ill and seemed to be on a constant dosage of super-strong antibiotics. I really felt for her. She was a sensitive, fragile, highly strung woman, who had the tendency to be a little on the snobby side. People who have never lived on the other side of the tracks seldom possess the empathy and understanding of those who have. It was a side of her I found difficult to deal with.

Having both revealed our imperfections, the relationship could move forward. We became sexually active, something she had not been for a very long time, due to her illness. I was impressed by the fact that she was from a family with both money and status. Her parents had a large home in Zimbabwe and split the year between their two properties. Kristin was refined, elegant and well-mannered. I began mixing in different circles; people with professions, tailored clothes and their own teeth! Initially I'd found myself mildly moist with sweat, unsure of how to behave or what to say. I started wearing shirts to dinner and made a conscious effort to improve my social skills and etiquette. I rapidly learnt a lot about how to conduct myself, and this had a knock-on effect with my business. I felt I was on the up.

Kristin was an aesthetic technician, administering Botox and similar cosmetic procedures. She mixed in the right circles and had clients both here and in Africa. The whole family were Botox-ed up, it was standard to them. She could make good money in a very short time. We were poles apart in personality; she certainly did not suffer from an addictive personality. She had one cigarette every six months and could happily drink half a glass of wine in a night. It was a state of affairs I struggled to comprehend but clearly outlined the difference in that respect.

Some of the Lytham garden parties were in a different league. Men in boaters and yachting shoes, cosmetically enhanced women and food that had been ordered in from exclusive local sources. One man had had his barbecue meat buried under the ground for thirty days prior to his soiree. These people were always immaculately turned out, their clothes reeked of money without being label loud. There wasn't an Adidas stripe or Lacoste crocodile in sight, unlike other circles, where two thirds of the feet are usually shod in the latest Adidas. Kristin knew all of the wealthy locals; I was impressed and wanted to be part of it all. I picked up a saying, "money talks but wealth whispers".

As my social circles changed and my business grew, I became acutely aware that my badly tattooed hand was not giving a very favourable impression and possibly even scared some customers away. I began the painful and arduous process of laser tattoo removal, which involved me making regular trips to Manchester. The lasering was agonising and the process slow; I had to leave three months healing time in between sessions. It took almost three years, as my tattoos were very deep and dark in colour. During those three years I wore a bandage over that hand, to shield my tattoos from the eyes of potential customers. A bandage says so much less about a person than a swath of homemade prison-like tattoos. The tattoo had been done under the influence of heroin and crack, not only me but also the tattooist, I didn't want the daily reminder. It took three years and cost a lot, but it was worth every penny. In some way I felt I was clearing away evidence of my dubious past.

Another way I have shed my old skin is by having my teeth fixed. I no longer look like a junkie poster boy and can smile with confidence. I've had all sorts done, crowns and implants and more. It's not been cheap to rectify and like the tattoos, it's been a lengthy and painful process. As soon as I got clean, I became acutely aware of my shameful smile. Most people do. Teeth are important; a smile speaks a thousand words.

The business had won a few national awards and competitions by now; I wanted to be able to represent myself, and my business, with pride. I'd been in the local papers and on local radio to publicise the business and its successes. In many ways I was moving up in the world, to a place I never expected to reach.

I'd never believed I would live beyond the age of thirty-four.

Kristin was very family-orientated; they were her world. There had been a family tragedy. Her brother's wife had died from a sudden heart attack during a school fete, leaving her brother with two very young children. Kristin took her role as aunt (and in part, surrogate mother) very seriously, I respected and admired that. I believe this family tragedy had softened her and she was grateful to meet someone who could be empathetic and caring. We had a good connection but she had a mile-wide streak of insecurity, triggered primarily by her health difficulties. So did I; it wasn't always a good combination.

My frequent travels and weekends away, performing service for my fellowship, caused horrendous problems between us. She'd get ideas into her head that I was being unfaithful, and no matter what I said or did she could not be dissuaded. In her head I had been found guilty of a crime and I was frequently accused, tried and convicted in my absence. There was nothing I could say or do to alter her verdict. It was an impossible situation. I, too, feared rejection and abandonment in a very major way, and the two of us would bounce off each other's weaknesses. A destructive pattern was developing. I hated being accused of things I hadn't done, but I refused to give up aspects of my life to appease her. I also hated the constant insecurity and turmoil that this dynamic created; it didn't feel secure. And security was something I craved more than anything.

The relationship frequently broke down and we wouldn't speak for weeks or even months at a time. It was painful and exhausting. I'd miss her and pine for her, even though I knew deep down it wasn't working. I hated feeling abandoned and rejected, it triggered off my childhood feelings of being defective and unlovable. It was a very painful time in my life. I became insecure and twisted around the relationship she had with her brother; they were very close. Which one of us was weirder. Who knows?

We had similar issues and it was not a pretty cocktail. I had the capacity to be as paranoid and insecure as she did; the difference was I had a 'programme' in my life. Working the steps and having a sponsor forced to me look at myself and attempt to rectify my errant behaviours. Kristin did not have a programme in her life. For anyone not familiar with 12-Step programmes, they are a set of simple and guiding principles by which to live. They include owning up to your past, making amends, correcting defective and destructive behaviour patterns and maintaining this on a daily basis. I'd become painfully aware, through years of inner work, that my own thinking can be off-key and unbalanced. Kristin had not been provided with this insight. She remained resolute that she was not the one with the problem.

In hindsight, I should have walked away after a few months, but I was in awe of her status, dignity and wealth. I had very little guilt-free freedom during that time. It did however fulfil a valuable function; I became aware that relationships are my Achilles heel and I began looking into other fellowships concerning co-dependency and relationships. This is a secondary issue that comes to light for many recovering addicts once they put the drugs down. I found support; I was certainly not alone in these matters.

I had the good fortune to travel to Africa twice during this relationship. Kristin's family owned a luxurious gated villa in Zimbabwe, complete with extensive grounds and a pool. The first trip was an unmitigated disaster. I'd flown over business class to Harare (business class on an African airline is not as expensive as it sounds). I felt very anxious, thousands of miles away from my comfort zone and very much in her territory. She had her own annexe in the grounds and it should have been idyllic, but we didn't connect and sexually things weren't going well, so we began to bicker and argue. The atmosphere was awful and we couldn't get past it. It was a real culture shock too. I'd entered a world where they had black servants and I struggled to not equate it with slavery. It turned out that their main man, called Friday, was treated pretty well, but initially it felt alien and harsh. I was a fish out of water. I lasted two days and decided to fly home. We parted on very bad terms. The relationship was over, or so I thought, and I was distraught. I cried for hours and hours on the flight home, shattered and broken. I got home and expressed this pain in a painting, which I later sold, called *When Two Worlds Collide*. Slowly, I began moving on with my life once again.

As was our pattern, we ended up getting back together several months later, enjoying some happy times again. My second trip to Zimbabwe was far more successful. We flew over together and went on a few romantic trips; I actually saw a bit of Africa that time. We set out on a remote safari in Mozambique, a country that borders Zimbabwe. We took a tiny twin-propped plane to an island in the middle of a huge lake – its only access. It was so beautiful it was verging on the trippy. A Jeep collected us from the remote airstrip and took us up the hill to a luxury five-star hotel, which overlooked the shores of the lake. Our balcony overlooked the water and giraffes and elephants regularly wandered past. It seemed like I was participating in a big budget feature film.

There was a small and spooky abandoned prison on the island. It had been used for political prisoners and would have once housed about twenty or so very unlucky souls. It was long abandoned and rusted through, but I found reading the graffiti etched into the crumbling walls both fascinating and chilling. The roof was constructed of tin sheeting and the heat was unbearable after a few minutes; the thought of being locked away in there was terrifying. I was so glad I'd never been a prisoner in Africa.

We did a safari and saw plenty of native species, but my African holy grail, the lion, evaded us. I was wandering along the lake shore one day when I found a baby elephant's skull. The teeth were loose, so I wiggled one out and brought it home. I still have that giant molar in a cabinet. Fishing was also a whole different kettle of fish because there were crocodiles and other lethal predators to consider. On the plane ride back to Zimbabwe I sat up front with the pilot as we flew over the amazing landscape of Africa, a dust storm swirling below us. A powerful and very memorable sight.

Throughout all of my relationships, I've always had children in the back of my mind. During my inner child work, I'd connected with this side of myself. Sometimes I'd walk past a school yard and tears would well up from deep within me. Kristin was unable to have children and this issue, on the whole, went unmentioned. To add insult to injury she once told me after the fact, that she'd had an ectopic pregnancy and underwent an operation to abort the foetus. I felt hurt by this. I know the pregnancy could never have carried full term, yet I felt betrayed and grief stricken. We managed to soldier on through, but I knew deep down that I wanted to have at least one child. It was an instinct I couldn't quash.

Throughout this relationship turmoil, Lucy continued to get more and more ill. After several very tough and unsuccessful operations at Christie's Hospital in Manchester, hope began to slip away. It was heart-breaking. She was now a doting grand-mother as well as mother; Anney had had a baby boy. Her daughters had been through so much and now it became clear that they would lose their mother, just as she had turned their lives around. It was very difficult as Lucy needed help and support from everyone, myself included, but Kristin couldn't understand and was wracked with jealousy if ever I visited. Lucy now had a new partner, but still Kristin could not be swayed into understanding. I wasn't about to abandon Lucy or the girls at such a time of need, so I ignored Kristin and put up with the endless arguments instead. I couldn't understand where Kristin was coming from. I kept saying, "but she's dying", even that fell on deaf ears. Of course, I could still care about Lucy without being in love with her. Kristin's jealousy and lack of compassion began to grind on me; it was becoming distasteful. Plus, I refused to give up my service commitments and travel plans. I wasn't ready to have my wings clipped.

Seeing Lucy go through so much pain and suffering was one of the most horrific things I've witnessed in recovery. It was traumatic to see her, especially when all hope had finally evaporated. There were no words of comfort I could offer, no chink of hope to hold on to. She was in so much pain, and on so much medication, that her physical condition was painful to witness. I wouldn't wish that on my worst enemy. Lucy stubbornly clung on, as was her way, outliving the doctors' most optimistic predictions. She refused to use a commode and clung on to her dignity until the bitter end. She could certainly be an unruly patient.

Lucy, her mother, father, daughters and new partner went through months of emotional anguish. She finally passed away in the local hospice, her fighting spirit the last thing to go. It seemed so unfair that someone who had hauled themselves out of the bowels of addiction and managed to bring their family back together, should then be taken so cruelly. Luckily, Lucy and I both believed in spirit and knew that it is merely the end of a chapter. I'll never forget the last time I went to see her. I sat on her back doorstep and sobbed. There was nothing anyone could do; it was terrible. I knew it would be the last time I'd see her.

Before Lucy 's funeral I went to the funeral directors and asked them to put a fellowship infinity coin into her hand. It is a big bronze disc with the infinity symbol etched onto it, for people who die clean in recovery. I was honoured and flattered to be asked to speak at her funeral. It was a big loss and tragedy for a lot of people. She was only 42, and had given so much and helped so many since coming into recovery. The ceremony was full, even Marley the dog was there in his Sunday best. It was a tough day for everyone, and I was devastated for the daughters and Lucy's parents. Lucy had chosen her own funeral music; as the curtains closed around her coffin at the very end, the theme music to *Star Trek* played out. "Space, the final frontier, to explore strange new worlds, to boldly go where no man has gone before." The coffin vanished from view, the music typical of her characteristic dry humour and wit. She had exited in true Lucy style.

I did a lot of grieving for Lucy, as did many others. A few months later I was at a UK fellowship convention in a place where I had gone with Lucy several times. She always loved a convention; the socialising, the people, the gossip. I was sitting in the main hall, listening to a share, when I felt a warm vibrating hand upon my head. I looked round, but no-one was there. Instantly I knew it was Lucy, her energy. She had returned to an old stomping ground and she was telling me that she was all right. It soothed me greatly. I've not heard from her since.

The business continued to grow and one day I came across an apartment for sale overlooking a lake and the coastline. It was a beautiful flat and a dream come true for me. I managed to get it at a very good price at auction, and I moved in quite quickly. I'd partly made the move with Kristin in mind; I'd finally have a place posh enough for her to move into. But it proved to be the last nail in our crazy coffin. I'd only been there a couple of days when she made one of her typical comments, "you'll probably find someone nice to share this place with one day." I was fuming, I'd jumped through hoops and bought the place with us in mind. It was the end, and we have hardly seen each since that day. I was, yet again, not so young, but free and single.

Chapter Sixteen

Making Amends

A crucial part of working the 12 Steps involves setting things right and making amends for the past. It's a vital and often rewarding piece of the healing process. The most significant of these amends often involves the addict's own family, who are are usually the people we have hurt the most. The difficulty with families is that they can often be the very same people who have hurt us the most too, at least for those who have experienced dysfunction and abuse. The process is messy and tangled up with childhood resentments and painful wounds. To fully feel the repentance required, it can take serious time to separate it from the harm done by others. Some of these people will also have passed away, which makes direct amends impossible. This process took place over many years, so I have brought together the fragmented instances. It is a path fraught with difficulty.

My heaviest burden of guilt, shame and remorse surrounded my beloved grandparents. They had only ever loved me, yet I had dragged them through my addiction regardless. They had given me the love and freedom to flourish as a child, yet I had failed to attend their funerals due to my addiction. I had begged, borrowed and stolen from them many times. I needed to release this guilt and shame, despite being unable to make a direct apology. An indirect amends was all I had.

I also carried a hefty weight of remorse towards poor Teddy. I wished I'd been more of a brother to him or somehow found a way to help him more. His death was so tragic and also so avoidable. He'd been using alone and he was lonely, so no-one had been there to revive him. Owing to his mental health issues he wasn't an easy person to help, but I couldn't let go of the fact that I should have tried harder. He was unpredictable and unhinged towards the end, but he was also kind, caring and fragile. I had realised he needed serious help.

I used to visit Hereford regularly, primarily to be an uncle to Alan's children, my niece and nephew. I'd take them for proper days out, feed them and treat them, whenever I could. With my grandparents and Teddy, one of the few things I could do was to make graveside amends. They are all buried in the same graveyard in Hereford, a few hundred yards apart. In Hereford, I would visit the dead as well as the living.

Due to my psychic experiences, I knew that I wasn't just talking to bones. I did this year after year and it would always be a mixture of saying I was sorry and asking for their help and blessings. After one such visit, I had a strong urge to visit my great aunt (my grandmother's sister). She was very elderly and always delighted to see me, although I didn't go as often as I would have liked. She was surprised and overjoyed about my visit. She had been in the attic sorting through things the day before and had found something she had to give me. She rooted out two old figurines, one male and one female, that had always stood abreast the fireplace at my grandparent's house. She said as soon as she found them, she just knew she had to give them to me. She handed them over. I remembered them well and I knew instantly that this was a message and a validation. My grandparents had sent a message to me. I felt I had been forgiven.

I also gave a donation to the local cancer hospice where they had both spent their last days and bought a memorial plaque in their honour. This plaque went up on a wall in the hospice. It was small gesture, but I knew it would have meant a lot to them. After a while I came to realise that repeatedly revisiting the graves was doing me no favours. Every time I went, I would go into a deep and painful remorse process, which wasn't exactly akin to moving forward with my life. I'd been stuck in this emotional recovery phase for way too long and I concluded it was time to move forward and spend less time looking back.

I very rarely go to the graves any more, but I still have those figurines watching over my life, and they will forever represent my grandmother and grandfather. The sign I received from my grandparents helped me to release my guilt and compartmentalise my regrets. I'm convinced a higher power orchestrated this. It was just what I needed, at just the right time.

Whenever I did visit the graveyard, I was always triggered about another shameful act I'd committed during my using. I'd sneaked into the church once and taken a wallet belonging to one of the groundsmen. The wallet had yielded me £80 in cash, which had seemed like manna from heaven at the time. The new clean me felt deeply ashamed and I now recognised the value of an honestly earned wage. I realised that the money did not merely equate to eight bags of heroin, to a junkie money is not really money. A tenner is a bag, gone in one hit, or a pipe, gone in a few sucks. The higher the amount of cash, the grander the weight or amount of drugs. I had now learnt to value money and the honest graft that goes into earning it, so I knew I needed to make amends for this crime too. I questioned several staff members over the years, trying to find out who the man may have been, but it was so long ago it was impossible to locate him. Eventually I settled on making an indirect amends. If ever I see a groundsman working at the church, I present him with £20, and I will do this until the debt has been paid in full. I make light of it, saying it is my way of thanking them for the great work that they do. There is no need for them to know the real truth and it's a creative way of setting the record straight.

My most challenging amends, for very different reasons, was the one I needed to make to my father (or stepfather). My feelings of guilt towards him were tangled up with the resentments I had about the harm and abuse he had inflicted upon me. It was a painful web to unravel. Early on in my recovery I'd phoned him occasionally, to let him know I was clean and doing well. Yet again I was seeking his approval and validation, but I failed to get what I so keenly sought. It became clear that he was getting on with his new life; he had a new family and two more children. After several calls I decided to leave the ball in his court and wait for him to call me instead. I did not hear back from him for fourteen years. This hurt, and my thoughts quickly turned to "fuck you"! I've heard from others that this is just the way he is, he's not a big one for staying in touch with anyone. This reassuring sentiment did little to placate my feelings of loathing and rejection. I knew he was responsible for many of my wounds.

A couple of years ago I decided to have another crack at dealing with this lingering unresolved issue. I'd done so much work around him and I felt I needed to act, to put things to rest, mainly for my own benefit. I put conscious effort into remembering the good times – the skills he had passed down, his mentoring and the fact that he been guarantor for my very first motorbike years after he had left the family home. In his own way he had still been there for me. The more work I'd done on my own damage and my own anger, the more I came to understand the rage that he had suffered from. He was carrying his own generational wounds. His childhood had been harsh and abusive. He was to remain accountable, but I felt with these new insights I could find room to forgive him. For my own sanity I was seeking resolution and an ending.

As part of this emotional recovery journey, I visited a well-known and infamously intense retreat on the south coast of England. It is best known for hosting its famous clients and for offering a unique and powerful healing environment. Set in a grand old house over-looking the sea, it provides a highly structured and deeply caring experience. I wasn't shocked by the place – after six solid months of the Lily Lodge Treat-ment, I was pretty much unshockable. For those who hadn't had this baptism of fire, the intense regime was both profound and overwhelming. The retreat runs on a very eclectic regime of meditation, therapy, re-enactment, assignment writing, visualisation, expression, art, shamanic drumming and rituals. It was a week-long therapeutic process with no television or technology. All connection to the outside world was removed and mobile phones are handed in on arrival. There were special meditation techniques that helped me to connect with my spirit guide. Yet again, wind within the trees became prominent for me and I got a sense of an ancient Native American spirit called Wise Winds. It was a vague vision, but I had the sense of his wild earthly presence.

The main issue that came up for me during that week was my father. The first morning was focused around releasing our anger and we spent hour after hour beating pillows with baseball bats. It was intense and the energy in the room was frenetic and powerful. The other clients were a mixed bag, from all walks of life. One was a psychiatrist for the criminally insane, another was a football agent and manager. Most who hadn't known what to expect were shell-shocked and intimidated by the rawness and vulnerability on display. It was a process that required courage but I was ready and pressed forward courageously. I was unfazed and at times led the way; I'd done this kind of work before, after all.

I was advised not to work for a few days afterwards and I felt so vulnerable by the end that I even stayed in a local B&B the night I left. I didn't want to drive; I was raw and still in pain. It was trippy walking out of the place, I'd stepped into another dimension and now I had step back out into the real world and it suddenly felt harsh and very sharp. In some ways I felt like I was going over old ground, but I'd also learnt new tools to help me go deeper than ever before. I continued to do online sessions with one of the teachers/counsellors from the project. This lady, who was also in recovery, helped me tremendously over coming years. I'd gained even deeper insights into my drives and difficulties.

As part of this ongoing journey I concluded that I needed to face my father because to some extent I was still living in fear of him. He had grown to almost mythical proportions in the darkness of my mind. I made a decision to meet up with him in person. Alan, who also hadn't seen him for years, came along too. For me it was all about facing my fears and looking my demons straight in the eye. We travelled to a pub near Chester and awaited his arrival. Alan, who hasn't done any of this work, was oblivious to the deep journey I had been on around this man. I didn't mention it to him. His ignorance sometimes seemed like bliss to me.

Eventually our father arrived. The man who stood before us was old, frail and failing. He'd cut himself shaving, lost his teeth, was balding with wispy white hair and was shorter than me. He looked thin, wizened and most surprisingly of all weak, almost vulnerable. I felt disdain as the myth of his almost god-like power dissolved before my eyes. His memory was beginning to fade and his mind was also weak. It was a shock. Despite his vulnerability, I felt a ball of disdain and animosity deep within me. Nothing of any significance was spoken about that day. It became clear that it wasn't on the agenda, he wasn't that kind of a man. But I had faced my fear – and seeing him in the flesh had dispelled some of my latent terror. I felt angry that such a weakling had ruled my fears for so long. As the conversation about trivialities rolled on, I was silently swearing inside, I had experienced a very different side to him as a child that was difficult to ignore. While I understand his shortcomings, he was still accountable.

Complex matters and motives aside, this giant of superhuman strength and power had been killed off. He was now a man I could push to the ground with a gentle shove. It's something I contemplated inwardly. The fact his mind was failing too was a shock to me and muddied the water, but I'm sure I could sense shame from him. He wouldn't look me in the eye at all and on the odd occasion I did gain eye contact, his eyes quickly slid away. I craved an apology; I wanted an acknowledgment of his behaviour and my suffering. It was not to be.

Our second meeting was equally unsatisfying. The third time we met, I did something that I hoped would prompt the resolution that I craved. I knew that I had not been an easy child to deal with and I clung on to the ways in which he had been a good father. I spoke to him outside the pub we met in and said, "I forgive you for the way you treated me and I'm sorry for the way I behaved too." I wanted him to meet my eyes and apologise for his part. What I got was a man who looked back at me bewildered, oblivious and confused. He replied a mere, "all right" in response, failing to grasp at my carefully laid out opportunity. I felt wounded and unseen all over again. It was not how I had envisaged the scenario playing out, he was not reading from my script. I was gutted. I had not considered that this man is a trained killer, he just doesn't go there with feelings and amends. However, some fragment must have dislodged in his mind, because later that day he rang Alan to ask if I was all right and was something the matter with me? It had triggered off a tell-tale feeling of discomfort within him.

I may never get the acknowledgment, apology and approval that I sought and craved and that's something I'll have to live with. He is still a heavy drinker and I've always wondered if he's an alcoholic. Either way, drink is his medicine. It's a very blurry line between heavy drinker and alcoholic. The drink may or may not be responsible for the decline in his mental faculties. His father was certainly an alcoholic, one who I believe attended a 12-Step fellowship for a number of years. It's not easy to break the generational cycle of addiction.

I had done what I set out to do – slayed my monster and faced my fears. There have been times in recovery when I have considered dragging him through the court system, so severe was the abuse at times. So strong was my desire for justice and closure. In the end, I settled for looking him straight in the eye.

A few years after my first healing retreat, I went back for a refresher weekend. During this time, I took part in a group meditation where we were asked to call on our guides to take us to the place where we really need to go. The meditation techniques used were powerful and lengthy, it was mentally and emotionally demanding. I was taken right back into my trauma. It was overwhelming and primal and I was literally convulsing with pain, wailing, breathless from crying, disorientated and bewildered. I was pulled out of group and talked back round in the staff dining room. I don't even know exactly where I went, or where I had just been. Over the next few days I began to recognise what was happening. I was releasing toxic pain and shame, and not just my own.

I had a powerful awareness it was not just my pain, but that it was generational. It wasn't only my pain and shame that I was releasing; it was pain and shame that stretched back over several previous generations. I believe there's a 'psychic cord' that attached me to previous generations and I was releasing their suffering too. Each generation had toxic shame beaten into them. I had broken the spell and released the pain for many generations. It hurt, but it was also cleansing and healing.

I felt love, clarity and connection opening up within me. It was a powerful and rewarding time. By releasing the bad, I had made space for the good. The love and the joy. I felt less of a victim. I became empowered and released. If I never see my father again, I know that I have done my part. I have apologised for my share and attempted to rebuild a bridge. His part is up to him. I have made efforts to embrace and acknowledge the good that he did. He provided for us. My mother said that every Christmas it was he who ensured we had a great pile of presents, because as a child he had gone without. It was he who worked hard to feed and clothe us. It was he who taught us skills and took us out onto the mountains and 'trained' us. He had tried, in his own way, to break the cycle and change the patterns of his childhood. He had fled the slums of Liverpool and excelled in the armed forces. His temper and his drinking led to him falling short, but for that I have found forgiveness. The fact that he had at least tried is in itself a worthy deed.

The process of forgiveness and forgiving around my mother has been ongoing. I realised early on that I had lingering resentments and shame around my mother and this was a barrier to truly connecting with her. I made an effort to move out of victim consciousness. Initially I found being around the family dynamics both traumatic and draining. I would regularly have to remove myself to the woods to regain my mental solace. My mother is a very warm, nurturing and loving person, but she also had a temper when we were younger, and she clung onto a toxic relationship that was damaging to us all. Relationships aside, she's a strong and spiritual woman and I'm glad she found some stability and happiness with Kirk. She has lived in the Wirral since leaving her flat with me about twenty years ago. Kirk died recently and she has struggled deeply with her grief, while also nursing Alan through serious health problems. It has taken time, but we now have a stronger connection than ever.

The closer I have come to her in recovery, the more I have come to empathise with her predicament as a young woman. She was unmarried and pregnant at eighteen, during a very different era, a time when this would have been stigmatised and denounced. As we grew up, single mothers were not common and what I read as weak would have been far more complicated than that. How would she have coped with three children, unsupported and alone? I've also come to fully comprehend what difficult and unmanageable children we must have been. All three of us were wild, angry addicts in the making.

Many amends involved faceless and untraceable victims. These needed dealing with by alternative means. I was a regular sneak thief and remembered taking a wage packet from the purse of an unknown woman. I'd sneaked into the back of the shop where she worked and grabbed a purse at random, without a thought that I could have been ruining that woman's week or month, maybe even rendering her unable to feed her children. I had no way of finding this individual or several others from similar thefts. I committed instead to give generously to those in low income jobs, such as waitresses. There was a waitress in Hereford who was telling me she had dropped her phone down the toilet and that she was skint and very upset about it. I was keen to repay my debt to society and gave her half of the money towards a new phone. I hope she didn't think I was hitting on her. Whatever she may have thought, my motive was pure.

I gave a similar tip to a therapist who had given me a beautiful hot stone massage. Again, I worried that she may have thought I was a weirdo or a pervert. I wasn't either, I promise! Looking back, I may have been a bit too hasty and over keen to absolve myself of my lingering guilt. Rightly or wrongly, I forged ahead.

My prolific shoplifting habits of old posed yet another problem. To some extent I had paid for these crimes by being imprisoned on numerous occasions, but this didn't feel an adequate solution to the new me. I also knew there had been many occasions when I had not been caught. I considered approaching the managers of the shops I had stolen from, for instance Woolworths and WH Smith's, to confess my crimes and negotiate a way of setting things right. After lengthy deliberation I decided not to risk that particular manoeuvre, as they may have felt inclined to press back-dated charges. It was unlikely but I decided that it would not benefit anyone. I conspired to tackle the issue from a different angle. I would buy textbooks for 12-Step newcomers and repay the debt that way. The ones who stayed with the fellowship would in turn stop committing crimes, so my actions would have a knock-on effect from a different direction. This gesture means a lot to newcomers too, simply that someone cares enough to buy them a book and has hope for them. When was the last time someone had given to them, without any expectation of reciprocation? This is something I continue to do.

I borrowed money from a very elderly aunt, who had been extremely kind to me for many years. She was a cool old bird in her seventies and I got her into U2; she even bought an album. We had a great connection and I probably brightened her day when I went to visit. As soon as I became drug dependent, I borrowed some money from her and never returned. She would have been very hurt by my actions. I spent hours hunting for her grave, to no avail. In the end I sat in the graveyard and spoke to her. I apologised and headed off into town to donate the equivalent money to a charity shop that supported a local cancer charity. I hope she was listening. I didn't wait around for the manager to come down and thank me. I didn't want the fuss, that wasn't what this was about. I strode away down the high street, feeling rather like Clint Eastwood, an unsung hero. Shining brightly with the light of goodness.

A crucial guideline in the making amends process includes a clause which states "except when to do so would injure them or others". This came into play when I went down to see Chloe and repay my debt to her parents. I knew I had taken money from them and I'd also written off a car they bought. I had a repayment figure in mind and a pocket full of money, and I was keen to get this debt replayed, but Chloe implored me not stir up the past as it would cause her problems in the present. Part of me was relieved I could now keep the money was earmarked for them, but the bigger part of me knew I had done them wrong, and that it needed to be put right. In the end I went there with Chloe, but I was very careful about how I worded my amends. I kept to a carefully worded apology and asked them if there was any way that I could put things right? They were happy to see me clean and doing so well. They said "just keep doing what you're doing, that is amends enough." It's a beautiful and common reaction to the amends process.

Despite Chloe's reservations I was glad I'd visited them. It's not something that many people do and I got the impression it had meant a lot to them. I had travelled a long way to see them and gone out of my way to visit. It's not an easy thing to do either; it takes great humility and even greater courage. It would be far easier to never see the people we have wronged ever again. We can't predict the response we will get, either. Most times the response is favourable, but it's impossible to know in advance. To show up and look people in the eyes is never easy.

In my early twenties, at the beginning of my descent into full-blown addiction, I had committed a crime I could not forgive myself for. I knew I could not leave this stone unturned; it was a painful amends that would take some courage. Sniff's family were like a family to me at that time, which made my wrongdoing all the more despicable. You see, I knew where their spare key was stashed and I also knew there was a cash box in the bottom of his parents' wardrobe. One day when I was craving heroin, I rooted out the key, sneaked into the house and stole all of the money from the cash tin. It was about £300, a lot of money in those days and probably their entire savings. When the money was discovered missing the police were called and the matter was taken very seriously. I was still going to the house despite being under suspicion. I had decided to front it out.

It was a heavy and shameful burden to carry, one that produced feelings that required more heroin to shut them away. Many addicts back themselves into such dark and shameful corners, that using to block away the guilt and shame rapidly becomes the only way too cope. Sniff's brother ended up being wrongly blamed, but even Sniff had been under suspicion. It caused tension and suspicion within the family. In a sense I got away with it, but I didn't really. I was living a deeply shameful lie. I'm sure Sniff suspected me, and it was this kind of conduct that began to drive a wedge between us. I could not look at myself in the mirror back then.

Most addicts have committed similar acts, living lies and tangling a stressful and secretive web of dishonesty. Over time, we become hardened to living this way, as the amount of guilt and shame we carry escalates both in size and severity. It's no way to live. When covering up actions such as these, our acting skills have no choice but to improve. This deed haunted me for many years and I confessed the truth to Sniff after my first time in rehab. He told me to forget about it, he was just happy to see me free from the smack. Good people are often so forgiving.

I also admitted that I'd made stories up about him, when I was trying to curry favour and persuade the police to release me. I'd told them he was expecting a big weed delivery on a certain day. It was total make believe but I'd do anything to build a rapport with my captors. He was busted but nothing was found. Unintentionally, I had nearly cost my friend a lengthy sentence – yet another shameful act I had carried out in the desperation of my addiction. It was a kind of grassing, but not quite, and any kind of grassing or betrayal is not easy to own up to. I had committed an absolute druggie no-no.

Sniff, being such a brother to me and an all-round good guy, told me to forget about both misdeeds and concentrate on keeping clean and staying well. That was all he wanted for me. It was a huge relief and he advised me not to mention it to his mum as she was going through a divorce at that time. Time ticked on and eventually I ended up using again, and for many years I blocked myself off from the shame I was carrying. After a few years clean again, it began playing on my mind and I knew an actual amends needed to be made. Thirty years after the crime had been committed, I got wind that Sniff was back in Hereford. I was still troubled by what I'd done. I hadn't gotten away with it at all. I hooked up with Sniff with the motive of going over to see his mum and repaying her the money. Sniff was living in the sticks at the time and I'd not yet told him of my plan.

I sat Sniff down and said I wanted to repay the money to his mum. I had the cash in my pocket. Initially he hated the idea and was dead set against it. He didn't want to upset his mother or rake up the past but I stood my ground. Eventually he agreed to phone his mum and tell her we were popping over to see her. We headed off in his old beat-up van to her humble little flat in Leominster and it felt quite surreal. This is a woman that I used to call mum, yet I hadn't seen her in nearly thirty years. I asked if we could speak in private and we went to sit in the garden. I told her the truth, it was me.

I asked if there was anything else I could do to put it right, as I handed her the £300. Tears swelled in her eyes and she buckled forward. I had touched her heart, in a good way. She didn't want to accept the money, saying it was such a long time ago, but there was no way I was leaving with that cash in my pocket. I persuaded her to keep it. She had tears running down her face as she told me, "I always knew you were a good person." It was a powerful moment and one of my most significant amends. I had restored something within her; her faith in human nature. I had stolen her dignity and now I had given it back. Sniff's fears that it was not a good idea had proven unfounded. She said it was strange, as she really needed the money at that moment in time. I'd returned a lot more than a bundle of cash that day. It's funny how these things sometimes work.

We headed off in contemplative silence. I bought fish and chips and we sat on a hilltop overlooking Hereford, eating our chippy tea as the sun went down. I'll always have a special place in my heart for Herefordshire and it always felt like home to me. I finally felt like I could put that particular portion of guilt and shame to rest. The sun set and I felt a deep sense of peace.

Another instance when I felt I had restored someone's faith in human nature was when I repaid my old boss for a caravan that I had stolen long ago. I'd sold his caravan while I was working for him in my early twenties and I'm sure he never expected to receive recompense. I set up a payment plan and paid my debt in full. When the last payment had been made, I spoke to him over the phone and could tell that he felt emotional and restored by the repayment. We had worked closely together for a couple of years and he must have felt betrayed by my actions back then. He never expected I would keep my word and keep up the payments. He was a tough hard-working businessman but I could tell I'd touched his heart.

Some past misdemeanours I chalked down to the dog eat dog world of addiction. There was an Asian guy who ran a restaurant and used to buy a lot of my stolen goods. I'd even steal to order for him and sometimes do the washing up if I was really desperate. One day I was feeling particularly bold (or desperate) and I persuaded him to invest in a cocaine business! I made him believe it was child's play and he would at least double his money. Unbelievably, (owing mainly to his opportunistic greed), he'd given me a £1000. Needless to say, it was like junkie Christmas. My plans of repaying him, of which I had good and honest intention, lasted only as long as my first hit. He did not get any money back, let alone double his punt. I avoided him for a while, before going back with a sob story about being busted and having to ditch the coke, adding that I'd done him a massive favour by leaving his name out of the police enquiry. It defies belief but I even managed to wangle another £500 out of him. I never ventured down that street again. It was all part of the game back then, two criminals both up to no good. Getting ripped off was one of the prizes in the wheel of fortune world I lived in, much of which I was on the receiving end of myself.

There were also drug dealers I owed money to. I wasn't really feeling the idea of running back to them with bundles of cash. I felt little would be gained by ploughing my clean money back into the world of drugs and crime, and I certainly didn't want to revisit many of these ruthless characters. I also needed to write off any such debt to myself. I put this money back into the fellowship, helping newcomers and those who were ready for change. I could think of no better way.

There was another area of my past behaviour that I carried shame about – the way I had treated my partners over the years. I hate to admit it, but I've had ongoing issues with controlling my temper and those closest to me often bore the brunt. There were instances where I'd slapped them and been verbally abusive. It's not an excuse but it's what I witnessed as a child and to some extent it came naturally to me for that reason. As I became more aware that my father had been repeating his patterns, my patterns came into clear focus too. I became even more determined not to repeat this cycle.

Part of breaking the pattern involved making amends for my past behaviour in this area. This involved digging up old ground and revisiting my past. My first proper girlfriend, Mitch, had been on the receiving end of my anger. My mother had bumped into her and had saved her number for me, so I called her and we met up in McDonald's in Hereford. She had two young sons by then and had been married. She looked older and well established but was not in the finest of fettle, having been recently divorced. She hadn't turned out to be an addict like me; she never was really. It was obvious from the outset that we had grown a long way apart.

The powerful bonding times of our misspent youth were a dim and distant memory to her. I apologised for my behaviour towards her and presented her with a painting I had recently produced, by way of amends. It was an image that meant a lot to me. I'd titled it *The Truth in Itself is the Paradox* and it was a spiralling tree painted in black on white, white on black. It was one of my pointillist labours of love and I'd spent hours on it. She accepted my painting and we separated on good terms. I don't think she had expected such a heartfelt gesture and it took her by surprise. It's not something that happens often in everyday life. I felt it ended the relationship on a far better note and gave closure to a messy time in my life. We had really loved each other at one time, when we'd both been very different people.

Then there was my Japanese girlfriend Koki. Tracing her was more problematic. I trawled the internet looking for her name and did a search of Japanese professors in an attempt to find her father. In the end, I had to accept that the quest was akin to finding a needle in a haystack. I had to take a step back and live with my guilt. I knew I had deceived, misled and used her. I'd also really loved her and had attempted to treat her with respect and tenderness at other times. I'd been devastated when she had left, that fateful day when the police somehow became involved. Looking back, it was the best thing that could have happened to her. I came to accept that this amends would have to be left on the shelf. These unmakeable amends are often the hardest to deal with.

I often wonder what became of her. She was naively looking for a good time and certainly had a wild side. The fact that she had made a beeline for someone like me speaks volumes. I'll never know if she descended into addiction or turned her life around and lived happily ever after. Is she dead, or does she live back in Japan surrounded by a loving family? I sincerely hope she found her way to a beautiful life and I have often sent this intention out to the universe.

The last serious girlfriend on my amends list was Chloe. We'd been through a lot together. I met up with her in Hereford while she was visiting her family. This was one amends I executed very badly. My focus was primarily on unburdening myself, as opposed to making her feel better. I sat her down and said, "I'm sorry, I used you," She looked very sad and hurt, saying,

"Well, actually I loved you." On the way home I realised that in my haste I'd chosen my words badly. I'd meant to express that I had ended up using her, due to my addiction, but I had loved her too. We may have had a very drug-orientated relationship, but we'd also had a real and genuine connection. I realised in that instance the importance of making a careful and thoughtful amends, with the emphasis being on them, rather than me. It's an instinct that doesn't always come naturally to me. It would also pay me well to remember that had she not come into my life when she did, I could well be dead by now. Amends don't always go as planned; it was a hard lesson to learn.

Chloe and I have stayed in contact since then and we wish each other nothing but the best. She turned her life around and has held down professional jobs that included the probation service. Luckily for her, she turned out not to be a full-bore addict, and succeeded in getting herself back on track. I've always made it clear to her that, should she ever end up needing help with her drug use, I will be there to help her. When I'd met her, it had forced me to straighten up my act. I wanted to keep her, which involved me cutting down on my injecting and prompted me to eventually sort myself out. She was a real catch for me, and I was desperate to keep her. I'm convinced I would have sunk further under the surface of life without her stabilising influence. She also gave me a reason to live – and most importantly of all, she loved me. I owe her a lot.

I've had an ongoing battle in recovery with my temper. After I slapped Lucy while I was in recovery, it forced me to take a long hard look at myself. Even though I had made an almost immediate amends to Lucy and we became firm friends again, I vowed to never get physical with a female in that way, ever again. So far, I've managed to uphold this intention. I never got physical with Kristin, despite the tempestuous and toxic nature of our relationship. It's not been easy and I've certainly had my moments, but I have always managed to restrain myself. I find women have the ability to hurt me more deeply than men. I'm sure it stems back to feeling unprotected by my mother as a child. It's a wound that takes time to fully heal.

I also considered the guilt I had around supplying drugs to the younger generation during my earlier using days. I had contributed to the drug problem and to people's addictions. I knew I'd sold speed to people far younger and more vulnerable than myself. In the end I came to realise that not everyone involved in the party scene turns out to be addicts; most don't, in fact. I know many people who possess an off switch that I was unable to locate. Those who are addicts will hunt out their drugs, regardless of me and my part. I'm not vindicating myself, but I eventually came to a place of acceptance around my actions. Addicts all tread their own painful paths, just as I have.

Nor were all my amends concerned with my using days. I've had my fair share of conflicts and scuffles in recovery too, owing to my pride and quick temper. Partaking in service, as part of the fellowship, can be extremely challenging. The fellowship after all is entirely run by recovering addicts, all of whom have shortcomings and issues. I've kicked off a few times, or left service positions and never returned. An ongoing process for me is to calm myself down and make amends whenever appropriate. On occasion other people have been out of order, acting on their issues, and I've had to find forgiveness for them.

After all of this amends work, of which I've given a snapshot and which took place over many years, I realised above all that I needed to forgive myself. I visited a Catholic priest during my early searching days and he told me I needed to forgive myself, above all else. I'm not a fan of, or a convert to, organised religion but I have flirted with it on occasion. In the end I have found my own way and my own spirituality. I can find traditional religions narrow minded and insular. I do not need to be saved because I do not attend church services. I don't judge people who go to church, so long as they don't pity me for being me. I think religion provides a valuable sense of community but I get this comfort and support from the fellowship. I have considered religion at times, but in the end I concluded that it isn't for me. I have followed my own spiritual path.

Slowly and with great difficulty I have managed to find forgiveness for myself; it often comes in waves. It's miraculous how being in recovery has transformed my life and turned my destiny around. Once I was a dead man walking, quite literally. I didn't escape my relentless using unscathed, I have lingering physical and mental health scars to bear but I have managed, with help, to rewrite my destiny. The amends process wasn't always about making me feel better. Some amends just can't be made and I've had to live with this unresolved guilt. The ongoing process also acts as a reminder of the things I did during my addiction. A reminder that I'm simply not terribly good at taking drugs. I have become the opposite of what I once was, as have many others. I am not alone. It's not been easy, but it's nothing short of miraculous.

Chapter Seventeen

Troubled Waters

During my trips abroad in service of the fellowship, I met a promising and attractive female from Slovakia. She was beautiful, tall, slim and distant and her vibe intrigued me. We kept in contact after I got back home, and slowly but surely I was hooked. The fact that she was so beautiful, and also so far away, triggered off my insecurities. It was a painful time. She was riddled with issues and went to more different recovery fellowships than I thought possible. Fellowships around food, money, debt, drugs, drink, relationships and sex. None of this intensity alarmed or deterred me.

Probably her main issue was around food; she was in early recovery from serious bulimia which had ravaged her body and damaged her insides. She worked a 12-Step recovery programme designed for those with chronic eating disorders. It's a very intense and strict regime, but it had probably saved her life. She was also a year or so clean from drugs and alcohol. She was a lot earlier on than me but she was so intense around recovery I tended to forget that. She could politely be called an assertive type, especially around her own needs. She could afford to be, she was very beautiful.

I went back and forth to see her many times. She was living at her grandmother's and life was very poor. I met her parents and she came over and met my mother. Our relationship was starting to deepen. Despite her apparent poverty and desperation, she always carried herself with dignity and even a little superiority. She was very slim and held harsh and brutal opinions around those who carried any extra weight, me included at times. It wasn't always easy to cope with. I tend to eat too much, whereas she weighed and measured every morsel that passed her lips. This did little to ease my relentless insecurity.

After about a year, she came over to live with me. She was much younger, and I had high hopes of finally gaining the children and family that I had long dreamed of. But she was a very changeable entity; one minute warm, the next minute icy cold. I was at times blissfully happy, but always slightly unsure. There were so many issues to contend with and her issues around sex, food and money were a constant drain on our emotional resources. Sex was tricky and nothing was simple and straightforward with her. She didn't work and I took her on some amazing holidays to Spain, Malta, New York and Barbados. She eventually got a job and decided promptly to move out. Due to constantly working on herself, she decided it would be a positive move for both of us; that way she could concentrate even more deeply on herself. She wanted to find herself and although I didn't want her to go, I allowed her the space she requested. I understood all about finding yourself in early recovery.

She promised it would only be for a few months. I was worried, but she persistently reassured me, taking me up on holiday offers and romantic meals. I felt we were still on solid ground. Then one day, she announced out of the blue that she felt we had a lack of chemistry and didn't fancy me any more. I could see she was upset too, and she claimed she still loved me. I felt like I'd been hit with a sledgehammer; suddenly she was gone from my life. I felt abandoned and more than a little used. I never did quite have a handle on her and now I had paid the ultimate price. She had been working a programme around sex and relationships too, and I felt I'd been cast aside due to that, in part. Apparently, she wanted to explore her sexuality. Before I met her, she'd been working as a high-class call girl for an exclusive escort agency and maybe this line of work accounted for her coldness and sexual issues. Either way, I felt used and it was one of the lowest points in my entire recovery. She had pushed all of my rejection, abandonment and betrayal buttons.

She had made a dream board and I wasn't on it. I'd spotted this a while back, but she had brushed it aside. My gut instinct had been screaming at me but I'd chosen to ignore it at my peril. I really suffered after that breakup because she'd been a powerful force in my life. On the negative side, she could be described as rigid and cold, but on the flipside this translated into her being determined and focused. She was capable of great warmth, and at other times an utterly chilling icy coldness. She was a being of enormous duality.

My dreams to start a family and leave some kind of legacy had been left in ruins. I was wounded and was forced yet again into doing some deep work on myself. I've never been more aware of how broken and shattered relationships can render me. They have the ability to hook into my core beliefs and emotionally tear me limb from limb. Her fluctuating temperature scale had traumatised me but nothing had prepared me for her brutal departure. I had to start over, yet again.

Inga had made me think far more carefully about what I ate. She was a very strict and righteous vegan and before she left, I'd booked a vegan cruise as a surprise for her. Suddenly I was left holding cruise tickets and no-one to go with. I thought about selling them but decided to go by myself and I met an amazing Croatian guy called Jesse. It was a surprisingly powerful and spiritual experience. I ended up really getting on with these totally out of this world folk as we island hopped around the Adriatic Sea. They came to stay with me for a week and I learnt a huge amount from them. Jesse lived the cleanest of lifestyles. It wasn't just about veganism, his essence was pure and as a result his spirit shone very bright. He was solid and strong in a gentle and quiet way. He left a lasting impression on me. I'd never met people like these before; it was a brand-new world.

As a result, I became a raw vegan over that summer and went to a few vegan food festivals. I invested in juicers, dehydrators and other new kitchen contraptions. I felt great for a while, but suddenly I was struck down with body-wide pain and swelling. I could hardly move and my feet and hands were like balloons. I'd aged fifty years overnight. It was baffling and scary. My condition worsened and I asked Jesse to travel over to help me. I was in the midst of a detoxifying healing crisis or a purging, possibly aggravated by my excessive consumption of dehydrated tomatoes. I now know that they are a member of the nightshade family and can antagonise arthritic conditions. I was diagnosed with psoriatic arthritis, along with gout in my feet. Jesse was convinced it was due to the acidity and toxins within my system. Feeling its morbidity also made me feel low emotionally.

Jesse put me on a strict juicing regime, I was making and drinking a few litres a day and he also wanted me to stop the prescribed painkillers that would only compound the problem. I had help and support from his mother who is a naturopathic doctor. He advised me on exercise, diet and much more. I took a leap of faith, ignoring all conventional medical advice.

I felt so ill and scared that it shook my faith in a higher power significantly. One night I lost the plot and took a baseball bat to an angel I had bought in early recovery. It was a huge pottery figure and I took great joy in smashing it to smithereens. Afterwards it only made me feel worse and looking at the fragments did little to lift my mood. It was my dark night of the soul. The next morning, I was sitting in my living room, which overlooks the lake, when a robin hopped in through the window and perched on the back of the chair opposite. He calmly sat there watching me, not remotely stressed or in any hurry to leave. I made myself some breakfast and still the robin sat happily opposite me. I had the feeling he was either my grandmother or an angelic presence, sent to comfort and reassure me. After a while, he hopped through to the kitchen. I opened a window and he flew away. It was an unusual and uplifting experience that I will never forget.

Slowly but surely over the course of several weeks my pain decreased and my mobility returned. I had seen a specialist and he'd recommended steroids, but I refrained from touching them, knowing they are little more than a quick fix sticking plaster. I managed to keep the business going while I recuperated and healed. I was using a combination of cannabis oils orally, which does have a mind-altering affect and was tricky to reconcile in recovery and abstinence terms. I really went out on a limb with it. It was as dangerous for me as it was healing.

But heal me it did in combination with the diet and other things Jesse and his mother had prescribed, and in hindsight I'm glad I took the risk. I returned to the NHS clinic a few months later and was horrified to look around the waiting room and see what I could so easily have become. I told the consultant what I was doing, and he was amazed at my improvement, although he couldn't endorse my methods. As I looked around at other patients, with their swollen steroid faces, pain management, weight problems and fatigue, I was hit by a tidal wave of gratitude. That could so easily have been my path and my life.

We are so seldom proactive around our own health and I am eternally grateful for the fact that I had met people like Jesse. Sadly, I didn't manage to sustain the raw veganism for very long and have been in and out of veganism ever since. Having said that, I fully believe in the ethos and science behind the entire lifestyle. In the end, I stopped the regime as I was taking it to the extreme and began teetering on the edge of both my recovery and my sanity. I'd gone from limping to running within a matter of 12 weeks, but I was in danger of taking things too far. Psychologically, I began suffering from anxiety and I became crippled by debilitating panic attacks.

I'm sure the damage I had done to my body, mind and soul through trauma and drug abuse had been dislodged and my mental health began to go into decline. I'd had short lived episodes of panic before, but they had become immobilising. Eventually I had to turn to conventional medicine to tackle these. I was prescribed a medicine and I realised that I had been mentally suffering for a very long time. Reluctantly I came to accept that conventional medicine also has a time and place and I resigned myself to an ongoing low dose. I'd also run this new medication by my sponsor and others with many years of strong recovery behind them, explaining how I was suffering and the options that lay in front of me. One person blew me away with her insight. "This medication might just be a recovery-based decision," she said.

Sometimes we suffer unnecessarily due to our unwillingness to medicate and try different avenues. Many of us are left with lingering and severe mental health problems; there are few heroin addicts who have not experienced some kind of trauma in their lives. Addiction is so often an attempt at self-medication. My persecuting internal voices had been bullying me for years, yet I was so used to them I didn't know there was another way. I had been plagued by suicidal thoughts and feelings of utter worthlessness for as long as I could remember. I don't suffer with this as severely since I began accepting that I needed outside help. Lots of people cope fine without any medication throughout their recovery, there are others who suffer deeply. Ranks of beautiful clean people have taken their own lives.

Chapter Eighteen

The Moral of the Story.

Addiction is literally a matter of life and death, and sadly death is a thread that winds its way through this book. Innumerable souls have been lost to this condition over the years, often in tragic and disturbing circumstances. When people died while I was knee deep in my own addiction, it seemed to matter little. Life was of little value back then and these things added to the drama factor of it all. It was part of the day to day unfolding of the chaos of addiction and never really hit home in the same way as when you are clean; it was merely par for the course. People regularly died of overdose, disease or suicide. It was to be expected and all part of the game. Life was such a living hell, I'd lost sight of how precious it could be.

Everyone was simply consumed with getting high or not getting sick. In fact, when someone did overdose, there was often a ripple of excitement as addicts rushed to get hold of the same lethally strong batch, which is an unfathomable scenario for a non-addict mind to comprehend. When someone overdosed in my presence, I was far more concerned with the legal ramifications of the situation than whether the person lived or died. It was a cut-throat world, inhabited by the spiritually dead.

I knew many people from my early days in Blacon and later at The Saracen's Head who had been drinkers and were extremely anti-smack back then, but heroin has the ability to take anyone out, and many later died of their addiction to it. It's not about will power or morals. If you have strong addictive tendencies, heroin will get a hold of you. It's tragic, the lives lost in search and maintenance of its warm, comfortable numbness.

Of course, for me Teddy was the most tragic of all, a death that did not pass me by, even from the depths of addiction. Drugs and addiction take mercy on no-one, mental health problems will grant you no clemency. It had also rendered him lonely and isolated, so there had been no-one there to save him. I wish I had been, but hindsight is a wonderful thing, though it can't be said I did not try. Teddy never had the opportunity of recovery that I did. I think of my mother, having lost one son to the condition, then having to watch her other two sons clutched in its powerful grip. I know of other families who have lost several siblings to the illness. It's a powerful force that can decimate entire families.

Many others died during my using years, but none hit me in any significant way. I was too numb. Then there were the numerous deaths during my two stints in rehab. Even though, on both occasions, we were sternly informed about the recovery stats, many simply refused to heed the warnings. Commonly, two thirds of people will relapse during the treatment process and ninety per cent of people will return to drugs within the first year. Due to the lowered drug tolerance, the chance of overdose is heightened.

Countless people who walked out of treatment were reported dead within days of leaving. However many times this happened, it didn't deter others from following suit and they too ended up proving this frightening statistic to be true. That's the tragic thing; even death is no deterrent.

Others would survive for longer and I'd see them about town looking desperate and destitute. Often these people would also be reported or rumoured dead within a period of time. Without exaggeration, hundreds have died over the years. People from all walks of life and from all classes and careers. From street urchins to the aristocracy, addiction does not discriminate. Rehabs fight a war of attrition every single day.

Even skilled workers within the field of addiction are not spared. I'm thinking of Cee and Mark, to name but two. Cee was a support worker in Lily Lodge and had driven me to a lot of meetings early on. We'd become friends, but slowly he drifted away from meetings and started spending too much time on dubious dating sites. Before long he was in the grips of sex addiction and was back on the drink and drugs in no time. One often leads to the other. Poor Cee didn't last long, and I attended his funeral soon afterwards. Mark was a hugely important mentor for me and a man I had untold respect for. He was an expert in the addiction field and had probably helped hundreds of people into meaningful recovery. But he did not take his own addiction seriously enough and ended up drinking after his return to Australia. He lasted a couple of years before dying of chronic alcoholism. It scared me – if it could take him, was anyone safe? I consoled myself with the fact that Mark had stopped attending 12-Step meetings, something I have never done. For me, his loss gave tragic meaning to the term irony.

It doesn't matter how much knowledge or clean time you have, in my opinion recovery is a process that requires ongoing commitment, perseverance and consistency. Working in the addiction field is also emotionally exhausting and workers are commonly known to suffer from burn out. Countless people have relapsed and disappeared. Some return, others have never been seen again. Witnessing the cruelty of addiction daily is of little deterrent.

There will always be a mystery surrounding the double suicide of Jay and Corey and it's something that will forever haunt many of the people who knew them well. One thing is certain about their story; relapse very seldom has a happy ending. Their deaths shocked many and will be spoken about for years to come, a catastrophe that acts as a powerful warning about the perils of relationships and co-dependency in early recovery. Many addicts have relapsed after entering relationships too soon, that's a fact but does not include everyone, I might add.

There are many people who relapse and survive for a while, but later go on to commit suicide. They can no longer stomach the hellish purgatory of addiction and decide to end their lives prematurely. The agony of addiction is even more painful when you know there is a way out and you have blown your chance. It is so very hard to come back from a relapse. I learnt that myself after ten years of tortuous using after cleaning up the first time. Using was never the same again, but

I couldn't find my way back to where I knew I belonged. I was beyond lucky to get back at all.

There are others who neglect their emotional recovery and end up mentally ill. Addicts are often people in pain, who have suffered great trauma. Some stay clean but cannot shake the mental health issues and sadness that still haunts them. I've seen many of these people banged up and drugged up in various mental health institutions. The hardcore medications handed out in such places are far from therapeutic, in my opinion. It is well documented that recovering addicts need to take extra care around their mental health, hence the daily maintenance and commitment to growth and development. Those who neglect this are a long way from happy and free. I've seen people written off and drugged up for life, doomed to shuffling the corridors of these infirmaries for an eternity. I can think of no more terrifying prospect.

There are a few people who do manage to buck the trend and succeed in living non-abstinent lives. They manage to pick up drink or recreational drugs and hold onto a reasonably manageable life. I believe these individuals do not have the some condition as me. They had a problem which they have somehow managed to resolve. I know I have the condition and have never fancied carrying out further experiments by chancing my luck with drink or soft drugs. I've attended fellowship meetings regularly the whole way through. It's a risk I don't want to take. It's like playing Russian roulette but having five bullets in a six-chamber gun. My roulette days are over; I just don't fancy the odds today.

I've been back to the formidable Blacon estate in recent years, to have a look around. It's had a lot of money thrown at it and the environment has changed, but I'm sure it has the same kind of characters, just a different generation up to much the same kind of stuff. I stood in front of the house we lived in and it looked small. I felt so detached and remote from the life I had once had. Walking around brought back plenty of minor memories but no major revelations or deep feelings. The area we lived in was called Poet's Corner and the old pub The Lord Byron had been knocked down and turned into some sort of housing for the elderly. The adventure playground was still there, thoroughly sanitised by modern health and safety standards. No longer could you climb to the top of the trees and swing about freely; it was all clips, harnesses and safety staff. Much of the wildness had been scrubbed away. Council estates are fascinating places, akin to microcosmic worlds.

Hereford was always closer to my heart than Chester. It was more rural and mellow and it also hosted some of my happier childhood memories. I've been back there many times and always visit my favourite historic hill that overlooks the city. I sit up there and listen to the trees, it's a sacred place. I'm always surprised by its smallness. The city centre is barely bigger than a small town but it's crammed with ancient historical tales. I love the mystical feeling of the place.

Alan has survived many turbulent times and has also suffered with his mental health over the years. He cleaned himself up and no longer has a drug problem but has been left with long-term physical health issues. He's now living a very different life, not far from our Mother. Alan, in his own way, committed to breaking the cycle. He vowed to never hit his children and he was a man of his word. His two children are doing well, looking forward to careers and to living normal, happy lives. Hopefully they have been spared the purgatory of addiction.

Sniff is now back in Hereford, a renowned tattoo artist with clients from all over the globe. He has his own healthy covering of tattoos and still manages to maintain his bohemian and off-grid lifestyle. I'm slightly jealous whenever I see him; he was just so much better at using drugs than me. He has always managed to avoid the slippery slope down into full-blown addiction. For two people so similar, we differ in that one very important way. As a result, our lives panned out to be very different indeed.

I've never managed to find my real father. It's a complete brick wall. I've hammered my mother with questions numerous times and she really doesn't know anything more about him. All we know is that he was in the regiment and was possibly Scottish. It's difficult to track people down within the very secretive Special Forces. I don't even know if he knows that I exist and it's been a tricky issue to work through. I'll always feel like I lack a certain sense of identity and that half of my genetic origins are unknown. Even for minor things like medical questionnaires I can provide no definitive answers. It leaves a hollow and empty space.

His absence left me with my stepfather, a man I have very mixed feeling towards. I know in my heart of hearts that he did his best with what he had at the time. He tried, educated us and loved us through doing and teaching us stuff. He was a powerful and highly capable father who in many ways I respected, but he also had a fatal flaw. He had a painfully brutal temper and liked a drink far too much.

My 12-Step fellowship has become a big part of my life – in fact, it has given me a life. It helped to mend my soul and provide me with spiritual awakening. I prefer spirituality to religion. Spirituality doesn't cause war and killing, as is so often the case with religion. I love the open-ended, all-encompassing scope of spirit. The spirituality of the fellowships has crossed borders and brought comfort to those living in conflict. I have seen it with my own eyes and heard about it from others – I'm thinking of both Bosnia and Northern Ireland. It has transformed lives all over the world; I have seen that too, many times over. It is a powerful, inclusive and healing force.

Through my experiences and knowledge, I have come to believe that many addicts possess the same acute sensitivity that I do. It's a sensitivity so painful that many are cajoled into taking drugs in an attempt to supress it. Add in a dose of trauma or abuse and we are easily overwhelmed, becoming tortured and tormented. I'm reminded of my very first memory, the butterfly's fluttering wings vibrating within me as a baby. For a child so sensitive to the world at large, violence and beatings quickly become unbearable, forcing an emotional shut down and later self-medication. The more I have got to know myself, the more I can forgive myself for descending into the bowels of addiction. I was frightened and vulnerable, seeking solace in a brutal world. The same is true for so many others.

Recently I have had to stare death in the face once more and consider my own mortality. I suffered a heart attack when I was home alone. I was taking out the bins when I started to feel very tired. I sat down to rest and a pain and numbness spread down my arm and around my heart. I instinctively knew what was happening, and massaged my own heart and visualised a bright white light while I waited for the paramedics to arrive. It transpired that my artery was ninety per cent clogged. Since then I have undergone heart surgery. It pervaded me with a frightening feeling of vulnerability.

My days of endless travel are probably behind me, due to my lingering health vulnerabilities, but I still continue to get away every January. I realised there were plenty of other places besides New York, and a couple of years ago decided to try Thailand instead. I knew someone who lived there; my first ever counsellor back in the '80s. Before long I'd added another item to my itinerary – why not hook up with a few women and maybe get laid? I began planning ahead, joined a Thai dating sites and met a girl called Pim. She seemed a bit different from a lot of the others and was more concerned as to whether I was a scammer. Apparently, the scam works both ways because men target girls to wangle money out of them. We got chatting and she was very straight-forward about wanting marriage and a child. It all sounded a bit full-on and scared me a bit, but something about her appealed to me. She seemed refreshingly honest. She is in her 30s, petite, beautiful with long flowing black hair. She shone with a natural beauty, unlike many of the others.

When I went over there, we met up and she looked just as good as her photos, if not better. She was concerned that I might just use her while on holiday. She had a good job in an ICU unit in a big hospital in Chiang Mai, working up to seventy hours a week. My experience with the Slovakian girl had left me fearful and sceptical of long-distance relationships. Pim gave me a book to read about Thai customs around relationships, marriage and culture. I was still afraid of being used and of her motives. After I returned home, I began missing her and within a month I flew back to see her again. I really liked her but I was worried. I slowly came to realise that there was a lot more to Pim.

A good few months later she came to stay for six months. We got to know each other a lot better and the relationship solidified. We had a fair few ups and downs, with some fraught moments, but we always ended up coming back together, stronger than before. The relationship began to gain a foundation of trust, acceptance and honesty. She was very up front in admitting that she wanted both love and security.

She is also strong and stands up for herself; she's no pushover or shrinking violet. I proposed to her in the car, driving up a bypass, "Well, do you want to get married then?" She took a few moments and said yes. "Well then, let's go and get you a ring," I replied. I'd already made enquiries with a mate of mine and we popped into his jewellers to choose her ring. She has a cheeky honesty about her and has learned to understand my sense of humour too. We finally negotiated a medium sized engagement ring. All in good humour and with a refreshing honesty.

I decided she was worth a touch of romance and we went up to the Lake District for the weekend. I'd booked a lovely room overlooking a lake from a boathouse. I knew she deserved a proper proposal and lowered myself onto one knee and asked her to marry me. She said no! She was joking, but she had got me back; she had started to embrace my sense of humour. We began planning the wedding; it was to be held in Thailand, in her parent's village in the mountains. I already knew she was desperate for a baby. Despite being only 34, she already felt her time was running out. I had long since given up on the dream of having a child, yet it had now become a distinct possibility. You can never know for sure what the future will hold.

Within a few weeks she came running into my office with a pregnancy testing kit in her hand. It was positive. We retested and the result was the same, we were having a baby! We both cried with joy. Shortly afterwards, we trekked off to Thailand for the wedding, which had all been arranged from the UK with the help of her parents and her village. A wedding over there is a community event and the entire village pitches in. It was a traditional Thai ceremony with hand tying, money pins and a huge village feast. Two of my good friends who live in Thailand came along, so I felt supported and not totally outnumbered. It was an honour to be a part of such a community occasion. The village is poor in money but rich in culture and community. Elders are respected and cared for.

We are now married and awaiting a baby. Scans have shown that the baby will be a boy. Pim is ridiculously happy, all her dreams have come true. As have mine. Within the space of a year I have gone from staring death in the face to awaiting the arrival of a brand-new life. A child we will call Benjamin.

With the ending of this chapter starts a new one; a new life. An end and a new beginning, coming together as one. I wonder if my son will lie in his pram as a baby and feel the butterflies flutter past, seeing their colour and sensing their vibrations? I sit here approaching my 19th anniversary of being clean, with one hand I stroke my heart, wondering how long it will beat. With the other, I stroke Pim's tummy, intrigued to meet a new human and hoping to invest in his future by instilling what I've learned about love, the dark and the light.

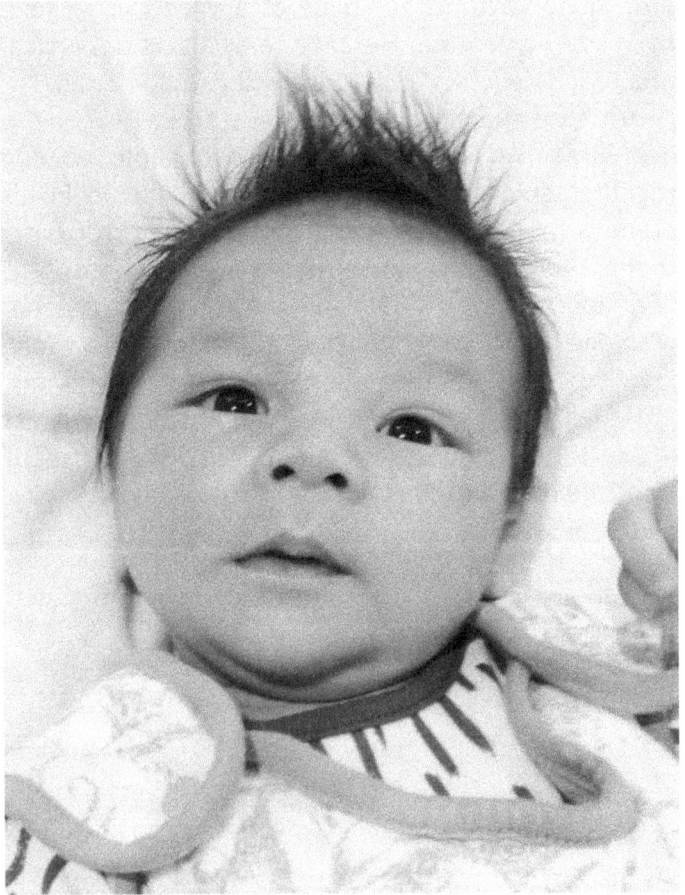
Benjamin Born Winter 2019

*9 7 8 1 8 3 9 7 5 0 4 4 1 *